*Cinderella Rockefeller*

AN AUTOBIOGRAPHY

# Cinderella Rockefeller

ISABEL LINCOLN ELMER

*Freundlich Books*

NEW YORK

Published by Freundlich Books
(A division of Lawrence Freundlich Publications, Inc.)
212 Fifth Avenue
New York, N.Y. 10010

LIBRARY OF CONGRESS CATALOGING-IN-PUBLICATION DATA
Elmer, Isabel Lincoln, 1927-
  Cinderella Rockefeller.

  Includes index.
  1. Elmer, Isabel Lincoln, 1927-
2. Christian biography—United States.  3. Community
of Jesus (Cape Cod, Mass.)  4. Rockefeller family.
I. Title.
BR1725.E47A3    1986      289.9 [B]        86-29163
ISBN 0-88191-052-X

Distributed to the trade by Kampmann & Company
9 East 40th Street
New York, N.Y. 10016
Manufactured in the United States of America

10   9   8   7   6   5   4   3   2   1

*To the memory of my mother,*
*Isabel Rockefeller Lincoln,*
*and to my spiritual mothers,*
*Cay Andersen and Judy Sorensen,*
*this book is dedicated.*

# *Prelude*

---

I OPENED MY EYES and noticed the light beginning to show under my window shade. Stretching comfortably in the little bed, I glanced over at the door to my grandparents' bedroom and wondered if Grandma was awake yet. The room I was in was like a dream—a special room which they had made over for my frequent visits. It had been Grandma's dressing room, but she had taken delight in making it over for a five-year-old—a delicate confection of white and pink. There were frilly white curtains at the two windows and a miniature easy chair, just big enough for me, covered in a bright pink chintz with little butterflies embossed in the material. My bed, also white, had some of those butterflies decorating it, as did the specially made bedspread.

But the high point of the room was the mantel over the tiny working fireplace! It too was white, showing up crisply against the pale pink walls, and in its center was a large clock that ticked with a comforting sound, day and night. At each end of the mantel stood a candlestick, white with bright gold rims, and lightly running up them were the ever-recurring butterflies. Best of all, there sat on the mantel an elf—a warm, brown stocking-knit figure barely a foot high, looking down at me with bright eyes and a whimsical smile.

I called him Brownie, and Grandma told me that he was a very special elf with magical abilities. I loved him and spent hours on the carpet, playing with him. The magic part happened during the night.

For when I awoke in the morning, I would find a surprise treat entwined in his arms. Now, squinting up at the mantel in the half light, I wondered what it was. Sometimes it was a chocolate kiss, sometimes a lollypop in the shape of an animal; occasionally, there would be a barrette for my uncompromisingly straight hair, or a handkerchief with my name embroidered on it—Bellita.

Just then, I heard that name whispered, and turned to see my grandmother, looking in. "Are you awake?" She had softly opened the door and was smiling down at me, like a grown-up Brownie. "How would you like to go for a walk *right now*? We could go through the rose gardens and see the sun rise. Want to do that?"

Instantly wide-awake, I nodded vigorously, slid out of bed, and went straight to my bureau. Eagerly, I climbed into my blue cotton shorts and white polo shirt, so quickly that the shirt went on back to front. I had problems, anyway, knowing backs from fronts, but I didn't care how I was dressed. When my parents were with me, my nursemaid organized me, but at my grandparents' house, I was on my own; no one came to dress me or tug a comb through my straight brown hair.

I loved these secret expeditions with my grandmother. She liked to get up early, before daybreak if possible, to go out and walk in the gardens, where she could be free and unobserved by the myriad gardeners and servants who would soon be at work.

As soon as I had latched my sandals, the two of us slipped out of my room and down the long corridor of the second floor of the house. At least six other bedrooms and suites, almost as vast as my grandparents', led off this corridor. As we tiptoed along in the dim light, the first door we passed was my Aunt Winifred's. I liked Aunt Win; I was her goddaughter, and she had always been kind to me, even letting me come into her room to watch her caring for her new baby daughter. She loved babies, and unlike the rest of the family, she insisted on bathing and tending her baby herself and would not allow a nurse to do any of it. I thought Aunt Win was pretty: she had rich, dark brown hair worn in an old-fashioned bun at the back of her head. Her hair and eyes were like my grandmother's, but there the resemblance ended. For while Grandma's eyes often sparkled with fun, there was a sad, haunted look about Aunt Win's. She loved coming back to the security of her parents' huge home, bringing her two little daughters with her.

Her younger sister Faith's room was catty-cornered across the hall.

At twenty-two, Faith was vibrant, tall, attractive, and full of life—very much my favorite aunt. She seemed to have inherited a good measure of her father's geniality, for the house always seemed to be full of her friends. But no matter how busy she was with them, she always had time for me.

There was a third aunt in the house, Gladys, the youngest, whose room was opposite my grandparents'. Aunt Glad was totally unpredictable—wildly happy one moment, and desperately miserable the next. She liked to do madcap things that made my grandparents deeply concerned—but which, for some reason, never really bothered me. Five-year-olds are surprisingly resilient; I got used to Aunt Glad's mood shifts and enjoyed the upswings.

Beyond Aunt Win's room were two guest rooms, and beyond that was a white, wooden swinging door that led to another long corridor with all the maids' rooms. This was forbidden territory to us children, but sometimes, if my sister and cousins and I were playing hide-and-seek in the forty-room house and were feeling daring, we would push open the door and run along the corridor, trying to find one of many little rooms unoccupied, to hide in. Each room had a neat white bed with an iron bedstead and a white porcelain basin on a stand. Interspersed between the rooms were bathrooms with huge bathtubs standing on cast iron legs. We seldom stayed long, as we would be scolded severely, if caught.

When my parents drove out to Greenwich to visit, they had a suite of rooms on the third floor, and there was also a big playroom up there for me and my sister and cousins. Uncle Avery no longer had a room there, for he now lived with his family in a renovated farmhouse, next door on the 400-acre estate.

We had reached the grand staircase that swept away from us in a shallow curve down to the first floor. The stairs were covered with a sapphire blue carpet, and the walls, which soared up above us to the third floor, were hung with tapestries. I clung to my grandmother's hand and stretched my other hand up to the polished banister. Even though the morning light was still dim, the mahogany gleamed, and under my fingers it felt smooth, silky, and strong.

I gave Grandma's hand a squeeze when we got to the bottom, and she looked down at me and smiled; it was hard to say who loved these dawn adventures more. Suddenly, I heard the sound of a piano being played in the distance, and listening hard, I thought I could make out one of Grandpa's favorite tunes, "The Blue Danube."

"Grandma," I whispered, "is Grandpa up, too?"

"Yes," she sighed, "he's been up all night. Your poor grandfather has so many worries. Today he has to go to Washington." I was shocked to see tears in her eyes, and said nothing as we proceeded along the ground-floor corridor. On our right was the breakfast room and the passage that led to the cavernous kitchen with massive gas stoves and the endless pantries, storerooms, and larders beyond, all silent now. The breakfast room was where we children had most of our meals with our nurses. We sat at a large table presided over by the housekeeper, Mrs. Hunt. Even this room was hung with tapestries, one showing a Roman goddess whose head was a mass of writhing snakes. Mrs. Hunt gravely informed us that if we did not eat all of our Brussels sprouts, the snakes would come down and get us. So we ate every one, keeping an eye on that tapestry all the while.

We turned left and headed down the hall, past an enormous living room that in spite of its size was a warm, friendly room, in which everyone, even the children, felt completely at home. I never understood why we were allowed to frolic in this room, but we certainly were, and played endless games of "house" all over the comfortable, cushioned sofas in front of the two birch log fires that crackled in the ornately carved marble fireplaces at either end of the room. We took turns being "mother," while the others pretended to be her children. Whenever it was my turn, I always chose to be "Grandma" instead, for she was the one to whom I felt closest.

To an outsider, I suppose it was a strange room in some ways, but to me nothing in it seemed strange. Aunt Faith played the organ, and my grandparents had one built into the corner for her that would have been large enough for a church, its silver pipes reaching almost to the high ceiling. Somehow, it did not seem at all out of place among the paintings, easy chairs of all kinds and sizes, and long, oak refectory tables behind the sofas, covered with neatly arrayed copies of the New York *Times* and the *Herald Tribune, Wall Street Journal, Daily News Graphic, Town and Country, London Illustrated News,* and *Country Life.* The magazines were a wonderful source of horse and dog pictures, which I used to cut out and paste into a scrapbook Grandma had given me.

Some living rooms are strictly for show; this one was the opposite—a living room that was truly lived in. It was the one room in which all of us could be together informally, quietly curled up in chairs or lolling amongst the cushions on one of the sofas, reading, knitting, doing embroidery, or perhaps waiting for afternoon tea. How I loved to hear the creaking wheels that signaled the approach of the tea cart. Just as the grandfather's clock in the front hall began to chime four, Oscar, the Swiss butler, would wheel it in, with two maids, in black silk uniforms and starched white caps and aprons, following behind.

On the cart, the big silver samovar was steaming and gleaming, and next to it was a three-tiered mahogany stand, laden with delicately thin, lettuce-and-tomato sandwiches with the crusts cut off, lacy cookies, and slices of pound cake—all so delicious that I often heard Grandma say, "Don't eat any more, Bellita; you'll spoil your supper." To an outsider, our living room may have seemed formal and imposing, but to us it was cozy—the very heart of our home.

Next came the music room, and I looked up at Grandma, to see if we were going to go in to see Grandpa, but she just shook her head. We continued on until we reached the solarium at the end of the corridor, walked quickly through it, and opened the door to the outside. Down the flight of marble steps we went, until at last we were in the garden. The air was cool and sweet, filled with birdsong and all the scents of early morning. Dew covered the grass and hung in droplets on wondrous spiders' webs. The sky was already pale with the approach of the sun, and streaked with a color that was almost peach. There was a rich smell of moist earth, and as we stole across the lawn, I felt the cool dampness of dew on my sandaled feet and could make out luminous blue patches of forget-me-nots everywhere.

Like escaping prisoners, we hurried toward the rose garden, and when we reached the wooden gate, we found, placed neatly beside it, a wicker basket containing Grandma's gardening gloves and a small pair of pruners. The gardeners knew of her early morning visits to her beloved roses and showed their affection by making these things ready for her, in case she should come. Soon my grandmother was happily snipping pink, white, and yellow roses, carefully telling me the name of each variety, as she laid it in her basket. Her favorites were the climbing roses, which she had trained to the cedar fence surrounding the rose garden, but these were not yet in bloom. Suddenly, I saw a shiny green-and-gold beetle climbing on one of the roses. "What's this?"

She looked at it and frowned. "Oh, dear, I'll have to tell Joe we've got a Japanese beetle." She went on to explain that these dreadful beetles were steadily advancing further and further north and had now reached southern Connecticut. By now Grandma's basket was full, the sun was up and turning golden, and it was time for us to retreat, before the garden and estate filled with men beginning their day's work. I had loved our foray into early morning, and now it was turning into a perfect June day.

For the first time, I remembered that I had not yet seen what treat Brownie had for me this morning, and now I was anxious to get back to my room and see what it was. Usually, I would get it and then slip into my grandparents' big mahogany four-poster and snuggle down between them, waiting for Oscar to bring breakfast for us all. There would be freshly-squeezed orange juice, hot oatmeal for me with a small glass of plump raisins beside it, soft-boiled eggs for my grandparents, and lovely thin toast in silver toast racks, like the English had it. And always there was homemade jam: yesterday's had been made from the wild strawberries, which grew in profusion beside the small roads that crisscrossed my grandparents' estate.

But today was different. Grandpa was going to Washington, where he had been summoned before the Stock Exchange Investigating Committee, and his private railroad car would soon be hitched to the Pennsylvania Railroad train headed for the capital. With his departure imminent, there would be no breakfast in bed this morning for the three of us. As we returned to the house, I ran ahead, bounding up the staircase and down the corridor, throwing open the door of my room, and dragging the little easy chair over to reach the mantel. There, in Brownie's arms, was—I couldn't believe it! A Mickey Mouse watch! The nicest present he had ever given me! Grandma had promised me a watch when I finally mastered the difficult task of tying my own shoes. This I had finally succeeded in doing the day before, but how did Brownie know?

I ran to find Grandma and tell her about this wonder. "Look!" I exclaimed, showing her the watch with the black strap and the big red-and-black mouse whose arms pointed out the time. "I wish Grandpa were here, so I could show him, too!" For I had heard the big black Cadillac crunching down the gravel driveway as it pulled away.

"So do I, Bellita," Grandma said softly, and I looked up; there were tears in her eyes again.

It hurt to look at her, so I looked at Mickey instead; his big hand was on the 12, his little hand on the 8. It was almost time for breakfast.

MANY YEARS WOULD PASS before I learned that Grandpa had been summoned before a Senate investigating committee to answer charges of stock manipulation, of which he was exonerated. Such things were discussed behind the closed velvet curtains of the library, and so carefully kept from my generation that I grew into young womanhood before fully realizing the extent of the enmity some people bore against the Rockefellers. Mine was an insulated and protected childhood— and my grandparents had the wherewithal to ensure that it remained that way.

*Cinderella Rockefeller*

AN AUTOBIOGRAPHY

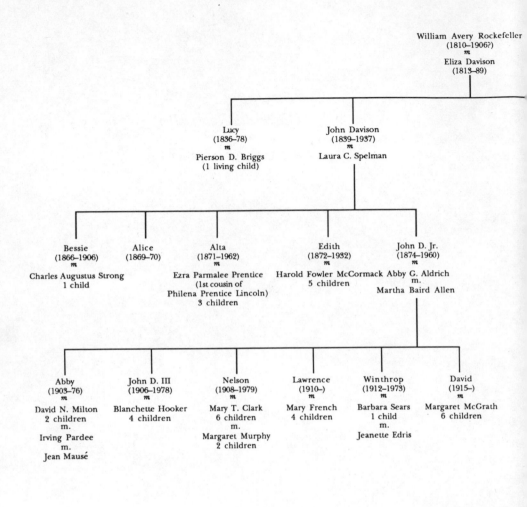

William Avery Rockefeller
(1810–1906?)
*m*
Eliza Davison
(1813–89)

Lucy
(1836–78)
*m*
Pierson D. Briggs
(1 living child)

John Davison
(1839–1937)
*m*
Laura C. Spelman

Bessie
(1866–1906)
*m*
Charles Augustus Strong
1 child

Alice
(1869–70)

Alta
(1871–1962)
*m*
Ezra Parmalee Prentice
(1st cousin of
Philena Prentice Lincoln)
3 children

Edith
(1872–1932)
*m*
Harold Fowler McCormack
5 children

John D. Jr.
(1874–1960)
*m*
Abby G. Aldrich
m.
Martha Baird Allen

Abby
(1903–76)
*m*
David N. Milton
2 children
m.
Irving Pardee
m.
Jean Mausé

John D. III
(1906–1978)
*m*
Blanchette Hooker
4 children

Nelson
(1908–1979)
*m*
Mary T. Clark
6 children
m.
Margaret Murphy
2 children

Lawrence
(1910–)
*m*
Mary French
4 children

Winthrop
(1912–1973)
*m*
Barbara Sears
1 child
m.
Jeanette Edris

David
(1915–)
*m*
Margaret McGrath
6 children

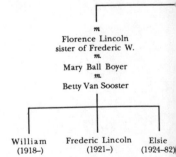

*m*
Florence Lincoln
sister of Frederic W.
*m.*
Mary Ball Boyer
*m.*
Betty Van Sooster

William
(1918–)

Frederic Lincoln
(1921–)

Elsie
(1924–82)

# 1

GRANDMA'S MAIDEN NAME was Isabel Stillman. She was the youngest daughter of the legendary James Stillman, chairman of the National City Bank of New York, and with J. P. Morgan and H. H. Harriman, one of the three most powerful financiers in America. Grandpa was Percy Rockefeller, the youngest son of William Rockefeller, who with his brother John D. had founded and controlled the Standard Oil Company.

Isabel and Percy met in 1895, when the latter was invited to a ten-day house party at the Stillmans' summer mansion, "Cote d'Or," on Narragansett Avenue in Newport. The house party immediately preceded the marriage of Isabel's older sister Elsie to Percy's older brother William G., and was to bring the rest of the Stillman and Rockefeller clans as close together as the two fathers had become during the past eleven years in business, since they met in 1884.

Isabel at nineteen was a superb horsewoman, either in the saddle or driving a carriage, and she was especially proud of her ability to handle a pair of thoroughbreds in harness. So when Percy was to be picked up at the train station, she would not hear of anyone else calling for him. Nor did she see any need for the two liveried footmen who were assigned to ride on steps behind the rear wheels of the carriage.

She must have found Percy quite attractive, for hardly had they started for home than she expertly—and gleefully—swerved to the left and the right, throwing each of the footmen off the back and leaving her and Percy unchaperoned. Never in his seventeen years had Percy met such a high-spirited girl, and he was instantly smitten.

Circumstances further conspired to foster this budding relationship, for everyone was preoccupied with wedding preparations. Isabel and Percy went everywhere together, laughing, talking, and sharing. For Isabel, this was a totally new experience. Never had she had anyone to confide in, and now here was a handsome young man who was not only interested in what she had to say, but who seemed to care very much for her. It was intoxicating, and it soon became love—the first she had ever known.

For Isabel had had a life that no one would envy, could they have seen beyond its surface. Unchecked power tended to twist the people who wielded it, and her father James Stillman was a twisted man. Stern, brooding, forever silent except when dropping sardonic remarks, he was known on Wall Street as "the man with the iron mask." He didn't care. He could crush anyone who spoke ill of him, and he often did. Barely forty when he had gained the helm of the National City Bank, his shrewd ability attracted the attention of the Rockefellers. They made him Standard Oil's banker, and as Standard Oil acquired controlling interest in many other companies, William brought them to his friend James at National City, which soon became the foremost bank of all the great industrial and financial combines at the turn of the century.

But if all went as smoothly as well-oiled machinery in the oak-paneled boardroom on Wall Street, such was not the case in the Stillman mansion uptown, or in their country home in Cornwall-on-the-Hudson. James Stillman had married a New York girl, Sarah Rumrill, who bore him five children. But she had done something to displease him, something so horrendous that he had banished her totally from the family, when their daughter Isabel, whom James had named for his sister, was still a small girl. Not only did Sarah vanish, but no one was ever allowed to speak her name or refer to her again. (Indeed, to this day, when her grandchildren mention her, their voices unconsciously drop, as if they are afraid of being punished.)

Isabel had thus been brought up entirely without a mother's tenderness and care, in a tyrannical household where each morning all the children and relatives, and every servant, had to line the hall of the house and bow or curtsy to James Stillman, as he left for his office. The

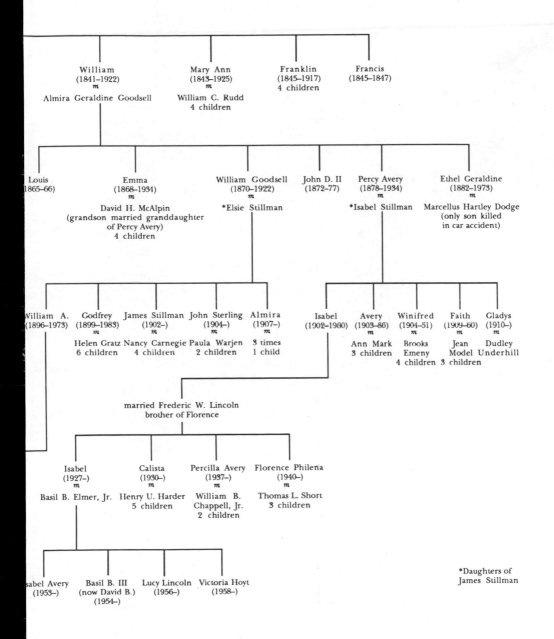

William
(1841–1922)
m
Almira Geraldine Goodsell

Mary Ann
(1843–1925)
m
William C. Rudd
4 children

Franklin
(1845–1917)
4 children

Francis
(1845–1847)

Louis
(1865–66)

Emma
(1868–1934)
m
David H. McAlpin
(grandson married granddaughter
of Percy Avery)
4 children

William Goodsell
(1870–1922)
m
*Elsie Stillman

John D. II
(1872–77)

Percy Avery
(1878–1934)
m
*Isabel Stillman

Ethel Geraldine
(1882–1973)
m
Marcellus Hartley Dodge
(only son killed
in car accident)

William A.
(1896–1973)

Godfrey
(1899–1983)
m
Helen Gratz
6 children

James Stillman
(1902–)
m
Nancy Carnegie
4 children

John Sterling
(1904–)
m
Paula Warjen
2 children

Almira
(1907–)
m
3 times
1 child

Isabel
(1902–1980)

Avery
(1903–86)
m
Ann Mark
3 children

Winifred
(1904–51)
m
Brooks
Emeny
4 children

Faith
(1909–60)
m
Jean
Model
3 children

Gladys
(1910–)
m
Dudley
Underhill

married Frederic W. Lincoln
brother of Florence

Isabel
(1927–)
m
Basil B. Elmer, Jr.

Calista
(1930–)
m
Henry U. Harder
5 children

Percilla Avery
(1937–)
m
William B.
Chappell, Jr.
2 children

Florence Philena
(1940–)
m
Thomas L. Short
3 children

Isabel Avery
(1953–)

Basil B. III
(now David B.)
(1954–)

Lucy Lincoln
(1956–)

Victoria Hoyt
(1958–)

*Daughters of
James Stillman

only sign that Isabel and her sister Elsie ever had of their mother's love was a mysterious package that each girl received through the mail with no return address. Each little box contained one beautiful teardrop diamond earring. They were a matched pair, and although there was nothing to show who had sent them, they both believed it could only have been their mother.

Percy's father, on the other hand, was just the opposite of Isabel's. An exceptionally charming man, William Rockefeller used his geniality to win key industry leaders to his point of view, as he consolidated many diversified corporations in common cause. He was the perfect balance to his brother, the brilliant but obsessive John D., who did not make friends easily and preferred to remain in the background. Together, beginning in 1866, they made an indomitable business combination, and with Henry Flagler, who joined them a year later, they forged Standard Oil into a monopoly that had absolute control over the oil industry in America, and indeed most of the world. And that control extended far beyond oil—into mining, shipping, real estate, and railroads.

The brothers Rockefeller were on the boards of many of the largest corporations in the country, and they expected these corporations to favor Standard Oil whenever possible. When this was not the case, off came the gloves, and some of the most ruthless in-fighting ever seen in boardrooms took place. Nor was this ruthlessness limited to the boardroom; other industrialists crossed the Rockefellers at their peril. Those who survived knew that they had been in the brawl of a lifetime, and those who didn't survive would often hate the Rockefellers for the rest of their lives.

William Rockefeller, for instance (according to my Uncle Avery), while on the board of the Chicago, Milwaukee & St. Paul Railroad, felt that line was not giving him a sufficient price break for transporting oil from the Twin Cities to the West Coast. When the other members of the board would not accommodate him, he built his own railroad, the Northern Pacific, paralleling their route. It wasn't profitable, but he didn't care; the Minneapolis & St. Paul was not getting Standard Oil's business.

While John D. would eventually become the better-known brother, it was William who put the deals together and cemented intercorporate relationships which eventually grew so powerful that in 1911, at the instigation of President Taft, the Supreme Court, under the Sherman

Antitrust Act of 1890, ordered the dissolution of Standard Oil, breaking it into thirty-nine different companies. In divesting himself of his Standard Oil holdings, William, whose real interest lay in the diversified corporate challenges of railroads and real estate, sold many of his oil shares to his brother, whose faith in the future of the internal combustion engine—and the gasoline and oil it would need—remained unshaken. So did the closeness of their relationship, which had begun in boyhood and was often referred to as almost mystical. William had picked and bought the land in Tarrytown for John D.'s famous estate, Pocantico Hills—and had then built his own, Rockwood Hall, next to it. In Manhattan, William's mansion was at 10 West 54th Street, while John D.'s was at 4 West 54th. And this exceptional closeness between the two families would continue down through the generations.

At home, Percy's father was as much in command as he was at the head of a boardroom table. And while Percy's upbringing may have been considerably more cheerful than Isabel's, still parental word was law: it was never challenged, never even silently questioned. But now, on this house party, with everyone's attention focused on the imminent marriage between their older brother Willliam G. and sister Elsie, nobody seemed to notice that this younger couple was fast developing a mutual attraction of their own.

The days were filled with sailing aboard the Stillman yacht, with riding, at which Percy was as adept as Isabel, and with outings of every description. And in the evenings, at magnificent balls illuminated by Mr. Edison's marvelous new incandescent lights, they danced and talked and danced some more. Everything Percy and Isabel saw and did and felt, they shared, each for the first time. And the bond between them grew stronger, until in ten unbroken days it had reached a point that might normally have taken many months.

As the wedding drew nigh, they asked to speak to their fathers together, in private. No one knows exactly what was said behind those doors; there are no diary accounts. But from the stories that have been passed down from generation to generation, one can imagine what probably took place. The initial reaction of James Stillman and William Rockefeller to Percy's request to court Isabel might have been a gentle, even humorous denial—"You two are much too young for courting. You're merely caught up in the excitement of your older brother and sister getting married, and infatuated with the idea of romance."

But when Percy and then Isabel made it clear that they were quite serious, the smiles of their fathers vanished. "Absolutely out of the question!" William might have thundered: "Isabel, you're two years older than Percy! And Percy, you *are* going to go to Yale! And it will be four years before you graduate! Not only is marriage unthinkable; I don't want you thinking about it, while you're supposed to be getting an education. If Isabel's father agrees, you are not to write her or speak to her, until you are finished!" Isabel's father did agree and laid the same stipulation upon his daughter.

The young people were crushed. Receiving the edict as if from a magistrate's bench, it never occurred to them to challenge it. The years passed slowly for Percy and Isabel, broken only by the occasional word or note transmitted by their older brother and sister. They remained faithful to each other, cherishing the memory of those ten wonderful days, and if anything, the bond between them grew stronger.

EXCEPT FOR ISABEL'S ABSENCE, Percy was happy at Yale. Immensely popular, he was elected Chairman of the Junior Prom—in those days the most prominent position an undergraduate could attain. In addition, he was manager of the football team, and in his final year was one of the very few to be "tapped" for the most prestigious of Yale's secret societies, Skull and Bones.

Percy graduated from Yale in 1900, and was immediately installed on the board of Standard Oil, alongside his father and his Uncle John. He demonstrated a remarkable gift for finance and management, and became a valuable asset to the trust, far beyond what might have been expected from one so young. But with this responsibility came pressure—so intense and unrelenting it had already proved more than his older brother William G. could bear.

Percy had his father's gift of geniality; men who met him instinctively took a liking to him, and he soon demonstrated that he had considerable business acumen to accompany his popularity. His father was immensely pleased with him and was now delighted to have him court his best friend's daughter. Needless to say, Percy and Isabel were delighted, too; they were married within a year.

Unfortunately, they were not allowed to live happily ever after. Their fathers, pleased as they were with the union, nevertheless continued to impose their benevolent dictatorship upon their offspring.

Percy and Isabel's first home was a mansion on East 72nd Street, just off Fifth Avenue, built and lavishly furnished for them by James Stillman. During the summer, they rented a house on the Hudson, near Tarrytown, to be near Percy's parents. As their children came one after another—my mother (the third Isabel) in 1902, Avery in 1903, Winifred in 1904, Faith in 1909, and Gladys in 1910—their parents felt the need for their own home in the country.

At this point, Percy's father William stepped in. He had been somewhat piqued by the grandiose generosity of James Stillman in providing the New York mansion, so when Isabel mentioned that she was looking forward one day to having a place in the country, he had plans drawn up for a magnificent estate in Greenwich, Connecticut, where he owned a vast tract of land. It was divided by Lake Avenue, and he gave the west half to William G. and Elsie and the east half to Percy and Isabel. The latter couple's estate of some 400 acres was known as Owenoke Farm, after the Indian tribe which had once lived and hunted there. Situated in beautiful, rolling countryside and covered with maple trees, elms, and oaks, it was an ideal setting for a growing family of young children, and right across the street were their five double-first cousins. As an added advantage, the New York, New Haven & Hartford Railroad station was less than fifteen minutes by carriage from their home, which enabled Percy to become one of the first men to commute daily from Greenwich to Wall Street. As other friends joined him, they had a private club car attached to the train, for their exclusive enjoyment.

William Rockefeller now determined to surpass James Stillman's gift of the splendiferous town house, and the Big House, as it came to be known in the family, gradually took form. It would have forty rooms on three floors, a red-tiled roof, and stone from the same quarry that had been used for the construction of the White House, a century before. The house faced north on a slight rise, and the main entrance was squarely in the middle, with an elegant, pillared porte-cochere, under which a carriage could dispatch its passengers in a rainstorm and not have them get wet. They would climb a broad flight of stone steps to the massive oak double doors, and upon entering would be confronted in the high-ceilinged foyer with the huge head of a stuffed buffalo. (No one ever told me how it got there, but I assumed William had shot it from a train window, while crossing the Great Plains.)

The first-floor rooms were all carpeted with oriental rugs, specially woven in Turkey for Owenoke. They gave a rich, blue haze to the long hall, the walls of which were hung with tapestry after priceless tapestry, collected by James Stillman. In addition to the living room, a library held shelves of books to the ceiling, a music room with Percy's piano, a solarium with bamboo furniture and french doors that let the summer air in but also permitted the enjoyment of sunshine in the middle of winter.

Away from the house, the long, graveled driveway that entered from Lake Avenue led to the stables and an enclosed riding ring. Across the driveway from the house was situated a large swimming pool, surrounded by flagstone, and an elaborate bathhouse, with separate wings for men and women. In addition, two clay tennis courts and two indoor squash courts were housed in a large, windowless cement building. (To these facilities, years later Percy and Isabel would add a wading pool and a large sandbox for the enjoyment of their grandchildren.)

With vistas of terraced gardens and lawns and shade trees, William Rockefeller had indeed created an idyllic place for his children and their children and *their* children. My mother and her brother and sisters and their cousins all loved to play there. The pool was big enough, and the stable endlessly fascinating, with its cavernous rooms holding the family carriages (and, later, automobiles) and the long narrow tack room, smelling of leather and saddle soap. In charge of it all, the head groom, Loren Conger, was an extremely gifted horse trader, as well as trainer. His enormously fat wife, Alice, kept half a dozen yapping Boston bull terriers. Loren, a good riding instructor, soon taught Percy and Isabel's children to ride as well as their parents, as they cantered over the endless bridle paths that laced the property.

Back in New York, James Stillman must have watched the creation of Owenoke with consternation. But he had already ensured that his own imprint would remain on the young family. For in addition to the tapestries and other art objects which he lavished on them, there occurred a significant episode at the birth of my mother, which spoke volumes. As James Stillman strode into the room to see his first granddaughter, he announced to all present that her name, too, would be Isabel, the same as her mother, whom he had named after his beloved sister who had died a premature death. He brooked no discussion on this point, never considering how Percy and Isabel would feel about it. Indeed, he had done the same thing a few days before to their older brother and sister, announcing that their newborn son would be named after himself: James Stillman Rockefeller. (So my mother became the third Isabel, as I would become the fourth, and my eldest daughter, the fifth.)

Young Isabel Rockefeller was a handsome, intelligent child, with clear blue eyes and fine-textured blond hair blowing about in soft waves. She had the long, strong Rockefeller nose and narrow face, and on it a spontaneous smile, which made everyone love her. As a child, despite the restrictions of a governess and a personal maid to dress her, she was very much a tomboy, riding and roaming freely on the estate, with her younger brother, Avery, and their first cousin, James. She was game to do anything the boys did—climbing trees, racing horses, or whatever, and they had their own little clubhouse hidden amongst the trees. But into this blissful existence came three younger sisters— two with ominous problems.

Winifred was a gloomy, unhappy child, unwilling to join in the boisterous games devised to outwit and escape from governesses; she tattletaled on the other children and generally cast a blight over everything. Things got so bad that one day Isabel and Avery decided to drown their wretched little sister by holding her head under an iron pipe that emerged from a rock and poured out fresh spring water. Fortunately, a hysterical governess rushed up in the nick of time to save Winifred from any harm, but for the rest of her life Isabel would carry a sense of guilt about how much she detested her morose younger sister.

Another, more serious source of unhappiness for the family came with the birth of Gladys in 1910. As a small child, she suffered from celiac disease, a rare disorder which meant that she could not digest or absorb fats, starches, or certain sugars. The disease was considered fatal, for at the time Gladys was born, no child had been known to survive it. Percy and Isabel consulted Dr. Emmet Holt, the most eminent pediatrician in New York, and through his perseverance and care their youngest child did survive. Regarded as something of a medical miracle, Gladys was seven before she was able to walk. The price of this miracle was that for years my grandmother devoted herself totally to her desperately sick daughter, who was cared for around the clock by a team of highly trained nurses. Indeed, she became so absorbed by this daily struggle for her daughter's survival that she neglected her other children. Never having had a mother of her own to love and care for her, she had no experience of how crucial a mother's love and attention were, or of how much she was hurting her other children by withholding it. How deeply this had wounded them was brought home to me when my Uncle Avery recalling it in his eighties, was practically brought to tears.

Percy, who himself had grown up in a loving family, tried to compensate for his wife's lack of attention, but his ever-pressing business commitments made it difficult to spend as much time with his children as he would have liked. Almost totally deprived of her mother's love, young Isabel would for the rest of her life find it almost impossible to express tenderness, and my sisters and I had to grow up without any of the usual show of affection. She could not bring herself to kiss my sisters and me; the most she could manage was sometimes to stroke our heads and brush our hair back from our faces with her fingers.

But if young Isabel never learned how to express physical affection, she developed an unusual gift for discerning the unspoken needs of others. And all her life she would be acutely sensitive to the needs of those around her, doing everything in her power to help them. And unlike her grandfathers, there would be no strings attached.

# 2

---

GRADUALLY, THE ABSENCE of a mother's love receded in importance in young Isabel's life, as she reached school age and was enrolled in Miss Ely's—a small private school in Greenwich for "young girls of good families." There she made a number of friends who also lived in large houses, including two sisters, Hope and Polly Lincoln, from North Maple Avenue, less than a mile away. As she grew older, she was allowed to ride her horse to school, and sometimes—with her parents' permission, of course—she would stop off at the Lincoln sisters' brown-shingled Victorian house on her way home.

For the Rockefeller families, the years passed pleasantly enough. Standard Oil, though forced to dissolve and diversify, was nonetheless booming, railroads were rapidly expanding, and real estate values were skyrocketing. War erupted in Europe, but in 1915 it was still an ocean away. On the nearby Boston Post Road more automobiles now sped by than carriages, and thanks to Henry Ford's assembly line, they were no longer the playthings of the rich. A Model T soon fell within reach of every hardworking family, and many of them reached for one.

Sadly, the time came when there were too few girls like Isabel to support Miss Ely's school, and it had to close. Suddenly, eighth-grader Isabel, a year too young to attend the Westover School in Middlebury, was left with no alternative but to attend the Greenwich public school. On the opening day, she rode to school on her horse, just as she always had—and found herself the object of merciless ridicule.

"Look at her, a Rockefeller, and she has to ride a horse to school! Her people are too stingy to drive her!"

Isabel was stunned. Never in her life had she been subjected to deliberate cruelty, and not knowing what else to do, she withdrew into herself. The other thirteen-year-olds intensified their persecution of the new girl, determined to make each day a misery. At home, Isabel tried to tell her parents what was happening, but they did not seem to understand. So she endured, and was profoundly grateful when at last she could go away to school. (The ordeal would, however, affect her for the rest of her life, leaving an unreasoning, implacable hatred of Greenwich.)

WESTOVER WAS A BREATH of fresh air. Here she found herself with girls of similar backgrounds, and here she truly came into her own. It turned out that Isabel Rockefeller had a natural gift for leadership. She did well in her studies and was the head of the undergraduate athletic association. Best of all, like her father, she made friends easily, and her room became the center in which the girls congregated.

As for boys, Isabel was too busy with her new life to pay much attention to them—at first. But then, over Christmas vacation of her junior year, when she was sixteen, that changed. On a cold, grey morning in early January, she had put on her dark green velvet skating outfit all trimmed with ermine, pulling it down over the hated plaster body cast which her parents, on the advice of their physician, had insisted that she wear for a year. At 5'10", Isabel was tall and growing still taller—and in danger of doing permanent damage to her spine. It must be kept straight at all times, until her body had a chance to catch up with itself, and the muscles and ligaments responsible to hold the spine in place could grow strong enough to do their job. The body cast was a radical solution—the best the doctor could come up with.

There may have been another factor at work, as well. It could be that Isabel, towering over her friends at Westover, was embarrassed by her height, and consciously or unconsciously stooped to minimize it, which could only make the problem worse. In any event, in another year she would grow to accept her stature and ignore it—and would incidentally have and maintain superb posture. But for now, the wretched body cast was a thing to be detested but endured without complaint. In that sense, it strengthened her character as much as her back, and in future years she would endure far greater adversity without flinching or self-pity. Hurrying now, she donned an ermine hat to cover her ears, and pulled on her thick leather gloves. Her Grandfather Stillman had sent her this beautiful skating outfit from Paris, and looking in the full-length mirror, she was pleased with the effect. Time to go—she ran down the graceful Owenoke staircase, along the hall, and out through the front doors, to join a cheerful, chattering group of girlfriends. Forming themselves into a human chain, with their arms round each others' waists so that they wouldn't fall on the ice-encrusted snow, the five young girls walked the half mile down to the frozen pond, singing as they went, their skates tied together and slung over their shoulders. Although it was extremely cold, nothing dimmed their enthusiasm. It was good to be alive!

When they reached the pond, they found that it had been swept clear of snow by some of the stable boys; indeed, there were already quite a number of people skating on the bumpy black ice. Isabel sat down on one of the logs that had been put beside the pond for that purpose and laced up her high brown skating boots. Quickly, she was out on the ice, taking long, graceful, gliding strides. Skating was one of her favorite sports, and she was good at it.

Round and round the pond she went, sometimes with one of her friends, sometimes alone, exhilarated by the exercise in the sharp, frosty air. Overhead, a group of shiny black crows circled the point, as if reluctant to land because the ice-sheathed branches were too cold and slippery to perch on. In one corner of the pond, a number of college men were loudly and and gleefully playing ice hockey, and Isabel recognized her cousin Godfrey racing down the ice, deftly stick-handling the hard black puck and shooting it into a makeshift goal.

When the young men tired of hockey, they usually joined the girls and skated in one long line, playing snap-the-whip. Isabel always hoped she would be near the end of the line, so that she would be one of the skaters catapulted off to shoot down the ice at tremendous speed when the whip cracked. Happily, she skated along, and was suddenly startled to see Godfrey racing toward her with his best friend, Freddy Lincoln, whose older sister had recently married Godfrey's older brother. Freddy was home on Christmas leave, for America had entered the European war now, and he had quit Princeton to join the cavalry. On and on they came, and as they drew level with her, Freddy swung his arm back and gave her a tremendous blow on her front with his fist. There was a dull thud and a shock that stopped Isabel in her tracks. She wasn't hurt—only astonished.

"There, you see?" shouted Godfrey, grinning. "I *told* you it wouldn't hurt her—she's fine!"

Freddy stood there, suddenly shocked and horrified at what he had done. Boasting that his young cousin wouldn't flinch, even if hit with great force, Godfrey had dared Freddy to do it. The latter had taken up the challenge, but now he was filled with remorse. How could he have hit a girl?

"Isabel," he finally stammered, "I'm so sorry! Please, please forgive me!"

Isabel laughed. "Oh, Freddy," she exclaimed, shaking her head, "it didn't hurt, and Godfrey knew it wouldn't! You see, I have to wear a horrid plaster cast to make me stand up straight, and that's why it didn't hurt. I was only a bit startled!"

Freddy thereupon made a half-serious bow and retreated, still ashamed. As he skated away from her—tall, handsome, abashed by his rudeness, but still charming—he took her heart with him. And it would remain his, through all the social whirl to come, and all the men who would court her.


WHO WAS THIS Freddy Lincoln? He was the older brother of her friend Hope from Miss Ely's. Beyond that, she knew very little about him, other than that his family lived on North Maple, and that his father was in shipping. Not until much later did she learn that he came from a long line of patriots. The first Lincoln, Samuel, was a Puritan who came over in 1637 and settled in the Massachusetts Bay Colony, in a place named for their home town in England, Hingham. He had seven surviving children, including two sons, Samuel and Mordecai. It was from Samuel that Freddy was descended; and on Mordecai's side, two centuries later, there would come a gifted young lawyer named Abraham.

From the beginning, the Lincolns distinguished themselves as responsible citizens, serving in the militia and taking active roles in the affairs of their town and colony. In 1768, Amos Lincoln left Hingham at the age of fourteen, going to Boston, where he apprenticed himself to a master builder. Five years later, he joined a secret association of patriots known as the Sons of Liberty and took part in the Boston Tea Party. He became a friend of Paul Revere, who in addition to being a silversmith of renown, would become the first manufacturer of copper in America, and the first to develop an open-hearth furnace. So sweet was the tone of the church bells that he cast, that more than seventy of them could still be heard in New England, two centuries later.

But in 1775, Revere was casting cannon, not church bells, for the Colonies were about to go to war, to fight for their independence. Amos Lincoln was one of the first to join that fight, being among the defenders at Bunker Hill. Subsequently, he saw action at Bennington and Brandywine Creek, wintered at Valley Forge, and fought at Monmouth, where he displayed a remarkable mix of courage and common sense and received a battlefield commission, becoming captain of artillery in Colonel Paul Revere's battalion. Subsequently, he would be assigned to Massachusett's governor, John Hancock, as his personal aide.

Colonel Revere had a daughter, with whom Captain Lincoln fell hopelessly in love. As soon as the war was over, he married Deborah Revere, and continued to work, as a carpenter and builder, among those who put up the State House on Boston Common. He and Deborah had a son, Louis, whose own son Frederic Walker Lincoln became mayor of Boston in 1858, at the age of forty-one. During the U. S. Civil War, he was credited with averting in Boston the kind of draft riots that had scourged New York City in 1863. On several occasions he was summoned to Washington for advice, staying in the White House as the guest of his distant cousin Abraham. Frederic Lincoln was to become the most popular mayor in Boston's history, being elected to an unequaled seven consecutive terms. His son, also Frederic Lincoln, committed the unthinkable, leaving Boston to head up the New York office of a prominent export-import firm, H. W. Peabody & Company. He was successful in this endeavor, but to his family's dismay, instead of marrying a proper Boston girl, he fell in love with and married a New York one, Philena Prentice. They moved to Greenwich about the same time that the Rockefellers did, and in time Frederic Lincoln III (Isabel's Freddy) was enrolled in the Class of '21 at Princeton.

At 6'2", Freddy had brown wavy hair, kindly blue eyes, and a gentle sense of humor that reminded many of his most famous relative; indeed, his friends nicknamed him "Abe," and elected him head of the student body at Pomfret School. In the fall of '17, he went down to Princeton, but America was now actively involved in the Great War, and recruiters were coming to all the campuses. Like his forebear Amos, Freddy responded spontaneously to the call of his country, leaving Princeton to enlist. An adept horseman, he chose the cavalry and soon found himself in a training camp at Plattsburg, New York.

When his parents learned what their only son had done without their approval, they were shocked—and infuriated. Using their considerable influence and connections, they arranged for Freddy to be transferred, just as his unit was about to ship out for France. He was assigned to Washington, where he served as a general's driver for the duration. He was not consulted in this decision; his own desires were of no account. Nor were they considered when, after the war was over and he was back at Princeton, his father pulled him out of college to assist him at H. W. Peabody, less than a semester before he was due to graduate. In fairness to his father, who was sixty-six at the time, there were no other sons to carry on the business, and neither was there inherited wealth. The future of the Lincolns—not only his parents, but also Freddy and his four sisters—depended entirely upon the fortunes of H. W. Peabody & Company. His father could neither afford to retire, as many of his friends had, nor could he any longer carry the burden alone.

ISABEL GRADUATED FROM WESTOVER in 1920, and it was time for her to make her debut in society. Officially, this was to introduce the debutante to her parents' friends, but in actuality it would ensure that she associated with young men and women on the approved "list." Isabel's mother, totally taken up with caring for ten-year-old Gladys, had neither the time nor the inclination to guide her daughter through the intricate and demanding ritual of the social season. Fortunately, her Aunt Elsie, across the street, did have the time, and was delighted to take charge of Isabel's debut.

Aunt Elsie loved parties and reveled in great functions, and with the aid of her efficient social secretary she set about organizing her niece's "coming out" year with energy and glee. In those days, it took at least one full year, or even two, to go to all the requisite balls and tea dances, join the Junior League to do good works, and visit Ivy League colleges on the weekends for a ceaseless round of parties. In glittering events and lavish parties, the New York season competed with the London season, but whereas entry to London society was almost entirely a matter of birth, in New York it also depended very much upon wealth.

Aunt Elsie was in her element, and the more she pushed her niece into the social whirl, the more Isabel grew to enjoy it. By then, the Rockefellers had become the best-known family dynasty in America, and anything that a Rockefeller did was sure to attract newspaper attention. This was especially true of tall, regal Isabel, the first Rockefeller debutante of her generation. And while the attention initially embarrassed her, eventually she took it as a matter of course, for every party, every escort, and every trip became an item in the social columns. The Sunday papers, in particular, concentrated on the dazzling festivities of the very rich, as they did their utmost to emulate and if possible surpass the aristocratic, traditional splendor of the English season.

Aunt Elsie even managed to arrange for Isabel to be presented to the King and Queen of England, at the Court of St. James's—the pinnacle to which social ambition could aspire. Isabel would never forget her presentation at court, the number of fittings she had to have for her special white gown, the arm-length white kid gloves with luxurious pearl buttons, the three white feathers that adorned her hair, and the special lessons in how to make a full court curtsy before Their Majesties. When the fabulous event finally occurred, the newspapers back home outdid themselves.

But double-page spreads in the tabloids did not social stature make, and secretly Isabel always felt socially inferior to the English, and also to the older established families of New York and Boston. Convinced that there was more to life than debutante parties, she began to plead with her parents to let her go to college. She had a bent for science and medicine, and given another time and place, she might well have become a doctor. As it was, her heart was set on going to Vassar.

But her parents would hear none of it. She had been to one of the finest finishing schools in the country, and they were of the opinion that it had indeed finished her schooling; further education was unnecessary and a waste of time. So Isabel had to abandon her dream of going to Vassar. But she refused to abandon her desire to learn, and she enrolled herself in a few carefully selected courses at Columbia's Teachers' College, staying in her parents' Park Avenue apartment. To their surprise, she not only persevered with her studies, but under the tutelage of Dr. Jean Broadhurst, who would be her lifelong mentor and friend, became an eminently capable bacteriologist.

By no means all of her time was spent at the microscope, for she grew to love a good party as much as her Aunt Elsie, and took delight in the attentions of the handsome young men who surrounded her. Four separate times with four handsome swains, she bore a flashing gem on the ring finger of her left hand, but each time she would hesitate before making it official and setting a date. And sure enough, each time she would meet someone else and have to extricate herself from the current engagement and embark on another. With practice, she became quite adept at this, and each time she would report to Freddy Lincoln, telling him in lavish detail about her new romance, how handsome her latest fiancé was and how much they enjoyed doing the same things together.

If Freddy felt a jealous response, he never let it show. All he did was nod kindly and say that if the new young man was going to make her happy, that was all that mattered. Smiling wanly, Isabel would hide the disappointment she felt that Freddy didn't object, let alone beg her not to get engaged to anyone else.

It seemed as though this might go on indefinitely, but after Christmas 1924, Isabel went down to "Overhills," the 3,000-acre plantation in North Carolina which her father and several of his friends had bought for fox hunting. Adjacent to Fort Bragg, a major army base, it was 35 miles east of the resort of Southern Pines. On the plantation they had built a forty-room clubhouse and a nine-hole golf course, but after a while her father built his own house, next to the clubhouse. This he called "The Covert," and here he could entertain his own houseguests privately. The Covert was managed by an impeccable English butler named Alabaster, who, no matter what the temperature or humidity, was always dressed in a cutaway coat, wing collar, black bow tie, and white gloves. Overhills was ideal fox-hunting country, and its pack of hounds could regularly be heard baying over the rolling countryside. Isabel loved to go down there, not only for the riding and quail shooting, but for the chance to relax with good friends, of whom there was always an abundance, to keep her and her latest fiancé company. This New Year's group was especially lively and cheerful, and it included the recently married Stapely and Polly Lincoln Wonham and Hope Lincoln Coombe, with her good-looking husband, Reggie. And as both his sisters were going to be there, Isabel also invited Freddy Lincoln.

One frosty evening, the house party was happily ensconced around a huge, blazing hearth in the living room. Everyone was tired but happy after a full day that had begun with a dawn fox hunt, followed by golf and an afternoon of quail shooting that had provided enough birds for dinner. Now they sat about, reading, gossiping, playing bridge, and yawning. Isabel was stretched out on a sofa, her long legs up on the cushions and a book open in her lap, when she heard Freddy's low voice in her ear: "Let's go for a walk."

"Oh, Freddy, no—it's too cold out, and I'm too tired! Besides, I've got to look after my guests."

"Isabel, come *now!*" Startled at the note of command in his voice, she set the book aside and glanced over at Hope, who had heard and now nodded approvingly. Reluctantly, Isabel got up and left the comfort of the hearth, went out in the hall and donned her heavy, fur-lined coat. She said nothing to her current fiancé, who was deeply involved in a bridge game and must have been quite confident that there was no reason for concern; after all, Isabel was wearing his four-carat sapphire engagement ring.

Freddy pushed open the heavy front door for her, and the two of them stepped out into the chill night air.

"Look!" Isabel exclaimed, "Look at our breath—it looks like white smoke!"

Laughing, they started puffing together, watching the clouds of their breath in the air. Above them, the moon was nearly full, and as they strolled along the edge of the golf course, Freddy took Isabel's hand.

"Listen," he whispered, and they stopped. The hooting of an owl broke the stillness of the night. She smiled up at him, and he drew her to him and kissed her. She kissed him back, and they stood embracing for a long time. "You know," he murmured, releasing her, "we belong together. We always have. Will you marry me?"

"Oh, yes, yes," she replied, tears in her eyes. Then she leaned back, cocked her head, and looked at him. "How long have you known?"

He chuckled. "Ever since that first day, skating on the pond, when I thumped you with my fist."

"Then *why* did you keep letting me get engaged to other people?"

He smiled. "You were having so much fun running to all those parties, I felt you had to get it out of your system. I wanted a real wife—not someone who was forever looking forward to the next party." He laughed. "I guess I can tell you now: my sisters kept a pretty close eye on you, whenever I was away." He sighed happily. "Well, it was worth the wait." They embraced again, holding one another till the moon and the stars and the hoot owl all seemed to vanish. Then, reluctantly, they walked back to the house, hand in hand.

# 3

---

ISABEL SAID NOTHING to her fiancé that night, nor did she break the news to him in the next few days before she sailed to Europe, accompanying her father on one of his two-month business trips, as she had several times before. But she determined to write him from the Continent, to give him ample opportunity to adjust, before she returned home.

Isabel loved the drive down to the Cunard pier, the first glimpse of the huge transatlantic liner, and the first of its deep-throated whistles. Their luggage had been sent ahead, and what awaited them now was a magnificent bon voyage party in their staterooms. A swarm of reporters and photographers was clustered at the foot of the gangway, but much as Isabel's father might have wanted to brush past them, Standard Oil was at last beginning to receive favorable treatment in the press, and he was loath to jeopardize it. He was, therefore, his most charming and gracious self, talking with them about his business trip to Europe, and when one of the photographers requested that he stand by the rail for a picture, he gladly obliged.

The picture appeared in the papers, and it showed Percy Rockefeller as he was—kindly and courteous, bespectacled, and going a bit bald. He was dressed in a conservative suit from his Saville Row tailor, and his grey-and-white cravat was adorned with a pearl stickpin, which gleamed in the sun. He was relaxed and smiling; one could almost catch the aroma of the bay rum he used after shaving.

At last the gentlemen of the press were satisfied, and Percy and Isabel now repaired to their adjoining staterooms, where friends were already celebrating their departure. Isabel's mother was there, and she had seen to it that there were many baskets of delicacies from her kitchen for the party—chicken sandwiches, deviled eggs, and the special sugar cookies that Mary the cook produced with unfailing skill. There was also hot cocoa and coffee to drink, and cool sarsaparilla. As usual, there was nothing alcoholic—nor would there have been, had Prohibition *not* been in effect, for the Percy Rockefellers strongly disapproved of drink.

The staterooms were jammed with happy well-wishers. Isabel's friends had arrived in force, including her oblivious fiancé. But the one face she wanted to see was not present. Freddy's father would not hear of his son leaving his work at H. W. Peabody to go to some frivolous farewell party.

The ship's high-pitched whistle now joined with its deep bass, to announce the last call for all visitors to disembark. At last the goodbyes were completed, their friends trooped down the gangway, and were now tiny figures, waving up at them. Isabel waved back, as tugs nudged the huge liner out of her berth. The clamor of the dock was soon behind them, and not long after, the tugs hooted farewell themselves. Isabel could feel the mighty engines of the liner far below decks, as they settled into the steady thrum that would accompany them for the next eight days.

In the haze of the weak noonday sun, they could just make out the Statue of Liberty, holding her torch high to welcome newcomers to America. For a while they just looked at her without speaking, and then Isabel put her hand on her father's arm and said, "I have something to tell you: I'm in love with Freddy Lincoln, and I'm going to marry him."

He turned to her, beaming. "Well, at last you're showing some good sense!"

She grinned, delighted at his response. "I can't tell you how happy I feel inside," she went on, "and how peaceful, too."

Her father put his arm around her. "And I can't tell *you* how long I've been waiting to hear you say that," he said softly, clearing his throat and looking away. "I like Freddy Lincoln; I always have. He's a good sportsman, and he'll be a good husband.'' His voice broke, as he added, ''I'm so happy for you, Isabel.''

They stood together at the rail without speaking, until well after land was no longer in sight.

IT WAS EARLY SPRING when they returned, and in June the engagement of Isabel Rockefeller to Frederic Walker Lincoln III was formally announced. The press had a field day. She was photographed, interviewed, and talked about everywhere, and headlines like

## LOVE IS WORTH MORE THAN MILLIONS

appeared on front pages everywhere. The wedding date was September 26, and as it approached, their ''almost royal romance'' caught the imagination of reporters and editors alike, and they outdid themselves in exuberant, gushing coverage of every detail of the forthcoming wedding.

For Isabel, the one great disappointment was that her mother, who had long planned a three-month Grand Tour of Europe for Isabel's three younger sisters, would not change her plans ''and disappoint the girls.''

This meant that she would have no part in all the elaborate preparation and planning for the wedding; indeed, she would arrive home barely ten days before the event itself.

Perhaps she was determined not to disappoint Gladys; possibly she was jealous of the fact that her glamorous, globetrotting daughter was clearly the favorite, not only of Percy, but also of her own father, James Stillman, who had doted on Isabel right up until his death. Another factor might have been that she simply did not feel up to coping with all the intricate social subtleties that would inevitably be involved, and which she was grateful to leave totally in the hands of her capable older sister, Elsie, and her redoubtable social secretary.

Whatever her mother's reasons, Isabel felt abandoned in her hour of greatest need by the one person she most wanted to share this precious time with. So deeply was she hurt, that she would never speak of this prenuptial period, which was traditionally one of the most exciting times in a young bride's life. She took her mother's deliberate absence as rejection—how else could she take it? And from that time forth, she would never feel close to her mother again.

THE ROCKEFELLER-LINCOLN UNION was to be unquestionably the wedding of the year, and arrangements proceeded on the scale of a royal wedding. According to the newspapers, seven thousand invitations were sent out, and some four thousand acceptances came back. Special trains had to be booked, to bring guests from New York to Greenwich, where they would be met by a fleet of limousines. Fortunately, Christ Church in Greenwich, of which the Rockefellers and their friends were at least nominal members, was of sufficient size to handle such a congregation. To perform the ceremony, Isabel had asked for her beloved rector from Westover days, Dr. John Lewis. But here, Freddy's mother began to take an active role in the planning, insisting that her own minister from First Presbyterian Church in New York should also take part.

The wedding day dawned crisp and clear, and as Isabel started down the aisle on her father's arm, she could see lilies everywhere. (Wadley & Smythe, New York's carriage-trade florists, had done the impossible, producing a churchful of Easter lilies in September.) Waiting at the altar were sixteen ushers in cutaways and striped trousers, and six bridesmaids in blue chiffon. Her sister Win, the maid of honor, wore pink chiffon, as did her sister-in-law Anna.

Isabel herself wore a magnificent gown of point-appliqué lace over white satin, and at the cuffs of long satin sleeves hung beautiful rose-point lace, which had been in the Lincoln family for generations, and which Freddy's mother had insisted that she wear. Her long veil, also of rose-point lace, had been bought by James Stillman for his daughter Elsie's wedding and was traditionally to be worn by every Stillman and Rockefeller bride thereafter.

At last she could see Freddy's beaming face, and standing next to him, his best man, Godfrey Rockefeller, was beaming, too. At that, Isabel herself grinned, recalling how Godfrey had come up to Freddy less than a week before, and told him, "Look, old sport, I don't know quite how to put this, but I'm frankly surprised that you didn't ask me to be an usher. After all, we've been—"

"Godfrey!" Freddy had interrupted him. "I assumed you knew that you were my best man! Couldn't possibly be anyone else!"

The church was filled to overflowing, and in the second pew on the bride's side was the legendary John D. Rockefeller, now eighty-six years old. At the reception at Owenoke afterward, he would take delight in telling everyone how pleased he was that his great-niece had chosen this day to get married—for on this day exactly 70 years before, he had started his first job.

THE NEW MRS. FREDERIC LINCOLN and her husband drove off in a car appropriately adorned with old shoes tied to the back, but when they reached their first night's destination in Hawthorne, New York, to their dismay they found the place mobbed with reporters—someone had leaked their destination. It was too late to change their plans, and so they spent a miserable first night. In the morning, they headed for the Adirondacks, specifically to an old log cabin on Upper Saranac Lake. Known simply as "The Cabin," it was the oldest dwelling in those old mountains, and President Cleveland had honeymooned there in 1886. Aunt Elsie rented it regularly, and here they had ten days of uninterrupted peace and quiet.

But only ten days, for Freddy's father would grant him no more. H. W. Peabody & Company had business for him to attend to in South America, and had booked passage for him aboard the liner S.S. *Essequibo*, sailing for Rio and points south on October 17. As he would be gone for a total of three months, Freddy insisted on taking his new bride with him, and down to the boat came all the family to see them off, as well as the usual retinue of reporters and photographers.

The trip began pleasantly enough, but after a few days Isabel found herself getting sicker and sicker. It was hard to believe her malady was *mal de mer*, for on all the many cruises she had taken, she had never once suffered from seasickness. Instead of getting better, it got worse, so that by the time they reached Buenos Aires, Freddy made her see a doctor, speculating that she might have contracted some tropical disease while they were in Chile.

Surprised when the doctor told them that he had good news for them, they were shocked at what it was: Isabel was pregnant. But how could she be? Soon after their engagement, while her mother was in Europe with Win, Faith, and Gladys, Isabel had gone to a gynecologist for a checkup. He had informed her that she had a tipped uterus, which would need to be straightened. It was a minor operation, but in the meantime she would be unable to conceive.

Obviously, the gynecologist's diagnosis could not have been more wrong, and Isabel would blame her mother for this: had she been home, she would have made sure her daughter went to the best gynecologist available—instead of someone who was apparently little more than a quack.

When they finally got back to New York and set up house in their little apartment, Isabel, constantly weak and sick, began her long struggle through the cold, raw winter. Freddy continued to be as kind and loving to her as he naturally would, but for the normally lively and energetic Isabel, the life of an invalid was a desolating experience.

One day in early spring, 1926, my mother woke with a high fever. Taking one look at her flushed face and burning eyes, Freddy rushed to the telephone and called her obstetrician, one of the best men in New York. The latter arrived as quickly as he could and examined Isabel carefully. Then he called Freddy out of the room and said quietly, "It's serious—very serious. I still don't know exactly what it is, but her temperature is 104°. We're going to try to save her, but there is no way we can save the baby."

Freddy was stunned, and the doctor told him to keep applying cold compresses, while he called for specialists. Soon the small apartment was crowded with consultants, oxygen apparatus, and a team of highly trained nurses. But still, no one could explain exactly what was the matter with her. At this point, Isabel's mother arrived and took command. With her, she brought Rossie, who had been the head nurse in charge of the team that for years had fought for Gladys's life and finally succeeded in saving her. Isabel's mother had come to rely on Rossie in many ways, and she had retained her services, more as a personal companion than for her medical expertise.

But expertise Rossie did indeed have, and noting Isabel's delirium, she announced that they had to get her temperature down *immediately*, by bathing her constantly in icewater. The whole family loved and trusted Rossie, and now, as she took command, calm and reassurance replaced chaos and despair. Isabel's mother rolled up her sleeves, too; her daughter's life was in jeopardy, just as Glad's had been years before, and she would not leave her side until the crisis was passed.

Though Isabel's eyes were closed and her mind wandering, her mother gently stroked her brow and spoke an unending flow of comforting words.

All day and long into the night, Rossie, the nurses, and the doctors worked on. They considered Isabel too ill to risk moving to the hospital, and although the best physicians, care, equipment were at hand, they still could not ascertain what was wrong.

Early the next morning, Rossie was looking down at the drawn face of her patient, when she thought she saw something like a rash on her forehead. Touching it, she found that the forehead was cool—the temperature had broken! Gently, she lifted the damp sheets and opened Isabel's nightgown, to find that she had indeed a rash all over—one that Rossie recognized at once as measles. Although it was not the three-day German variety that was so devastating to a fetus, the conventional strain nonetheless could be quite dangerous, whenever it attacked adults. But Isabel's temperature was down, and she was going to recover. Rossie sent a nurse to summon the exhausted doctor, who had retired for a brief sleep; together they examined and concluded that indeed the worst was over.

Their relief was shortlived. No sooner had the fever broken, and the crisis ended, than they found themselves plunged into another: Isabel suddenly went into labor. Frantically, the nurses scrambled about, gathering towels and sheets, and boiling water to sterilize whatever instruments might be needed. The labor was short and violent, and Isabel was already so weakened that beyond a few drops of chloroform on a gauze pad, the docters could not risk administering any anesthetic.

Freddy and Isabel's mother were at her bedside, as she gasped and screamed in agony. At that point, they would gladly have given their lives for hers, if possible, but there was nothing they could do, no one to whom they could turn.

An incubator was rushed in, for if the tiny baby, barely seven months in the womb, lived, it would weigh no more than four pounds. Suddenly, amidst the gasps of pain and the curt commands of the doctors, another sound was heard: the cry of a newborn babe. Isabel heard it and looked at the doctor, who smiled and told her that she had a new son. "Oh, please, please let me have him," she begged.

But Isabel's mother, now that her daughter was safe, took charge. "No!" she commanded. "Certainly not! You are much too ill. The

baby may not be here with you,'' she announced in a voice that brooked
no challenge.

"But I heard him cry,'' sobbed Isabel. "I want my baby! Just let me
hold him for a moment!"

Her mother refused, and the doctors acceded to the senior
Rockefeller's demand. Freddy Lincoln said nothing, anxious only that
Isabel should have the best care possible.

Despite everything that was against him, the baby seemed to be
doing well. But the next morning, without consulting her daughter
or the doctors, Isabel's mother summoned an ambulance and had
the prematurely born infant taken to the hospital. It was a cold,
windy April morning, and the little flame of life was snuffed out
on the way. Years later, Isabel would speculate that her mother
was concerned about avoiding even the breath of scandal. If the baby
lived, there was bound to be gossip, and some might judge her for having left her daughter without maternal supervision for three months
before the wedding.

"If only I could have held him,'' Isabel would say wistfully, when
she recalled the painful incident, "my son, my only son.'' And then
she would say no more.

The tiny body of the next—and last—Frederic Walker Lincoln was
laid to rest under a yew tree in the Lincoln family graveyard in
Woodlawn Cemetery in Yonkers. There was no headstone, not even a
marker in the ground. Isabel wanted one, with just his name on it and
the date. But her mother would not allow it, and her grief-stricken
in-laws bowed to her will.

Isabel, however, would never forget him—nor forgive her mother
for what had happened.

# 4

---

DAZED WITH SHOCK and grief over losing their first child, Isabel and Freddy picked up the pieces of their life and carried on. Freddy had plenty to keep him busy at H. W. Peabody, and Isabel turned with renewed interest to Dr. Broadhurst's laboratory. But life has a way of evening things out: to their surprise, within a year Isabel was pregnant again —this time with me.

Once again, as her delivery time approached, things began to happen quickly. That August in 1927, my parents were living on the Owenoke estate, in the "Corner House"—a small colonial farmhouse that my grandparents had given their daughter and her new husband. Late one afternoon, when my father arrived home from work, my mother informed him that she did not feel well and suspected that her labor was imminent. Immediately, they called Grandma Rockefeller, who said that she would be by with the limousine as quickly as possible, and she went to alert Gus, their chauffeur. Once again, Grandma was taking charge, which was fine with my parents; indeed, it never occurred to them that it could have been otherwise.

Gus drove into New York as rapidly as he could without jolting his passengers, and within an hour they were pulling up at the entrance to Miss Lippincott's Sanitarium (the only place to have a baby). My mother was whisked off to her room, and my father settled down with the evening newspaper, while Grandma took out her knitting. Five minutes later, my father noticed a figure being hurriedly wheeled down the hall, and went back to his paper; it couldn't be Isabel, who had just arrived. A few more minutes passed, and he looked up to see a white-smocked doctor smiling down at him. "Mr. Lincoln? You have a new baby daughter!"

"*What?*"

"Yes, your wife's fine, and she's just had a healthy eight-pound girl; would you like to see her?"

"You bet!" said my father, jumping to his feet, and Grandma was right behind him.

My mother was already back in her room and holding me by her side. Overjoyed to see us, my father came over and kissed her cheek, and looked down at me. "You were certainly in a hurry!" he exclaimed, chuckling, and he would repeat those words to me many times over the years.

Just then, Grandma, standing behind him, spoke. "Her name is Isabel," she said. It was not a suggestion; it was a declaration of fact—just as it had been when James Stillman pronounced those words to my grandmother, when my mother was born.

My mother just nodded, and my father said nothing, as Grandma now bent over me. Perhaps because of guilt over what had happened with the first baby, or over her neglect of my mother during the Gladys years—possibly because I was now the fourth Isabel and the third in a direct mother-daughter chain—whatever her motivation, Grandma had determined that I would be her own, special grandchild, to love and to cherish. She may also have sensed intuitively that I could be the means of repairing the broken relationship with her daughter and of making up to her for all the years of neglect.


FOR THE NEXT THREE WEEKS (which in those days was the normal period for postnatal convalescence), my mother rested and enjoyed her sojourn at Miss Lippincott's. My father came to see her every day after work, often bringing flowers, and it was to be one of the happier times in their young married lives. Even the bill for my arrival brought a smile: it was only $90. Everything had gone so smoothly that the doctors, perhaps because they had charged a staggering $10,000 for the previous delivery (which even with today's insurance coverage would be exorbitant), charged only a nominal amount. It may also have been out of guilt, when they realized that my young parents, and not my grandparents, had had to pay the first bill. For such was the control exercised over my parents by both of their families that whatever money they would inherit would not be theirs until after the death of their parents. They had to make a go of it on Freddy's salary, which though sufficient for their daily needs, was hardly enough for sudden emergencies. The public, of course, had no awareness of this and naturally assumed that anyone bearing the family name must be—rich as Rockefeller.

At the end of August, Grandma's car arrived to bring my mother and me and my baby nurse home. No sooner had we pulled up at the Corner House than I started screaming—and there was nothing that anyone could do to persuade me to stop. According to my mother's account, I apparently kept this up day and night, driving everyone to distraction. Both my parents lost a lot of sleep, and my father became so rundown that he caught a cold which developed into pneumonia with complications of pleurisy—providing his mother with just the opportunity she had been waiting for.

For Grandma Lincoln had never been happy with her only son's marriage. It is doubtful that she would have been pleased with anyone he married, but she considered my mother superficial, as well as a social newcomer, like all the Rockefellers. Proud of her membership in the D.A.R. (the Daughters of the American Revolution), she traced her own lineage back through the Prentice family, whose patriot strain was at least as long as the Lincolns'. In addition, the Prentices had always put great stock in the development of the intellect; Grandma Lincoln and her brothers and sister spoke Greek and Latin at the dinner table. Small wonder, then, that she looked down her nose at the flighty young Rockefeller woman who had captured her beloved Freddy.

Not that my mother particularly cared what she thought, for she had a strong will and character of her own. The contest between the two would go on for years. Like a mother hen, Grandma Lincoln wanted her children as close about her as possible, even to the point of insisting that they and their spouses come to her for dinner every Sunday evening *and* every Thursday evening, without fail. My father and his four sisters never questioned this, but my mother felt no such obligation, and as often as she dared, she begged off with excuses of ill health.

Were this the extent of Grandma Lincoln's possessiveness, it would be extreme but not bizarre. But she went further. The moment my father developed fluid in his lungs, she decided that she had been patient long enough. Suddenly one morning, she appeared with her car and chauffeur, packed him up, and took him with her, convinced that only she could properly nurse him back to health.

My mother was furious, and especially so, because her own mother, who would have been a match for her mother-in-law, was off again in Europe, with her three sisters. Of this Grandma Lincoln was well aware, and she quickly capitalized on her advantage, taking her son north to Maine, to recuperate in the peace and quiet of the summer home they had rented at the social resort of Prout's Neck.

Years later, recalling this episode, my mother would declare through thin lips that, had she then possessed any money of her own, she would have left my father at that moment. As it was, beside herself with anger and hurt, she was left alone to care for her squalling daughter. And she *was* alone, for like the Lincolns, practically everyone had fled the dreadful humidity of Greenwich in late August.

But all was not lost. For her Aunt Elsie, who had provided help and support to her in the past, now sensed that something was terribly wrong. She came back to Greenwich to see how my mother was, and in the first five minutes, my mother, sobbing, told her what had happened, and Aunt Elsie, outraged, fired off a telegram to my father, commanding him to return to his wife and baby. At once, my father left his mother and came home, and Aunt Elsie, knowing just what this fragile marriage now needed, sent the three of us off to The Cabin in the Adirondacks. The instant I was on board the train, I stopped screaming, and never screamed again—as an infant.

AS THE NIGHTS GREW COLDER and the leaves started to turn, my father became well enough to return to work, and we moved back to Greenwich. Grandma Rockefeller arrived from Europe with my three aunts, and life settled into a routine that would remain unchanged for the next two years. Between Grandma Lincoln and Grandma Rockefeller, the struggle for control over my parents continued unabated. We spent the summers in the Corner House at Owenoke, and the winters in an apartment in New York, directly across the street from my father's parents.

My earliest personal recollection of the Lincolns was of Grandpa Lincoln giving me a beautiful set of pastel chalks, when I was two and a half. He promptly showed me how to use them, seating me on his knee and drawing me a picture of a police dog that really did look like our dog Kebo (named after one of the ships that sailed to South America for H. W. Peabody & Company).

Grandma Lincoln had perfect posture, as befitted her social status. She was proud of her intellectual pursuits, but she also put great emphasis on regular religious observance and instruction, undoubtedly influenced by the fact that she numbered among her ancestors the Reverend Solomon Prentice. This eighteenth-century worthy had been galvanized into the ministry by America's first great evangelist, George Whitefield; indeed, he had become so ardent a Christian that he had lost two churches through excess of fervor. Ever since then, the Prentice family held daily prayers, and in my father's childhood, Grandma Lincoln insisted that he attend church four times on Sundays (with the inevitable result that, as an adult, he refused to go to church at all).

With the birth of her first child, Grandma Lincoln lost most of her hearing, and this affliction was to torment her for the rest of her life. She had a little tortoiseshell box that she used as a hearing aid, and if you spoke directly into it, she could hear you. But as she grew older and could not hear other people's conversations, she became suspicious, convinced that they were talking about her.

But there was another side to Grandma Lincoln, which gave balance to her portrait. For there was often a twinkle in her eye, and the charm evident in my father and his four sisters must have come from her. I remember her taking me to church (we would ride down Fifth Avenue on the open upper level of the double-decker bus), and to the American Museum of Natural History. But in addition to feeding the spirit and the mind, she did not neglect the body; after a sufficiency of gazing at dusty dinosaur skeletons, she would indulge me with an enormous banana split. And at her formal Sunday dinners for the family, she loved to take a hard roll, break it in half, pull out the soft inside, knead it into tiny figures, put them back into their hollowed-out "cave," and then make up a story about them.

IN THAT SUMMER OF '29, the American economy was booming, and the Roaring Twenties gave every indication of becoming the Roaring Thirties. My parents' friends were making killings in the stock market—but their good fortune did not appear to extend to us. For while the import-export firm of H. W. Peabody & Company was successful, its profits were hardly excessive. Grandpa Lincoln's partner grew too old to carry on and had to retire, which suddenly put a tremendous financial burden on the shoulders of Grandpa Lincoln, who was himself now seventy-three. For he had to buy out his partner's half of the business, and it took every cent he had. No matter; the profits, though not large, were adequate. . . .

And then came September and the long-overdue correction in the skyrocketing stock market, culminating on Black Tuesday—October 29th, 1929. On that day the stock market crashed, and investors who had leveraged their capital to the hilt, buying on 10 percent margin, found themselves totally wiped out. The plunge would continue for two years, until all listed securities had lost an average of two-thirds their value. The economic catastrophe spread rapidly around the world. Currencies collapsed, banking systems failed, and all manufacturing, and therefore exporting and importing, withered. The Great Depression, which would last nearly a decade, had begun. Almost every American was profoundly affected by it, and many lives were forever changed.

The immense, unrelenting strain that it put on H. W. Peabody & Company proved more than Grandpa Lincoln's weakened heart could bear. In April of 1931, he died, and his widow was forced to move into a smaller, less expensive apartment, on 62nd Street, just off Park Avenue. She insisted that my parents also give up their apartment and move in across the street from her, which they did. Now my father had to carry on alone at H. W. Peabody, and if anything, the pressure increased, for his mother, his sisters, and his own family were depending on him. He developed a spastic colon and would be plagued with stomach trouble for the rest of his life.

The one bright spot in these dark years was the birth of my first baby sister, in January of 1930. She was named Calista—a Lincoln name since mine had come from the Rockefeller side—and she arrived six weeks early. She needed blood, and my father donated it, and intuitively I sensed that thereafter she was my father's favorite—a place which had been uncontestably mine.

There was something else about Cal—she was exceptionally beautiful. She had huge blue eyes and, according to my parents and their friends, the cutest dimples anyone had ever seen. But her crowning glory was her radiant blond curls; they were natural, and they were everywhere. And people were practically speechless when they admired them—but not entirely speechless, unfortunately. Day in and day out, I heard about those marvelous curls and instinctively reached up to my own straight and stringy hair.

As soon as she was old enough, our nurses would take us for walks together in Central Park. In her white fur jacket, Cal would be so stunning that people passing by would invariably stop and exclaim at her beauty. I wore a fur coat, too, on these little strolls, but mine was brown. I would smile at these strangers as hard as I could, but they never seemed to notice me, and after a while I stopped smiling.

The worst, though, was the response of my grandmothers—*my* grandmothers—to Cal. I was especially devastated by Grandma Rockefeller, who had created the pink-and-white bedroom for me and had let me climb up on her and Grandpa's big four-poster and share breakfast with them, who had taken me on secret garden excursions, and who loved to tell me fairy stories. In so many ways, Grandma Rockefeller had let her young namesake know that she was special. . . and now she was actually planning to have a full-length portrait painted of Cal, who was only three. I was almost twice as old as Cal, and yet it had never occurred to Grandma to have one painted of me. Every afternoon at two o'clock, the lady portrait artist would arrive at our apartment, push aside the shiny mahogany dining room table, and set up a wooden box in its place. Cal, who was already as charming as she was beautiful, would come and pose on the box in the lovely salmon-pink party dress that my mother had ordered for her from Paris. With a broad collar of rose-point lace, the dress was made of the finest organdy and hung in soft pleats about her, showing off the cute little dimples in her knees. Seemingly aware of what a breathtaking vision she made, Cal would stand with her elbows bent and her hands behind her back, smiling her adorable smile. It got so I could hardly bear to look at her.

I kept hoping that the artist would tell me that she was going to put me in the picture, too, but she never did. Finally, one dismal afternoon in March, it all became too much. This dumb painting was taking forever! I sat in my room, pasting pictures in my scrapbook for what seemed like hours, listening for the sound of the dining room table being put back. At last the session was over, and the front door closed. Hurrying into the dining room, I shouted, "Cal! You've got to come to my room right away!" I ran down the hall, knowing that she would follow, as fast as her chubby little legs with their adorable, dimpled knees could carry her. When we reached my room, I quietly closed the door behind us. Our Scottish nannies, who shared these rooms with us, were both in the kitchen, having their afternoon tea—a leisurely, indispensable ritual that would keep them occupied for at least another twenty minutes.

"Sit down on the floor, Cal," I said, and she did so, trusting me completely. Until now, I had given her no reason not to; in fact, despite the difference in our personalities—mine unsure, awkward, and easily hurt; hers sweet-tempered and serenely confident that everyone loved her—we got along surprisingly well.

In the bathroom was a small stepstool that I used to stand on, to brush my teeth. I pulled it into the bedroom, over to my nurse Mina's bureau, and climbed up on it, to reach her top drawer. I wasn't tall enough to see in the drawer, but I could feel what was in there, and soon found what I wanted: her wicker sewing basket that she used for mending. In it was a pair of sharp scissors, much sharper than the ones I used to cut out clothes for my paper dolls, and these I quickly extracted.

"Now, Cal," I said to her softly but urgently, "I'm afraid that there are some bees' nests in your hair. We've really got to get them out, before the bees wake up and sting you."

Cal looked at me, her eyes widening. She had been stung by a bee last summer, and was terrified to even hear one buzzing. "Oh, Bel," she whispered, so as not to wake the bees, "help me! Please help me!"

I nodded reassuringly, and putting my finger to my lips, whispered back: "You can't see where they are, but I can, and I'll cut them out for you." Relief flooded over her, and she whimpered gratefully, as I began my work. "Don't worry; it'll be all right," I soothed her, "just close your eyes and sit perfectly still."

She did as I bid her, and I knelt beside her, my heart pounding, for by this time I had convinced myself that I was actually saving my little sister from a deadly swarm. *Snip, snip, snip*—blond curls cascaded to the floor. It was so much easier than I had imagined! Everywhere I saw a curl, I snipped, and in no time, we were in the middle of a soft, golden ring of them.

On and on I went, until Cal's scalp started to show through, and I stopped to survey my handiwork. "The bees are almost out," I comforted her, but now as I walked around her, reality began to assail me. Cal looked awful! All her curls were gone—and most of the rest of her hair, too. But hadn't she pleaded with me to save her from the bees?

I picked up one of the curls and made a half-hearted attempt to stick it back on her head, but it fell limply to the floor. And now the full impact of what I had done hit me. Frantically, I gathered up the curls and stuffed them under the corner of the brown rug. Waves of fear and guilt swept over me. "Cal!" I cried. "I love you! I love you!" I ran to her and hugged her, but it was too late.

Just then, Mina opened the door. For a moment, she was too stunned to speak, then she wailed, *"Help, help, help!"* In an instant, my mother was at the door, with Isa the cook, and Anne the chambermaid. They just stared, as thunderstruck as Mina had been.

At last my mother came into the room and scooped Cal up in her arms. There were tears in her eyes; it was the only time I had ever seen her cry. She carried Cal out of the room, and Mina and Isa and Anne followed her, leaving me alone and desolate.

I was never punished for this episode, never given a chance to sob and say I was sorry and be forgiven. No one ever mentioned it again, nor could I bear to bring it up myself. I was left with a crushing burden of guilt and with the unspoken—and unresolved—jealousy which had prompted the act.

Years passed, and while it receded from my conscious memory, it remained present in my unconscious, and many years passed before I would again know inner peace.

# 5
---

THROUGH THE PILLOW I could hear the muffled sound of train wheels in the night, as the Pullman coach gently rocked its other passengers to sleep. But there was no way that I would sleep this night, for nothing on earth was more exciting than an overnight train ride. My grandmother had forbidden me to raise the window shade next to the lower bunk in our drawing room, for if I did, I would stay up all night, watching the little stations come and go, the crossing barriers dinging their lonely warnings, and the weary baggage handlers moving the huge wagons down the platforms when we stopped. She knew that I would be enthralled by the steam escaping from beneath the train, and the night conductor's distant ''Booard!'' as he swung his lantern to signal the engineer. She knew that I would count the chugs of the steam engine, as it tried to gather momentum on the icy rails, and would be watching to see at what moment I could first detect our forward motion. And she was right, for I lay with my head against the pillow, peering out through the three-inch sliver of window; somehow that shade seemed to get stuck just short of going *all* the way down.

We were on our way to Overhills, in North Carolina, where my parents had first spoken of their love for one another. It was March of 1933 (two months after the curl incident), and my parents were on another steamship to South America. There would be little pleasure on this cruise, for the Depression had reached its nadir, and H. W.

Peabody & Company was failing. With staggering debts and bankruptcy imminent, my father was embarked on an emergency damage-control mission, selling or closing its branch offices in all foreign countries save England, in a desperate effort to keep the company afloat.

They would be gone three months, and Grandma Rockefeller decided to take Cal and me and Mina down to Overhills, until they returned. We were in two drawing rooms at opposite ends of the same train car—Grandma and me in one, and Cal and the nurse Mina in the other. As the night hours passed, the silhouettes of the trees flying by began to have leaves; we were in Virginia now, where spring was several weeks ahead of back home, and I could almost smell the honeysuckle and the Southern pines that were so much a part of Overhills. I couldn't wait to get there! The horses, the dogs, the good food, the gently undulating countryside all covered with pine and scrub oak. . . Overhills was my idea of heaven on earth.

I must have dozed off, for now the sky was definitely lightening, and I could make out colors; dawn would soon be here, and I wasn't tired at all. At last the sun rose, and while I couldn't see it, because it was on the other side of the train, I could see the long shadows it cast. Any moment now, the train would begin to slow, and we would hear the magical call of the conductor: "Raleigh, Raleigh!" That was our signal to get up and get dressed, for our stop, Sanford, was the next on the main line from New York to Palm Beach, and there was just time to get ready. Sure enough, the telephone poles did seem to be passing by more slowly, and now I heard the whoosh of air, as the door at the end of the car opened. "Raleigh," called the conductor in a tone which would awaken but not startle, and I quickly pulled the shade all the way down, before Grandma, who preferred the upper berth, could peer down into mine. The train was in the Raleigh yard now, shunting back and forth, collecting other cars from other trains with passengers bound for Palm Beach. I finished dressing and looked up at Grandma, who nodded her approval, as she bent to tie my shoes. We both looked forward to the day when I could tie my own without help. As she finished, we pulled out, and now she left to make sure that her other charges were ready and the porter alerted.

Before we knew it, the telephone poles once again began passing more slowly. I pressed my head against the window, to see as far ahead as possible and catch the first glimpse of the approaching platform. There it was, and the little white sign on the end read

*Sanford*—at last! With great commotion, we got off the train. There was Mr. Bruce waiting for us, grinning from ear to ear. He had originally come to handle the horses and hounds, but he and his wife Thelma were soon given the responsibility for the overall management of Overhills, and indeed, with his genial disposition and courtly manner, he seemed the embodiment of the Southern plantation owner. Needless to say, he got on famously with my grandparents—and me, too. Now, as I jumped down from the train, spurning the porter's proffered hand, he swept me up in his arms and exclaimed, "Good to see you, Miss Bel! Patches, the pony, is going to be awfully glad to see you, too."

"Oh, and am I going to be glad to see him!" I almost shouted.

Taking our bags from the station platform, he loaded them into the back of the wood-paneled Ford station wagon, which I had always assumed was made expressly for this purpose. When he was finished, we all piled in, and set off on the hour-long drive. I loved this drive every bit as much as the train ride, and watched with rapt attention as each familiar landmark passed. We were in tobacco country now, and in the distance I could see the big curing barns, where the leaves would be hung to age. It was poor country; the barns leaned and sagged, and the houses were dilapidated, with scrawny hens running about, worn-out cars rusting away in back, and an occasional tethered goat struggling to find some grass in the sandy soil.

On and on we drove, over the hills and dales, which I assumed had given the plantation its name. Finally, we reached the red clay road that meant there were only five more minutes to go. I could now make out the tall water tower in the distance, and on the left appeared the club's massive white hunting stables, with doors and windows trimmed in red and black. More than thirty horses were stabled here, with at least as many hounds kenneled beyond. We turned right and headed in on the Overhills road, passing the riding stables and twenty more horses on the right. My grandfather's interest in horseflesh had never faded, and he had introduced a Western quarterhorse strain into their bloodline. As a result, the Overhills riding horses were somewhat smaller and more agile than the hunters—and ideally suited to the local conditions. The ponies my cousins and I rode were also kept here; they were of all colors—bay, sorrel, grey, and piebald. My favorite, Patches, was covered with brown-and-white patches—hence his name.

The road turned left now, and went over an old railroad right-of-way. This spur ran from Sanford to Fayetteville and was still in use. Twice a day, just before noon and late in the evening, the little engine would slowly pull a baggage car, two passenger cars (one for whites and one for blacks), and a caboose by, stopping at the tiny Overhills station if there was mail to pick up or a passenger to let off. There were times when my grandfather and his friends would have their private railroad cars brought to the siding here, but I never saw them. My cousins and I were mainly interested in the train, to see if it would flatten the pennies that we carefully laid out on the track.

Now the the clubhouse loomed ahead, and I let out a cheer, which Cal copied, though she could not see above the dashboard. Beyond it, on the left was Grandpa's house, The Covert, and beyond that was the house Grandma herself had built when Grandpa complained of the unceasing racket all their grandchildren made. This house, in which we could make all the noise we wanted to, she named "Croatan," for the local Indian tribe that had once inhabited these parts. I always loved that name, for the mystery that surrounded it. Legend had it that the Croatans had helped Sir Walter Raleigh's lost colony of Roanoke, when their supplies had run out. And indeed, three centuries later, a number of their tribal descendants had blue eyes.

The station wagon slowed and came to a stop in the circular drive in front of Croatan—a gracious, red brick house with black tiled roof, very much in the style of Colonial Williamsburg, the restoration of which the Rockefeller family had recently undertaken. And like those Williamsburg buildings, Croatan, for all its size, was surprisingly intimate and inviting; the two-story columns around the front entrance supported an overhanging porch, and the square patio in front was covered with a carpet of pine needles that softened the tread of approaching visitors. The other side of the house, the south side, had a a magnificent flagstone terrace running its entire length, and it looked out on a lawn that receded into a forest of tall pines. Floor-to-ceiling bay windows let in much sunlight, and the overall feeling of the place was one of utter tranquillity—which was exactly what my grandmother had in mind. She had built it with her own money, inherited from her father, and she had not stinted, for with the exception of a small trust, whatever was left when she died would go, not to her children, but back to her three brothers and their sons. Thus had James Stillman ensured that none of the capital that he had worked so hard to accumulate would wind up in the hands of the Rockefellers, who had married two of his daughters. The house had seven bedrooms, most with their own sleeping porches, for my grandmother liked the refreshing feeling of sleeping almost, but not really, outside. In addition, part of the attic roof was cut away, so that four lucky people could actually sleep under the stars (and quickly roll their beds back to the wall, if it started to rain). In the dining room were two tables, one for children and one for adults, which could seat eight people each, and against the wall was a long, polished sideboard with two gleaming copper warming trays, for meals at Overhills were always self-service. But, as at Owenoke, the most delightful room in the house was the living room. It was sixty feet long and thirty feet wide, and at the end with the bowed window, at least three people could stretch out full-length on the window seat and peacefully read. The sofas and easy chairs were comfortable, and there was a Steinway grand piano, as well as a card table and a Victrola, on which we played Strauss waltzes. Truly, it was a room for living in, and we all loved to congregate there. Indeed, the more the merrier, for the big room seemed to amplify the glow of its huge hearth when all my cousins and aunts and uncles were present.

I flung open the door to the station wagon and leaped out, running across the patio with its thick covering of pine needles, and bursting into the front hall, where I barely noticed the imposing portrait of the great Robert E. Lee. The Civil War—or rather, the War for Southern Independence, as it was still referred to locally—may have been over for more than sixty years, but it might have been fought yesterday the way some folks felt. When my grandmother's neighbors discovered that her daughter had married a *Lincoln*, some of them actually became hostile. It was then that she acquired the large, handsome portrait of General Lee, hanging it in the place of most prominence, and the ruffled feelings of some of her neighbors were smoothed down.

Straight through to the kitchen I dashed, to bury myself in the warm, ample embrace of Croatan's chief cook, Aunt Rosetta. She had been born a slave more than seventy years before, and was now responsible for all the household help, whose husbands worked on the plantation. She always wore a red bandanna, and she had a wonderful, mothering quality about her that made me and all my cousins instantly love and trust her. And needless to say, no one, before or since, could hold a candle to her when it came to Southern fried chicken and baking powder biscuits.

My grandmother also loved her, and indeed she took a special interest in each of the servants, asking after their families and taking time to really listen to their response. For she genuinely cared—and they knew it and cared back. Nor was her concern limited to conversation; appalled by the extreme poverty in that backcountry area of North Carolina, she had put more than a little of James Stillman's money to good use, building and staffing a sanitorium for neglected, tubercular children. Naming it the Preventorium, she let it be known far and wide that any child needing food, medicine, and first-class care would be welcome there, for as long as was necessary. Many gratefully took up her offer, and throughout her life my grandmother would receive thanks from people who, as children, had benefited from their treatment at the Preventorium.

Another of my grandmother's special interests at Overhills was an Indian, whom she had discovered living alone in a wigwam in the Adirondack Mountains. She had arranged for him to teach her children and her niece and nephews about the lore of the woods, and the animals and birds that lived there. As he grew older, she became concerned that this gentle hermit, who had such a way with children, would perish in the prolonged icy blasts of winter in upper New York State, for he had made no provision against the cold. She offered to bring him down to North Carolina for the winter, give him a place to stay, and take him back to his beloved mountains in the spring. He thought about this for a few days and agreed, and now "Dan-Dan, the Indian man," as he was always known to us, lived in a room over Croatan's garage each winter, and was one of the people we most looked forward to seeing.

Perhaps because of her spontaneous, instinctive kindness to all with whom she came in contact, and because, instead of merely deploring a needy situation, she did something practical to remedy it, my grandmother was loved and respected by blacks and whites alike in that secluded area of North Carolina. And she, in turn, loved it more than any other place on earth.

There was so much for a five-year-old to see and do at Overhills!

Riding Patches was one of my favorite things, and going for nature walks with Dan-Dan, and swimming in the pond, and playing any number of games with my cousins Pat and Anne, and Betty Brooks (Aunt Win's daughter). But best of all were my secret, early morning adventures with Grandma. Long before the others were up, she would take me for a "fairy-walk" by the edge of the golf course, just at sunup, when the wooded glen was still dark with mystery. Here she would tell me fairy tales, and as we walked, we would look for their tiny footprints in the pristine, sparkling dew.

A different kind of excitement awaited us on those mornings when there was a hunt. Then we were not the only ones up early; indeed, the hunters were up before we were, to be off at the crack of dawn, when the fox's scent was the freshest. Grandma and I would hurry to the garage and climb into the station wagon, asking Mr. Bruce which way he thought the hunt had gone. Then we would tear along the dirt roads, to see if we could intercept the hunt and catch a glimpse of the grand pageant as it thundered by. Grandma was as adept at driving motor cars, as she was at handling teams of horses, and we were usually able to get a good view.

Before anyone came in sight, we could hear the piercing sound of the hunting horn and the baying of the hounds. Soon, through the woodland underbrush, there would be flashes of white, brown, and black, as the hounds tracked and crisscrossed, trying to follow the scent. After them came the first horseman, the Master of the Hunt, magnificent in hard black velvet cap, scarlet coat with black velvet collar, pale fawn britches and shiny black leather boots up to his knees. At his neck a starched white stock gleamed in the morning sun. Two men called "whips" rode on the extreme left and right of the main body of hunters, acting as guides and keeping the group together. All the horsemen wore scarlet, while the jackets of the women riders were black.

The ground reverberated to the pounding of the horses' hooves as they passed, and I would get scared. Then Grandma put her arm around me and said, "Don't worry, Bellita; they'll soon be gone."

"But the poor fox—"

She smiled and shook her head. "Your grandfather doesn't kill foxes. He'll make sure they let him go, when they've had a good run."

I nodded, but I still felt sorry for the fox, for I could imagine how it must have felt, being chased by all those dogs and earth-shaking horses. Indeed, my imagination was especially vivid, when it came to things that scared me—like the night train that passed through Overhills: how I wished I could get to sleep before I heard it! That eerie whistle made my hair stand on end, and for some reason it made me think of the convicts we sometimes saw working on the roads, their legs chained together, as they swung their pickaxes. And the vision of the convicts made me think of the Lindbergh kidnapping. I wasn't supposed to know about that; if the grown-ups were discussing it (and the danger of one of the Rockefeller children being kidnapped), they immediately changed the subject when I came into the room. But I could hardly miss hearing the New York newsboys yelling, "Extra, extra! Read all about it! New clue in the Lindbergh case!"

Such was my imagination that I was convinced that two escaped convicts were coming after me, to kidnap me and make their getaway on the midnight train. If I scared myself badly enough with such thoughts, I would have to get up and go downstairs, to find a grown-up or at least a light. But the worst scare of all was grounded in reality, as most "worst" scares are. Grandma was a meticulous housekeeper and kept an eye on all areas of Croatan. One day she decided to visit the room over the garage, where Dan-Dan slept. To her shock, she found the room infested with bedbugs, and immediately gave orders that what furniture there was in the room should be brought out and burned, bed, bedding, and all. I was with her and saw the mounting pile being soaked with kerosene and set alight. Suddenly it all began to seethe with black bugs trying to escape the flames and being shriveled up and killed. My eyes widened and my mouth fell open, and I began screaming with terror, convinced that this angry swarm of bugs was after me. For more than a week, this wide-awake nightmare recurred: I would sit bolt upright in bed, shrieking, until Grandma took me into her huge bed, and there I gradually relaxed, cozy and protected.

Yet so far did the good at Overhills outweigh the bad, that almost all the happiest memories of my childhood were centered there. And this three-month sojourn with my grandmother and Cal, until my parents' return from South America, was the happiest of all. In fact, its memory was one of the few things I had to smile about, in the cumulative tragedy of the months to come.

# 6

WITH THE COMING OF SUMMER, my parents returned from South America and again rented a summer home in Greenwich, not far from Owenoke. On the surface, our life was pleasant enough—but with my family, you could never be sure of the surface. The year was 1933, the Depression was grinding on, and with mills and factories all over the world shut down, nobody was importing or exporting much of anything. Despite all the efforts of my father, H. W. Peabody & Company was dying. My grandfather, who had always been fond of his son-in-law, must have helped him substantially for the firm to have lasted as long as it had, when so many others had gone under. Perhaps, if the Depression had lasted only one year or even two, it might have survived. But it was now in its third year, with no glimmer of hope that things would get any better.

The despair and the struggle went on, and my mother, who believed in shielding children from all worry and tragedy, never explained to me why my father kept coming home later and later, and why he hardly ever smiled anymore. I knew something was wrong, as children usually do, and the fact that she wouldn't talk about it, only made it worse, because I felt that I mustn't mention it, either. And so at night, I would lie in my bed and hear my father go into their bathroom which was next to my room and be sick to his stomach. Night after night, he suffered in wretched agony—and nobody said anything about it in the morning. Perhaps because of this, and perhaps to keep her mother happy, my mother always agreed to Grandma's increasingly frequent requests for her Bellita to come and visit. Possibly, after the curl-cutting incident and with Cal continuing to grow more adorable by the day, she wanted to make sure that I got my share of being special. Whatever the reason for these visits, I loved them. Grandma was delighted to give me her undivided attention by the hour. We did everything together, and she was always interested in what I had to say. I began to think of her almost as if she were my own mother, while she, incapable of showing affection to her own daughter, more than made up for it with her granddaughter.

I loved Grandma's house, too, from the small turtles she kept in a tank in the room adjoining her flower room, to the enormous kitchen, with its battery of black gas stoves, soapstone sinks, marble pastry counters, massive wooden butcher's block, and pots and pans hanging in orderly rows from the ceiling. Mary, the plump Irish cook, was in charge here, and she would greet me with a sample of her latest batch of molasses cookies.

I ate most of my meals in the breakfast room, and with the exception of those special breakfasts in their bedroom, the only time I ate with my grandparents was Sunday dinner, in the great dining room which could seat fifty dinner guests. If my parents were home, they would, of course, join us for this weekly get-together, which always struck me as a grand affair. Often, I would be issued a specially made linen bib and napkin for my lap, to protect my best Parisian dress.

The menu had come down from Grandpa's father, and it never varied from Sunday to Sunday: rare roast beef from a standing rib, crisp Yorkshire pudding, fluffy mashed potatoes, French-cut string beans, rich gravy, fresh-baked rolls with sweet butter, and for dessert, vanilla ice cream with a luscious chocolate sauce that turned hard the moment it touched the ice cream.

The meal was served by Oscar, assisted by two maids; so good were they at their jobs that we hardly noticed them. In fact, we lived surrounded by servants moving quietly about us, keeping everything spotless and attending to every need we might have, usually before we realized it ourselves. We were all fond of them, and my grandparents spent a good deal of time talking with them and making sure they themselves were not in any need, with the result that their staff loved them and would often stay with them for their whole lives. One such was Grandma's much-loved companion, Rossie, who had originally come as Aunt Gladys's nurse, many years before.

Thanks to Rossie's wisdom and the unflagging care of her and Grandma and the other nurses, Aunt Glad had defied medical history and become the first victim of celiac disease to survive. But the years-long affliction had taken a frightful toll of her mental balance. She was now subject to savage mood swings from extreme depression to wild hilarity. She lived at Owenoke, although she was frequently gone for long, unexplained absences (which, I learned later, were for treatment in a private sanitarium).

One day, when I was five, my cousin Ann and I were playing in the living room, when Aunt Glad, dressed in slacks and a silk blouse, came in and asked, "I've got to go to the drugstore, to pick something up; would you like to come with me? We'll put the top down."

Ann and I looked at each other, our eyes widening: we had, of course, seen the beautiful, midnight-blue Packard convertible in the garage. We knew that it was Aunt Glad's, but we had never seen her driving it; usually, when she went out, it was in the big Cadillac, with Gus, the chauffeur, behind the wheel.

"Yes, yes!" we replied in unison.

"Good!" She laughed. "I'll call the garage and have them get the car ready. I'll meet you out in front in a minute." She bent toward us and lowered her voice. "And, um—since this is an adventure, don't tell anyone." We nodded, and she hurried off.

We tiptoed down the long hall to the front door and eased it open. Hardly were we outside when the Packard pulled up, its long hood gleaming in the sun and its whitewall tires crunching on the gravel. Aunt Glad looked radiant and very chic, wearing a pair of the sunglasses that had just come into fashion. She patted the seat beside her, and we hurried around the car and got in.

As soon as the door was shut, she exclaimed, "Let's see how fast we can go!" and she jammed her foot down on the accelerator. The huge eight-cylinder engine roared in response, and the rear wheels sent gravel flying, as the open car gathered momentum. By the time we got to the turn at the end of the drive, we were traveling so fast that the car's rear end swung out wildly on the loose stones, while Aunt Glad grappled with the steering wheel, to bring it under control. She did not use the brakes; deceleration was not what she had in mind.

Once we were on the firm pavement of Lake Avenue, she cried,

"Now we can *really* go!" and above us, the limbs of the overhanging shade trees faded into a green blur.

This wasn't fun any longer, and Ann and I clung to one another in terror, afraid that we would be thrown out as the car passed the corners that Aunt Glad took with all tires squealing. Suddenly, Aunt Glad did hit the brakes, bringing the car to a screeching halt—in front of the drugstore.

"I'll only be a moment," she reassured us with a smile, apparently oblivious to our quaking, speechless condition. And with that, she got out and strode into the drugstore, the picture of casual elegance in her tailored slacks.

Ann and I looked at one another in stunned disbelief. Aunt Glad seemed so calm, so composed. Maybe that was the way grown-ups were supposed to drive convertibles. As we sat there in the sun, with birds chirping in the trees and shoppers strolling along the sidewalk, we began to wonder if we hadn't just been scaredy-cats.

Aunt Glad came out with a little package and got in the car. But instead of starting up, she turned to us and opened the parcel, pulling out a small triangular bottle. "Know what this is?"' We shook our heads. "Nail polish—*platinum* nail polish!" she whispered. "Want me to do your nails?"

Again Ann and I looked at each other, not knowing what to say. Aunt Glad was acting so strange. . . . We knew Grandma would be furious; she did not approve of adults painting themselves with lipstick or nail polish. But we were with Aunt Glad in her car, with no other way of getting home, and there was no telling what she would do if she got angry with us. Slowly, silently, we nodded.

With infinite care, Aunt Glad undid the bottle, and using the tiny brush attached to the top, one by one she patiently did our nails, until they glistened a pearly silver in the sun. Then she started the car and drove home in a quiet, even sedate manner.

As we turned into the drive to the house, I was startled to see the entire family gathered on the front steps—Grandma and Grandpa, my parents, Ann's parents from across the street, Aunt Win and Aunt Faith—and no one was smiling. Indeed, everyone looked grim or angry, and my mother was sobbing and being held by my father, who now, with Uncle Avery, rushed down to the car and lifted Ann and me out, not bothering to open the door. And then, as my mother hugged me to her, Grandpa, normally so gentle, went over to Aunt Glad, his eyes blazing: "You are never to take any of my grandchildren with you in the car!" he thundered. *"Never!* Is that understood?"

For a moment, I thought he was going to strike her. Never had I seen him so angry, and neither apparently had Aunt Glad, for she nodded meekly. With that, we were taken inside, and the incident was never spoken of again. But I could not forget it, and the thing I remembered most was my mother's embrace, for she hardly ever touched me. Looking back, I would decide that, for the sake of that hug, the ride was almost worth it.


IN THE FALL OF 1933, my parents again went abroad, this time to England, in a last-ditch effort to save H. W. Peabody, by shutting down and liquidating the assets of its British offices. Once again, I was living with Grandma Rockefeller, but not at Owenoke or down at Overhills; this time we were in New York, at Grandpa's elegant apartment at 300 Park Avenue. For I had turned six, and it was time for me to start school. I was enrolled at Miss Chapin's, one of Manhattan's two most exclusive private schools for young ladies. It was arranged that I would be driven to school and picked up as soon as school was over. My school uniform had already arrived—a light green jumper worn over a long-sleeved white blouse.

On the morning of opening day, I awoke with a deep dread of the unknown. What would school be like? Would the other girls like me? Probably not, I decided, dawdling as long as possible, brushing my teeth and washing my face. At length, I emerged from the bathroom and into my grandparents' bedroom. I had spent the night snuggled between them in their huge bed, as I often did when we were in New York, for my fear of being kidnapped had grown worse. By now, the Lindbergh case had thoroughly alarmed all the Rockefeller adults, and while they did their best to conceal their concern, the children knew. They sounded so serious, as they warned us *never* to speak to strangers or go out in the street alone. I even knew what kidnappers looked like: half pirate and half outlaw, they had patches over one eye and red bandannas pulled up over their noses.

Now I looked around my grandparents' bedroom longingly, as if I were saying goodbye to an old friend. It was so cozy, decorated in Wedgwood blue and soft rose—

"Bellita, come over here." My grandmother's quiet request cut across my thoughts. She was sitting at the beautiful, petite French desk that her father had given her, and she motioned to the little Chippendale chair beside it, which she had had made just for me. I loved her desk; it was beautifully crafted and delicate and had all sorts of cubbyholes and tiny drawers. It even had a secret drawer, and I knew the secret: how to pull out another drawer, press a concealed button, and watch the secret drawer slide open. My grandmother had never lost her delight in secret, magical things, and this desk was one of her treasures. I crossed the room and sat down next to her.

She took up a pen and some paper and announced, "Bellita, since you are starting school today, you must start using your real name. Here is how you write it: you start with an *I*, like this, and—"

"But Bellita's my real name, Grandma! That's what you and Mummy call me, and I've known how to write it for a year!"

"Your name is *Isabel*," she said with a firmness which she never used with me. Occasionally, I had heard her use it with others—but only rarely, for no one crossed her. In this, she was every bit James Stillman's daughter.

I was as shocked at her tone as if she had slapped me across the face. "Now give me your hand, child," she went on evenly, with just the trace of ice in her voice, "and I will show you how to form the letters." She took my hand, put the pen in it, and started to make an *I*.

I jerked my hand away. This could not be happening! Bellita was my mother's special name for me, the name which she had always called me, ever since I could remember, and Grandma had adopted it, too. In fact, *everyone* called me Bellita; it was even monogrammed on my towels!

Mustering all the authority of my six years, I declared: "Grandma, my name *is* Bellita." And I was surprised at the firmness with which it came out.

My grandmother was surprised, too; this was the first time I had ever defied her. Her eyes narrowed. "Your name is Isabel, and it always has been!" she exclaimed, her voice rising. "Bellita is just a childish nickname, and other children have a habit of picking up nicknames and making them stick, sometimes all through life. That is not going to happen with you," she emphasized. "Now give me your hand, and I will teach you how to write your real name."

She took my hand and held it so firmly that I could not wrench it away. "*You* are Isabel!" I screamed, "and *Mummy* is Isabel! I am *Bellita*!" And I started crying and shaking.

"You stop that tantrum this instant!" my grandmother commanded, sticking the pen in my hand and making it spell the hated latters. I was in such panic that my sobs came in spasmodic gulps.

"There!" she said through thin lips, when the job was completed. But we were not finished. "Now you do it. On your own," and her other arm was clamped around my waist, so there was no escape.

Wailing my grief and unable to see the paper through my tears, I somehow satisfied her, and she released me, admonishing me to hurry up and eat my breakfast.

I ran across the black-and-white marble squares of the hallway and into the dining room. There, everything was the same as ever, but one look at the steaming dish of oatmeal that Oscar put in front of me, and a wave of nausea engulfed me, to the point where I had to fight to keep from throwing up. Over and over, I kept repeating: "I won't be Isabel, I won't be Isabel," as if the words were some magical chant, and if I said them often enough, they would come true. Oscar saw the turmoil I was in and was powerless to help me. "Try to eat some toast, Miss Bellita," he said gently, and hearing my name—my real name, the one that my grandmother had tried to take from me—I started sobbing afresh.

On the drive to school, I was in such a daze that, when we got to Miss Chapin's, Gus had to come around and open the door for me. Grandma did not get out; in fact, she sat with her head back, so that no one, glancing in, could see her.

I got out, and as I started up the stone steps, an "old girl" who had been at the school several years, offered to take me upstairs, to the first-grade room. I nodded my gratitude, and as she took me by the hand and led me up through the big red door of the main entrance, I could hear Gus pulling away behind me. I had never felt so alone.

But the first-grade room was cheerful and bright, with three low, light green tables, surrounded by ten small chairs that were little bigger than footstools. On them sat young girls in uniforms just like mine, and the walls held pictures of little girls watering plants and playing with puppies and skipping down the street.

"This is your teacher," said the old girl. "Her name is Miss Jayne." I reached my hand up to a smiling young woman and curtsied as I had been taught. Miss Jayne pointed to an empty chair and told me to take a seat and wait for her to call the roll. After what seemed like forever, a clanging bell rang in the hall, and Miss Jayne started calling out our names. "Caroline Abel?"

"Present," replied a small blond girl, two stools away.

"Helen Anderson?"

"Present."

The list went on, until Miss Jayne read: "Isabel Lincoln?" There was no answer. "Isabel Lincoln?" she called again. Still no answer—it was not my name, and I was not going to answer it. My grandmother had done this. She must have called the school, to make sure they did it her way. Just as she made sure everyone did things her way. Well, I would not answer, and I could feel myself becoming like iron inside.

Miss Jayne continued the rest of the roll call, and when she was finished, she came over to talk with me. With the utmost kindness, she tried to break the deadlock. And then she tried firmness, but nothing worked. My will was set, one inherited trait that had not weakened with succeeding generations.

For two months, I refused to answer to Isabel, nor would I write it. And then my parents came home, and I astonished my mother by flinging myself into her arms and starting to cry when she called me Bellita.

I started to tell her what had happened, but my grandmother, who was there, would not let me finish. Proudly, she explained that on my first morning at school, she had changed my name from Bellita to Isabel and insisted that at school I should be known only as Isabel.

My mother sighed sadly. She wouldn't dream of disagreeing with her mother's wishes, but she now understood the depth of shock I had received, and she went to see Miss Jayne. She liked her and was comforted by her concern, for it turned out that I had a mild form of dyslexia, and tended to read words backward. They decided that Miss Jayne might come over after school to give me special help.

For two years, Miss Jayne spent three afternoons a week working with me, and in time her love and understanding pierced my desperate isolation. Sadly, I came to accept that, however much I might hate it, my name was Isabel, and there was not a thing I could do about it.

# 7

---

PERCY ROCKEFELLER'S father, William, had been the personable dealmaker, while his uncle John D. had been a visionary with the ruthless tenacity to see the vision become a reality. The two brothers made an unbeatable combination, but of the next generation only Percy seemed to have the knack. With his father's charm, he made business friends easily, and he shared his father's uncanny ability to be in the right place at the right time—with the right price.

Two other of Percy's qualities were equally rare: he was a man of utter integrity, whose word was truly his bond, and he could work—long and hard and patiently, without taking his eye off his goal. For Percy, five years had not been too long to wait for a girl, if she were the right one. That was the way he approached life: if a deal or a merger was right, it was worth working and waiting for.

Nevertheless, he was not his father's initial choice to succeed him; that honor fell to the eldest son and namesake, William G. But the pressure—the concentration that was required, and the courage, to say nothing of the towering expectations of his father and uncle—proved more than William G. could bear. He took solace in the conventional avenues of escape, where many good men have gone who were overmatched by the responsibilities thrust upon them.

And so the lot fell to Percy, fresh out of Yale in 1900, and installed on the board of Standard Oil at the age of twenty-two. Somehow, he took the strain and even thrived on it, becoming a key strategist at the heart of the Rockefeller empire. And with James Stillman backing his play, his father-in-law, who owned the National City Bank, he gained the reputation of having turned tens of millions of dollars into hundreds of millions. At the height of his career, on the board of directors of fifty-one corporations, Percy was regarded as the only true entrepreneur among his generation of Rockefellers, for his interests ranged far beyond oil, railroads, and banking—into nitrates, copper, matches, industrial alcohol, and steel.

And then came the Depression. Few saw its approach, and fewer still were prepared for it. No respecter of persons, it struck like a tornado, cutting down the large and the small alike. It was no joke about Wall Street millionaires, throwing themselves out of office windows. And for every man who "fell" out of his window, there would be several incidents of cars "accidentally" running into concrete bridge abutments at high rates of speed. After having had money for so long that they took it for granted, to face the tale of the ticker tape and realize that one was suddenly penniless—often proved more than a man could bear.

At Yale, Percy had been tapped for Skull and Bones, the most prestigious of the handful of secret societies. Perhaps only a dozen men from each senior class were accorded this honor, and in those days it was regarded as a sacred trust. These young men took a solemn, lifelong vow to help one another in times of adversity or in the event of an emergency. It is unlikely that any of them ever imagined that the emergency would be financial, for nearly all came from old-money families that had never known want. Indeed, it is unlikely that they could even imagine themselves in adversity, for all were confident of achieving success in their chosen fields of endeavor. And they had; in the ensuing thirty years, many of Percy's Skull and Bones brothers had risen to positions of prominence, patriarchs of their clans, much as Percy himself had become.

And then, as in the twinkling of an eye, all that changed. All at once, those old-money families were on the verge of not just bankruptcy, but annihilation. . . . Everything would go, the country house, the town house, the summer house, the yacht, the stables, the indoor tennis court, the clubs, the trips, the private schools, *everything*. Only one man stood between them and unspeakable disaster: Percy Rockefeller.

And so, some thirty years after the night they had sworn their oath of eternal fraternity, Percy honored his word. His friends did not need just a few thousand to tide them over; they needed millions. And while they all fervently promised to repay him, he knew that they never could.

He did not have the huge sums that they needed in ready cash, and as a delay of even a day or two could spell disaster—the only thing he could do was sell stock, for whatever he could get for it. So Percy sold his stocks across the board—dumped them, really—so much so fast that it had the effect of further depressing a stock market that had already lost countless billions.

The federal government looked at him askance. Why would the shrewdest businessman in the country suddenly practically give his stock away? He must be driving the market down for a purpose, probably to buy back in at the artificially low prices that would result. To do such a thing at any time was unethical, but to do it at a time when the entire nation was on the ropes. . . .

In 1932, Grandpa was summoned to Washington, to appear before the Senate's Stock Exchange Investigating Committee, to answer charges of stock manipulation. It was before this trip that he had stayed up all night, playing waltzes, the last of which I had heard that early morning, as Grandma and I slipped out to the cutting garden. Once he explained his motives to the Senators on the committee, he was totally exonerated. But the summons before this national tribunal capped three years of relentless, unbelievable stress, and it broke his health. Thereafter, he would be plagued by stomach problems, and his doctors now told him he must drastically curtail the work schedule that had been his life. He pleaded with them that he was only fifty-six, but they told him that, if he did not cut down, he would not live to see fifty-seven.

One evening after supper, in September of 1934, not long after my seventh birthday, I was staying at Owenoke with Grandpa and Grandma. Four-year-old Cal and I were playing Lotto on the oriental rug in front of the living room fireplace. Our parents were spending a long weekend at The Cabin in the Adirondacks, to celebrate their ninth anniversary, and the big house seemed oddly quiet and empty. There was no sign of servants anywhere; in fact, it was so still that I became aware that I could not hear *anything*, and for that matter, I could not even detect the faint scent of Grandma's rosewater that used to linger in the living room. We knew that Grandpa had left for tests at Doctors' Hospital in New York City the previous morning, but he had left cheerful and energetic, assuring us that he and Grandma would be back tomorrow morning. And before he went, he had played on the floor with us, which he hardly ever did, getting down on all fours and giving us "horsey rides."

Increasingly apprehensive, I decided to investigate and find out what was happening and where everyone was. I left the living room and went along the hall—still no one and not a sound. With a growing sense of dread, I reached the great stairway and started up. Suddenly, I did hear a noise, and looking up I was shocked to see Rossie flying downstairs toward me, her usually neat red-orange hair flying in all directions, her blue eyes glassy. When she reached me, she stopped and blurted out: "Your Grandpa—Bellita, your Grandpa is dead!"

Then she hurried on down the stairs, and I stared numbly after her. Grandpa, dead? No! It couldn't be! But as she disappeared into the kitchen, I instantly felt icy cold; it was true. I would never see Grandpa again, never eat toast with him and Grandma in their big bed—tears welled up in my eyes, and my throat couldn't swallow. Wishing my parents were home, I dimly sensed that things would never be the same again. And they never were.

The next morning, waiting for my parents, I sat in the front hall so I would be sure to see them the moment they arrived. The antique horsehair-stuffed chair was uncomfortable and scratchy, but I stayed in it anyway, swinging my legs back and forth, telling myself that things would be all right, as soon as they got there. At last, I heard the car in the driveway, and then the front door opened. My father looked tired and crumpled and somehow shorter than usual, and my mother was exhausted; her eyes were red, and there were dark shadows under them. I ran to them and hugged them, and they held me close, without speaking. Then I noticed something else: there were little red marks on my mother's face and hands.

"Mummy, what's the matter with your face?"

"What? What do you mean?" she asked and then smiled wanly, as she remembered. "Bedbugs. In our mattress on the night boat down from Albany."

They went off to find Rossie, and I went into the living room, looking down at the place where Cal and I had played horsey with Grandpa, two days before. My parents were home, but things were not all right.

When it was time for bed, we had seen very little of the grown-ups, who spent much of the time conferring out of earshot. Mina took Cal and me up to bed, and I was upset to learn that, instead of sleeping in my own little pink-and-white room, or in Grandma's big bed, I would be off in the nursery alone, while Cal slept in Mina's room. Mina tucked me in, turned out the light, and left. I lay there in the darkness, unable to sleep. Slowly, carefully, I felt around the bottom of my bed with my foot . . . and sure enough, I could feel them: *bedbugs*! The whole bed was crawling with them, just like the ones I had seen burning at Overhills!

I screamed in the darkness—but no one came. Screaming and screaming to no avail, I leaped out of bed and frantically groped about in the dark for the light switch on the wall. Finding it at last, I turned on the light and went over to inspect the bed. I could not find a single bed-bug. "What a silly girl you are, Bellita," I said out loud, imitating the tone a grown-up might use. "Now you put that bed back together again, and I don't want to hear another word of this bedbug nonsense."

I did as I had told myself, turned out the light, and got back in bed. And everything was fine—at first. But those bedbugs were devilishly smart. Not only did they hide in a place known only to bedbugs the moment the light came on, but they knew when and how to steal out of hiding, so as not to alarm their prey.

There, I felt one with my left foot—moving so slightly that at first I could not even be sure I'd felt it. Ever so slowly, I shifted my foot to the edge of the bed, hoping against hope that I would feel nothing more. But down in the crevice, where the covers were tucked in to the edge of the bed, there was another—and another, and more on the other side of the bed, and now they were all there back again, swarming all over me and biting me; I could even feel blood on my legs.

Again I started screaming, and this time Mina arrived, throwing on the switch, as she came in. Together, we examined every inch of the bed and under the bed, and the corners of the room. There was not one bed-bug to be seen anywhere. Finally, Mina, who was dead tired herself, got me to go back to bed, by promising to sit with me, until I was asleep.

In my mind, bedbugs were somehow messengers of death—Grandpa's, and perhaps mine next—and every night for the next six months this horrible, wide-awake nightmare would repeat itself. Grandma tried to help, even giving me a little flashlight to keep under my pillow and check under the covers with, the moment I thought I felt anything. But the bedbugs had grown smarter; now they would hide the moment they felt me reach for it.

Half a century ago, it did not occur to medical science that, when a young child went through the trauma of the death of a loved one, it was crucially important for them to talk about their feelings, work through their grief, and come into an acceptance of the reality. The prevailing wisdom of that day was just the opposite: don't mention the death in front of the child, or in any way refer to the person who had died, and the child would not suffer the pain of the loss.

But children know, and if they are denied any outlet for expressing their grief, their subconscious must then cope with it as best it can. And sometimes internalized trauma manifests itself in strange ways. Aside from the nightly ordeal of the "death-bugs," I became somehow convinced that there was evil connected to the letter $K$; indeed, it got so bad that I refused to speak to one of my classmates, because her name was Katherine. Miss Jayne, who continued to come by after school to tutor me, worked long and patiently with me, to help me see that $K$ was merely a tool of communication, no different from $L$ or $M$. But my grandmother's seemingly harmless fascination with fairies and the magic spells they wove had done its work; I knew the evil power of $K$, even if Miss Jayne didn't, and it would be a long time before I would see it her way.

And Grandma? She now clung to me as though I could somehow save her from the depths of the grief in which she was drowning. With my mother's blessing, I moved over to her New York apartment, but there was nothing I could do to relieve the awful heaviness that seemed to drag her down. I had never thought of her as old, for she had no grey hair and had always been so active. But now, even though she was only fifty-eight, everything seemed a great effort to her, and she began walking with a cane.

The only time Grandma ever seemed her old self, during that autumn of 1934, was on Saturdays. Grandpa had loved his undergraduate years at Yale, and had become manager of the varsity football team. As an alumnus, he had maintained close ties with the football coaches and their teams, and since New Haven was little more than an hour away by the Boston Post Road, he and Grandma had faithfully made the pilgrimage, whenever the Elis were playing in the Yale Bowl. For the past two seasons, I had been included in that tradition, and nowhere else had I seen Grandma and Grandpa have so much fun together.

Now, perhaps because it had meant so much to Grandpa, Grandma was determined that she and I would carry on. And so we did, and it was every bit as much of a production: Gus would drive us up in the big Cadillac, tucking the fur lap robe about us, and we would arrive outside the stadium early enough to join the other pregame picnickers. Mary the cook would have made us a lunch of cold fried chicken, hot homemade soup in a Thermos, tasty sandwiches, and, always, rich chocolate cake. On the way into the Bowl, Grandma would buy me a program and a blue chrysanthemum, and would answer my questions about football, as best she could. Throughout, I would cheer wildly for the blue team, and she often grew quite enthusiastic herself, and neither of us mentioned the one we loved, who used to sit between us.

The last Bowl game of the season, against Harvard that year, was on a chill November afternoon, so cold that we could see our breath, and we appreciated the extra Thermos of beef bouillon that Mary had packed. Just before the end of the game, when the Yale coach was making sure that all the substitutes who deserved to win varsity letters got into the game, she took me down on the field. We went up behind the players on the bench, and she spoke briefly to the coach, who smiled and nodded. Then, one by one, she went along the bench, getting the stars of the Yale team to autograph my program. I was thrilled, and could not believe how lucky I was!

We left a few minutes before the game was over, to be ahead of the mob that would shortly be exiting. Clutching my autographed treasure with both hands, I exclaimed, "Grandma, this was the best game ever!"

She smiled vaguely in reply, but she was not looking at me. Her gaze was on the ivy-covered stadium, which was now burnished green-gold in the last rays of the setting sun. We could barely make out the last strains of the alma mater, "For God, for country, and for Yale," and at the top of the Bowl the pennants were still bright against the gathering darkness. I had no idea that this would be the last game we would ever see together. But Grandma knew.

That Christmas, she drew her family close about her at Owenoke. We had come from New York to stay for the holidays. Aunt Faith and Aunt Glad were there, and Uncle Avery and his wife Anna and my cousins Pat and Ann and Joanie who lived next door to Owenoke. Also there was Aunt Win with her two daughters. My Uncle Brooks, however, was in Japan, on another extended business trip. In all, it was quite a gathering, and it did much to help Grandma get through her first Christmas as a widow.

As for me, with so many cousins to play with—skating outside and playing hide-and-seek inside—it was heaven! I was especially fond of Aunt Win's daughter, Betty Brooks, who at five was just two years younger than me and so happy, all the time. Our fun slowed down a bit after the New Year, when both Pat and Ann came down with chicken pox, but that had the happy effect of quarantining the rest of us, so that we did not have to go back to school right away. What a joy to be playing in Owenoke, while everyone else was back at school!

One morning, while we were all having breakfast under the watchful eye of the housekeeper Mrs. Hunt, she looked very hard at Betty Brooks and said to her nurse Helen, "Whatever is the matter with Betty Brooks's eyes?"

I had noticed earlier that they were red and swollen, and had assumed that she must be getting sties, from which I, too, frequently suffered. Now, looking more closely, I had to admit that they looked worse than mine usually did.

"I'll talk to her mother," Helen replied, "but I'm sure there's nothing wrong with her. She's such a live wire that if anything *were* wrong, we'd know it instantly." She told Aunt Win a little while later, and shortly after that, a doctor came. Then other doctors came, and there were more closed counsels among the grown-ups.

It developed that Betty Brooks had nephrosis, a gradual, irreversible deterioration of the kidneys, for which the doctors could do little more than watch and wait. As the weeks went by, we cousins also watched—in numb horror, as she began to swell. Every part of her body became bloated, until she could no longer walk and had to be in a wheelchair. Finally, in July, she died in the hospital, a month before her sixth birthday. We cousins were appalled and terrified; it was as though death had broken into our playroom world and tortured and killed one of us.

My mother tried to calm me down, telling me that Betty Brooks had gone to be with the angels.

"But," I wailed, "what about her poor tummy? Is it still so big?"
"No, dear. The doctors operated on her in the hospital and let out all the fluid that had been building up for months. They did everything they could to help her, but God wanted her instead, so she has gone to be with the angels."

Shocked, I speculated on what would happen if God suddenly decided He wanted *me*. Would I swell up all over and go to be with the angels? Such were the thoughts that tormented me, as my preoccupation with death was rekindled. But I never shared them with anyone.

Death seemed to have become the invisible, uninvited houseguest at Owenoke, and Aunt Win, who had always been a gloomy and anxious person, now became positively morose. And to make matters worse, her husband, Brooks, remained in Japan, where, despite Aunt Win's pleading, he had chosen to stay throughout their daughter's long and tragic illness. Nor did the sun and warm weather of summer bring any relief; what it brought instead was the sudden death by stroke of Aunt Elsie, Grandma's lively and sociable sister who lived across the street. All of us were stunned, but my mother was the most severely affected, for her aunt had been the one person in whom she could confide, the one who had guided her through her debutante years and her wedding, and who had intervened just in time to save her marriage.

As for me, so morbid was my obsession with our invisible houseguest, that I was certain I had seen Aunt Elsie come into the house, go upstairs to the closed room on the second floor, lie down in the huge four-poster that had once belonged to her father-in-law, draw the dark red curtains round herself, and die. (Fifty years later, when I asked my Uncle Avery why Aunt Elsie had come over to Owenoke to die, he was shocked that I should think such a thing, assuring me that she had, of course, died in her own home. Needless to say, he was not half so shocked, as I was; that period of my life had begun to sound like a Gothic novel.)


FOR THAT SUMMER OF 1935, my parents had again taken a furnished summer rental close by Owenoke, to be near Grandma, and once again I somehow managed to get poison ivy all over myself. This time, it was not clumsy carelessness; I was almost eight and knew very well what those shiny three-leaved plants looked like. And being extremely allergic to them, I avoided them like the plague. But there was no way of avoiding their fumes, if someone happened to be burning underbrush with a lot of poison ivy in it. And someone must have been doing just that, for I came home with the worst case I had ever had. I had the itching rash all over my legs, arms, stomach, and back, and even in my mouth and under the lids of my eyes. They had had to call the doctor, and now, sobbing in misery, I was covered from head to foot in pink calamine lotion, with gauze over the places where it was so bad that it was oozing.

Every few hours, my mother came in to change my nightgown and adjust the fan. The shades were down, because my eyes were so painful, but there was enough light to see the ugly brass bed and wicker furniture. How I wished we were at Owenoke, or at home in our apartment in New York! If we hadn't been here in this awful place, I wouldn't have gotten poison ivy—

"Bellita? Are you awake?" my mother whispered, having gently opened the door and peered in.

"Yes, Mummy," I answered dismally, tears coming to my eyes. And then I smiled; as happy as I was most times with Grandma, when I was sick it was my mother I wanted, and no one else. Whenever I was sick enough to be in bed, my mother would enter the sickroom, smelling faintly of Chanel No. 5, that most elegant of elegant scents, and she would sit on the side of the bed and give me a long and soothing alcohol back rub. She was a wonderful back rubber, and she always finished off by powdering me with cool, comfort-smelling Johnson's Baby Powder. Then she would read to me for as long as I liked. Years later, it would occur to me that the only time my mother could really relate to small children was when they were ill. Then she knew exactly what they needed to make them feel better, and she would allow no one else to do it. It struck me that her own mother may have had exactly the same problem, for poor, desperately sick little Glad had been the only one of her children for whom Grandma had been able to pour herself out unstintingly.

But there could be no back rub today, because of the wretched poison ivy. But still she came and sat beside me. "Bellita," she began, and I was instantly worried, because her voice was breaking with emotion. "Bellita, Grandma is ill, and I'm afraid she is not going to get better." She paused and struggled to regain control.

The invisible houseguest, I thought. The others weren't enough for him; he had to take Grandma, too. He would not leave until he had destroyed Owenoke. I took my mother's hand and squeezed it with both of mine, trying to help her, as much as she was trying to help me.

She cleared her throat and said very matter-of-factly, as if to an adult: "Grandma is dying of cancer. She had it once years ago, but the doctors thought they had removed it all. They hadn't; it came back last fall, just after Grandpa died. And since she did not want to go on living without him, she told no one about it. Finally, the pain got so bad, she had to, and now it's too late to save her."

So *that* was why she had started walking with a cane! And why she had been in bed the last few times I had gone to see her. And why we had rented this house, instead of simply staying at Owenoke. Then I started to cry. Grandma didn't care about me; if she did, she wouldn't want to die and go away to be with the angels!

My mother put her hand on my cheek—about the only place she could touch me, without aggravating the poison ivy—and shook her head. "I hate to see you so miserable; I just wish there was something I could do." She was willing to suffer herself, but she could not bear her children to. She sat for a while with her hand on my brow, until my crying subsided. Then, with a sigh, she got up. "Try to go to sleep now," she said softly, closing the door behind her.

I lay on my bed, feeling not the least bit sleepy. *Why* did Grandma have to die? The tears started to come again, and in my anguish I tossed my head this way and that—and happened to notice up on the wicker bookshelf the blue leather-bound Bible with gold-edged pages that my Grandmother Lincoln had given me when I was christened. How did *that* get there? I thought it was tucked away in a box somewhere, back in the New York apartment. Funny that it should be there.... My parents never went to church; in fact, the only time I had heard either of them mention God, other than in muttered swearing, which we children were not supposed to hear, was when Mummy had told me about God wanting Betty Brooks to be with Him.

With difficulty, I got out of bed and made my way stiffly and painfully across the room. Taking down the Bible, I opened it and noticed that Grandma Lincoln had written something on the flyleaf. I squinted in the half light to see what it said: "He shall give His angels charge over thee, to keep thee in all thy ways."

Not quite sure what that meant, but feeling somehow comforted by it, I took the Bible back to bed, switched on the night-table light, and started to read. I began at the beginning, on the first page of Genesis, and read about how God created heaven and earth. A lot of it was over my head, but in some obscure way it made me feel good, so I kept on reading.

WHEN I RECOVERED from poison ivy, my parents sent Cal and me up to the Adirondacks with our nurse Mina, where we joined our cousins, Pat, Ann, and Joanie, with whom we often spent much of our summer vacations. Their father, Uncle Avery, had rented a camp for the summer on Lake Regis, near Lake Placid, and there we had a marvelous time, hiking, swimming, mountain climbing, and exploring the lake by canoe.

One rainy afternoon we were indoors, playing "Hearts." As we sat on the floor, playing cards, we were so cold our teeth were chattering, and finally Pat, who at eleven was the oldest and also the only boy in the group, got up. "This is stupid, sitting here shivering! I'm going to make a fire." And with that, he took some wood and some kindling from the two piles by the fireplace and set to work. There was a stack of old yellowed newspapers there, too, and he took the top section and started to wad it up. All at once, he stopped still, and his eyes widened, as he looked at the page in his hand. One by one, we fell silent and looked at him. His face was ashen.

"What is it, Pat?" I cried.

Instead of answering, he just handed the paper to me. There at the top was the headline:

## ISABEL ROCKEFELLER DEAD AT 59

I started to cry, as did the others, when they saw it. "It can't be true!" I cried. "They would have told us!"

"I'm going to call my father," said Pat. "He'll tell me," and he walked over to the wooden box telephone on the wall, picked up the receiver, and cranked the handle. At last the operator at the central exchange answered, and he was able to get through. He told Uncle Avery about the newspaper, and then listened a long time, nodding and occasionally brushing a tear.

When he was finished, he hung up the phone and held his eyes. Then he looked up and said, "It's true. They were waiting until they could come up here, so they could tell us themselves." He paused. "They're sorry we had to find out this way."

No one said anything, and after a while we picked up the cards and started to play again, as the rain continued to stream down the windowpanes.

MY PARENTS EVENTUALLY did come up to the camp, and they took me out on an overnight canoe trip to a small island covered with pines. My father set up the tent, while my mother gathered firewood, and I found dry sticks and leaves for kindling. Then my father got a fire going, and my mother, who barely knew how to boil water back home, made supper. She loved camp cooking and was good at it; we had grilled lamb chops and baked potatoes and canned peas and Hydrox cookies, polished off with a metal mug full of hot cocoa. This last was a camping specialty, made by mixing a heaping spoonful of Whitman's powdered chocolate in a small amount of condensed milk and stirring it in the mug until it made a thick ball, and then pouring in boiling water.

This was the best time of all, sitting around the campfire after a good meal, listening to the snapping wood and watching the flames, and sipping our cocoa. I loved being with Mummy and Poppy, all cozy around the fire, and I wondered if this would be the time that they would talk to me about Grandma. In less than a year, four members of our family had died, and her death was the hardest of all.

I couldn't bring it up, but I kept hoping that they would. Only they never did. And gradually, even though we were as close then as we had ever been (or would be), I began to feel very alone.

# 8

THE DEPRESSION had bottomed out by the winter of 1936-37, but there it stayed. There was no upturn, no light at the end of the tunnel, no relief from the numbing economic winter that America was shivering through. But as bad as things were at home, abroad they were even worse: governments were falling, there was civil war in Spain, and the evil specter of Nazism had begun to spread beyond Germany.

Importing and exporting remained at a standstill, and despite all my father's efforts, the Lincoln family business, H. W. Peabody & Company, went the way that so many similar firms had gone long before. By liquidating all its holdings to pay its debts, my father was able to avoid the stigma of bankruptcy. But now he was out of work—and unable to find any; the men whom he approached assumed that he, being married to a Rockefeller, didn't need the income as much as others. So day after day, month after month, he would go out job hunting and come back even more withdrawn than the day before.

There was one place, however, where his business skills were essential—in the settling of my grandparents' estate. This was a miserable time for all of us who had loved Owenoke. There was no one to buy it, and so, to everyone's sorrow, the great home was torn down, the land divided into lots and sold, and my grandparents' furnishings auctioned off by Parke-Bernet. For years, I could not pass by that gravel driveway without a lump rising in my throat.

There was one compensation: now, for the first time in their lives, my parents had money of their own. The year before, we had moved out of our small apartment in New York, and into a duplex penthouse that occupied the entire top floor of 50 East 77th Street, between Madison and Park. Surrounded by a private terrace, it had fifteen rooms, not including maids' quarters, and was so opulent that I was embarrassed to invite my friends home. In fact, it never did feel like home to me, and I found myself longing for the cozy little apartment that we had left behind.

Money also meant that my parents no longer had to rent a summer home in Greenwich; they could build their own, and in the summer of '37, as I approached my tenth birthday, they began drawing up plans. My mother had never liked Greenwich, but it had meant much to my father, who had grown up there and whose mother still had a home there, and so Greenwich it would be. They picked a lot in Deer Park, so called because my great uncle William G. Rockefeller had once used the land as a deer sanctuary. It was a development now, of some thirty houses, each situated on a lot of at least three acres. Like our new apartment, it seemed to be far more home than we needed, and in my heart it never took the place of Owenoke.

With both Rockefeller grandparents dead, the center of our family life now gravitated toward the Lincolns. My parents continued to have dinner with my father's mother every Thursday and Sunday evening that they were in New York, and for me there were ten Lincoln cousins more or less my age. Two in particular, Hopie Wonham and Lee Coombe, I grew close to, coming out to Greenwich on winter weekends to spend the day with them. Gradually, they began to fill the void left by my grandparents' death, and as the months passed, I began to spend more and more time with Lee.

A lighthearted blonde who made friends easily, Lee was bright, inquisitive, and full of fun. Our personalities seemed to mesh perfectly: if one said, "Let's go climb a tree!" the other would instantly respond, "Oh, yes, lets!"; neither one of us was more often the instigator than the other. With the coming of summer, my parents continued to rent a house in Greenwich, until their own would be ready to move into, which meant that Lee and I could spend all our free time together, and we did, running, climbing, swimming—and talking. There was an old oak tree that we loved, and we would spend hours high up in its limbs, talking about all the things that were so important to girls about to enter their teens. That tree became our clubhouse, and we made a solemn pact that we would continue to climb it together, even when we were ancient—as old as eighteen.

The summer that I was ten, my parents told me with great joy that they were going to have another baby. Outwardly, I was thrilled and excited at the prospect, but inside I grew increasingly apprehensive. The arrival of adorable Cal had been bad enough; what if the new baby were—a *boy?* If that happened, he would be the center of their world, and I would be totally replaced. I was in agony, and of course I couldn't tell anyone—except Lee; to her, I told everything. It didn't help; the closer the time came, the more difficult I became; I was driving my mother to tears, until she begged me to behave and stop causing so much trouble.

As it turned out, I had done a lot of agonizing for nothing. The new baby arrived squarely on my father's birthday in October. Only instead of being Frederic the fourth, she was Percilla Avery Lincoln. Named for my Grandpa Rockefeller, she would be affectionately known as Percy, from then on. Lee and I were together almost constantly now, playing field hockey on Sundays and listening to gripping radio dramas like "The Shadow." In fact, the only time we were apart was when I was at school in New York, and she was in Greenwich, and on those evenings we would tie up our families' telephones for hours, until our fathers would roar at us to hang up. But for the most part, our parents found our attachment amusing, our mothers even buying us identical outfits, as if we were twins. And actually, we looked the part, for although Lee was a year older, we were the same size and build. Sometimes we would bind ourselves together with a length of chain that we had found, so that we would have to walk exactly in step and sit down and stand up simultaneously—until we got to laughing so hard that it was hopeless.

When we were eleven and twelve, as a pledge of our friendship, we gave each other silver lockets and chains, which bore our photographs. It had taken us months of saving our allowances to purchase them, and we promised each other that we would never take them off.

In the fall of 1939, just after my twelfth birthday, my parents, again full of joy, told me of the expected arrival of another baby sister or brother. This time I felt no apprehension whatever; Lee had become so much a part of my life, and I of hers, that it didn't matter, not even if it were a little boy. And so little Posy became the fourth daughter of

Freddy and Isabel. Posy was not her real name; like Bellita, it was a name my mother had given her at birth, because she looked like a posy. The truth was that for a year and a half my parents could not agree on what her real name should be, finally settling on Florence Philena, for my father's mother. But Posy was the name that stuck.

The following summer, Lee's family and ours planned, as usual, to take their vacations together, going for the third year in a row to a guest ranch out in Cody, Wyoming. I could hardly wait; Lee and I were both horse-crazy, as girls that age are often wont to be, and we loved nothing more than to ride and ride. The high-pommeled Western saddles meant that you didn't have to post, so we would go exploring for hours, often taking box lunches with us, and stopping for a swim in the roaring Shoshone River, if it got too hot. Occasionally, at our parents' insistence, we would include our kid sisters in our adventures, but usually we would be off and away, before anyone could think to say, "Now you two be sure to take Cal and Hopie with you."

This year, shortly before we were due to leave, my mother called me into the library. This room, bright and cheerful, with hunting prints on the walls and shelves of books up to the ceiling, was the heart of our new home—the place where all of us got together. I used to go in there when no one else was around, curl up on the end of the sofa that was covered in a chintz of daffodil yellow and leaf green, and thumb through a comic book or Mummy's *New Yorker*, or *Field & Stream*. The books didn't interest me yet; they were mostly novels—Hemingway, Marquand, Steinbeck, Waugh—and picture books about hunting and fishing.

To my surprise, Lee's mother, Aunt Hope, was in the library, too; they were having coffee, and my mother motioned me to join them. "Bel," she said cheerily (too cheerily), "Lee and Aunt Hope are not going to be able to come to Wyoming this year; Lee's having trouble with her leg, and yesterday Aunt Hope took her to a specialist in New York. The doctors want her to stay home, so that they can treat it." She was smiling, as if this were good news, and I should be smiling, too.

I didn't feel like smiling. Wyoming without Lee would be a dud, but I was more worried about her. I knew she'd been having pain above her kneecap, and recently she had stumbled twice, walking with me. But if she had to miss Wyoming, which she loved as much as I did, then it was a lot more serious than they were letting on.

"How bad is it?" I asked, straight out.

"Oh, they're just going to do some tests and some special therapy," my mother said, dismissing it, as if it were no more serious than the car going in for an overhaul. As usual, the grown-ups in our family had obviously decided that the children were not to know anything—for their own good, of course.

But Aunt Hope blew it. "Bel," she said, trying to emulate my mother's light tone, but with a quaver in her voice, "why don't you take that locket off, just for now?"

My mouth fell open, and I just stared at her. She was unable to meet my gaze, and when I could speak, I exploded: "No! I will not take it off! Not now, not ever!" And tears springing to my eyes, I fled from the room.

We did go to Wyoming, and without Lee it was a dud. My parents did their best to cheer me up, but I would not be consoled. I counted the days, until we could board the train home, and the whole family was relieved when that day finally came. It was a three-day trip, but this time there was no thrill to watching the prairie scenery pass by at night; I was too concerned about my best friend.

Lee was in Memorial Hospital when we got home, and as soon as I could, I went over to see her. I filled her in about Wyoming, making it sound so awful that she laughed. Soon I was laughing, too, for the first time in weeks, and I promised to come see her every afternoon, after school. And I did, telling her about school, and the gossip of our friends, and bringing her the movie magazines for which we had now developed a passion. Not once, in all those visits, did we ever mention her illness or her therapy.

Eventually, they let her come home—on crutches and wearing a brace. She was not the least bit sorry for herself, not even when the medicine she was taking made her feel sick. Always her attitude was: "This is only temporary; I'll soon be well again," and her smile, which had always been bright, was now radiant.

For Christmas vacation 1940, right after the 25th, the Coombes family came down to Overhills with us. It was an unusually balmy season, and we found that we could go out with only a sweater on, instead of a heavy winter coat. There were cardinals singing everywhere, and while we used to make a game of counting them, this year we had to give up, there were so many.

No mention was made of riding; instead, my father taught Lee and me how to handle a shotgun and introduced us to skeet-shooting, which we could do, standing still. As we banged away at the gliding, fast-receding clay pigeons, and Lee's father took pictures of her from every conceivable angle, I found myself getting annoyed at all the fuss he was making (and the attention she was getting). But the picture-taking went on throughout the vacation, and finally it dawned on me what they were doing: storing up memories of Lee. I did not start dreaming of bedbugs then, but I was every bit as depressed. And there was no one, no one, to talk to.

When we went back to New York, Lee returned to the hospital. She was coughing now, a lot, and I sensed that she was getting worse. Then they let her go home to Greenwich, and for the first time since I had known her, I was unable to see her when I wanted to. Each weekend, I pleaded with my parents to drive me up to Greenwich to see her, as we always had, but invariably they would say that this was not the right weekend, that she was not feeling strong enough to see anyone. And I supposed that was true, for even on the phone she tired quickly, and was no longer able to carry on even short calls, let alone the marathon sessions we used to love.

By March, the strain of Lee's deteriorating condition—and what it was also doing to Aunt Hope and to me—got to my parents. My father loved his sister very much, and my mother—well, it was always easier for her to accept suffering for herself than to see one of her children afflicted. They decided to go down to Jamaica for a week's respite, leaving Cal and me in the care of a very proper, live-in chaperone named Miss Taylor, while nurse Mina took care of Percy and Posy.

One Saturday morning, I awoke early, cutting-garden early, with the strangest but absolutely certain conviction that this day I was going to see Lee. I didn't know how; I just knew that I was going to do it. There would be no asking permission, because I would just be told it was out of the question. I didn't let anyone know where I was going, didn't even leave a note; they would only have tried to stop me. I just got dressed, took all my allowance money out of its secret box, and set out, leaving the apartment around seven o'clock, before anyone else was up.

Down on the street, the air was crisp and clear, and taking a deep breath, I turned right and headed east on 77th. I had never been anywhere in New York alone, but I was thirteen; I could figure out what to do. I took the Lexington Avenue subway down to Grand Central Station, and bought a round-trip ticket to Greenwich on the next eastbound New York, New Haven & Hartford train. It didn't leave for twenty-five minutes; I had time for a glass of orange juice and some toast and, I figured, just enough money. I would need cab fare from the station to the Coombes' house and possibly back, but that wouldn't be more than two dollars. At the worst, I wouldn't have the nickel for the subway home. No matter, it was only 35 blocks.

The train was mostly empty, it being early Saturday morning, and I had no trouble getting a seat by the window. As the train started to move, I pressed my forehead against the cool glass and stared into the passing darkness and thought about Lee. I fingered the locket at my neck, and knew that she still wore hers.

Lee . . . images of horseback riding and swimming, skating and tree climbing flashed through my mind. So many things we had done together, so many things we felt the same way about. . . . I felt the tears welling up and determined not to give in to them. I was going to visit Lee, to let her know that her friend still cared—so her friend had better be smiling and not all red-eyed.

The train emerged from the underground somewhere above Manhattan, and now the pale, early morning sunlight was reflected in the windows of the borough tenement houses. I had a lot to smile about, I scolded myself, as a grown-up might have. Lee had been about the best thing that had ever happened to me. She had come into my life after the deaths of all those people I loved, at a time when I was totally alone and miserable and unsure of myself, with no one to talk to or trust. She had lifted me out of despair—out of my self, really—and helped me to become almost another person, someone with courage and confidence, who loved life and could not wait for the next adventure. Someone who was not afraid to embark on a solo voyage like this one. If Lee had not come into my life, what a sad sack I would have been! I probably would have grown up gloomy and fearful—and I thought then of poor Aunt Win.

But Lee *had* come along, someone who loved and trusted me, as I did her, someone to share dreams and hopes and frustrations with, someone to just *be there*, on the other end of the phone or the opposite tree limb, someone who was patient and who understood. . . . I felt the tears coming again and fought them down. Lee would need me now, as I had so often needed her.

The train pulled into Greenwich, and I got off and asked the station master where I might get a taxi. Scratching his white hair, he nodded in the direction of the street behind the station. "I reckon you might find old Tom getting a cup of coffee in the diner."

I thanked him, walked around the station, and sure enough there was an old cab, parked in front the the diner. As there was only one man at the counter, I figured it had to be him, so I went up and asked him in my oldest voice: "Excuse me, sir, but would you give me a ride to Lake Avenue?"

His eyebrows went up, as he looked at me, and then he nodded. "Sure, if you've got the fare; I never give free rides on Saturdays."

"How much would it be?"

"A dollar and a quarter—maybe more, depending on how far we have to go out Lake Avenue."

That was more than I had counted on. As I mentally calculated how much I could afford, he was watching my face and now added, "Of course, seeing how it *is* Saturday, and there'll be nothing stirring in this town for another hour, I suppose I could give you the special thirteen-and-under discount. You thirteen-and-under?" I nodded, and he smiled. "Well, then, it will be a dollar even." Behind the counter, the red-haired waitress in the white uniform, who had been listening to all of this, smiled and nodded her approval at him.

"I accept," I said, "only can we go soon? I'm sort of in a hurry."

"Just as soon as I finish Josie's delicious coffee," and with that, he took a last big gulp and got up from the stool.

He opened the back door of the old cab and held it for me, then got in and started it up. I gave him the address, and we started off. "You visiting family?" he asked, keeping his eyes on the road and not looking up in the rearview mirror.

"No, a sick friend," and I didn't volunteer any more, so that he would understand I didn't want to talk about it. We rode in silence the rest of the way.

When we arrived at Lee's home, a lovely old white clapboard house set back among shade trees, I thanked him and gave him a dime tip, as I had seen my father do.

He thanked me, and getting out of the cab to open the door for me, asked, "Would you like me to wait?"

"No, though it won't be a long visit. I don't know exactly how long I'll be inside. Besides, I couldn't afford to pay you for your time."

"Well, I might just wait a spell anyway, on my own. This town hasn't even had its first cup of coffee yet."

I shrugged. "Suit yourself. Anyway, thanks again," and I turned and headed up the walk to the front door.

But now, standing in front of it, a wave of fear swept over me. No one knew I was coming; what if they didn't let me see her. . . . To cut off the thought, I reached out and grabbed the lion-head brass knocker and rapped it three times. It made a loud, hollow noise; if anyone was still sleeping inside, or in the houses on either side, they wouldn't be now.

Eventually, the door opened, and there was Aunt Hope, a faded blue wrapper clutched about her. She looked as if she had not been asleep all night.

"Bel!" she exclaimed, her eyes widening. "What are you doing here?"

"I've come to see Lee."

"But you can't! You can't see her today; she's not at all well."

"I'm sorry, Aunt Hope; I've got to see her," and I pushed past her and went upstairs to my friend's bedroom.

When I opened the door, though the shades were still down and there were no lights on, I sensed that she was awake. "Hi, Lee," I said, grinning. "I've come to see you."

My eyes were growing accustomed to the darkness, and I could see her now. She could barely rise up from her pillows, but she gave me the most beautiful smile. "I knew you'd come," she said softly, "I *knew* it." With a sigh, she sank back on her bed and struggled to catch her breath. "Come here," she whispered. "I want to see you. I can't turn the light on; it gives me headaches."

I went to her side, and she reached for my hand and took it in hers. It was so thin and light. . . . We held hands, not speaking. Minutes passed, and neither of us moved. And I had the strangest thought: I am in the presence of an angel. God is here.

At length, I sensed that it was time to go. Taking my hand from hers, I said gently, "Goodbye, Lee. Goodbye," and I turned away, so she couldn't see me.

"Goodbye, Bel," she said, closing her eyes and falling back into the pillow.

Lee died four days later. When Mina told me, I didn't cry; my desolation was beyond tears. No one had expected her to go so quickly, and my parents hurried back from Jamaica for the funeral. It was a small funeral, just for the immediate family, and the little chapel of Christ Church was banked with the gardenias that Lee loved. Their fragrance filled the air, as we sang Lee's favorite hymn and mine, "Fairest Lord Jesus."

I do not know how I got through that afternoon—how any of us did, for that matter. But I did not realize how hard it had hit my parents, until the following weekend. My father had taken me out to Greenwich for the weekend, and the two of us were having lunch. The soup course was served, and as he picked up his spoon, he started to silently weep. I had never seen him cry before (and I never would again, though the image of his grief would remain with me forever). It was more than I could bear; my heart breaking, I ran to my room, threw myself down on my bed and cried and cried.

Thirteen, apparently, was the age in our family at which children were judged old enough to begin to share in the adult world. Or perhaps because Lee and I had been so close, my parents felt I deserved an explanation. Whatever their reasons, they now finally told me the truth about Lee's condition. She had died of bone cancer. When Aunt Hope had first taken her to the New York specialist, he had given her a terrible choice: the disease was invariably fatal, but there was the remotest chance that if the cancer had not already spread, they might be able to save her by amputating her leg. Aunt Hope and Uncle Reggie decided against amputating, and it seemed, in retrospect, to be the right decision: a young boy with the same condition was diagnosed on the same day as Lee. In his case, they did amputate, and he died six weeks after Lee.

Cancer—how I hated that ruthless, malevolent killer! That evil force, torturing and destroying those I loved! Science did not really understand it, and so no one, not even the loved ones of those suffering from it, talked about it. I vowed, then, that I would discover a cure for cancer, if it took the rest of my life. My mother had often worked in a research lab; so would I. And from then on, I planned all my courses in school and college with that one goal in mind.

I was not the only one whom Lee's death had left with an abiding hatred of cancer; her father, a senior officer of the Hanover Bank, now threw all of his energies into raising funds for a cancer research and treatment center, to be connected with Memorial Hospital. It became a life's crusade for him, and he prevailed upon Alfred P. Sloan, the chairman of General Motors, and Charles Kettering, the inventor of the electric starter for automobiles, to put up most of the money for it. Indeed, Uncle Reggie would become world-famous for his fund-raising work and promotion on behalf of cancer research, and for three decades he would serve as chairman of the Memorial Sloan-Kettering Center.

At one of their board meetings, they gave him a special tribute for the work he had done, in memory of his daughter "whom we all grew to love so well, when she was a patient here. It can truly be said that she carries on in spirit, a character which was so outstanding in her life."

Yes, Lee, I thought, as I read that, your life brought so much joy to mine, and now your death will bring life to so many others.

It was a comforting thought—but it did little to dispel the numbing ache in my heart. Time was supposed to heal all wounds, but the process was dreadfully slow, during that summer of '41. Still, events were taking shape over the eastern horizon that would soon command our undivided attention. My father saw the gathering clouds sooner than most, but his warnings fell on deaf ears.

# 9

---

To be successful in the export-import business, my father had had to be acutely sensitive to shifts in political and economic climates in different countries. For what happened in one country would eventually have a direct effect on others, and anticipating that effect was what gave a world trader his edge. On his many trips abroad, my father had always made a point of consulting with those who could give him the best appraisal of what the future might hold in store. And so, after World War I, he had not been surprised by the runaway inflation that wiped out the stabilizing middle class of one European nation after another, toppling their governments and paving the way for chaos and totalitarianism. He had predicted the rise of Nazism and Bolshevism, and he viewed with profound misgivings the emerging dominance of the warrior caste in Japan.

He tried to warn his friends, his contacts in Washington, anyone who would listen, that a global war was coming that would eclipse that of 1914-1918, which had supposedly made the world "safe for democracy." But America did not want to think about war. At long last emerging from the economic nightmare of the Depression, all she wanted to do was look up into the sunshine. "Get their factories running again," his friends said. "Get their people back to work, earning wages and spending money, and everything will be all right. It's working for us, and it will work for them."

In 1938 when Hitler decided that Germany needed more *lebensraum* and only Czechoslovakia could provide it, my father decided that I was old enough to share his and my mother's concern. He bought me a scrapbook, and every afternoon after school, I was to take that morning's *Herald Tribune*, cut out the overseas articles he and my mother had underlined, and paste them in. In this way, I did come to know what they were talking about at the dinner table, as in shocked tones they discussed Hitler's nonaggression pact with Stalin, and his subsequent invasion of Poland. Soon all Europe was at war again, and as the Luftwaffe began to attack London, those were not just trading partners who were being bombed; many were longtime personal friends. And for all my father's former detestation of Roosevelt, he was grateful for the long-range vision of "that man in the White House," whose Lend-Lease destroyers were all that kept the U-boats from tightening the noose around England's neck.

IN THE MEANTIME, on the other side of the world, Japan had built a fleet of aircraft carriers to rival our own. The Battle of Britain had demonstrated, for those with eyes to see it, the strategic importance of air superiority. Aircraft carriers—mobile air bases, capable of moving 500 miles in a single day—were the weapons of tomorrow, as revolutionary as the tank had been in trench warfare. Nor was Japan building these radical new ships to defend her homeland; theirs was a blue-water navy whose sole purpose was the projection of force thousands of sea miles from the Land of the Rising Sun.

That September of '41, my father went out to the Mayo Clinic in Minnesota for a thorough checkup in hopes of getting some specific relief for his ulcerated digestive tract. He came back, disgusted; the sum total of their collective wisdom was that he should give up coffee. But he was even more incensed at the sublime, head-in-the-sand isolationism that he had encountered in the Midwest. "Isabel," he practically shouted at my mother at the dinner table, "those, those—*people* out there think we are back in the nineteenth century! According to them, if the Europeans want to kill each other off, let them. All they care about is how well the wheat is doing, and whether Minnesota has a chance of beating Ohio State this year!" My mother just nodded and said nothing. "Well," he said, not losing any steam, "there *is* something I can do; I'm going to enlist. Now. I'm not going to wait until they have to call me."

*William Rockefeller, Elsie Lyons, John D. Rockefeller, Moravia, New York, 1921.*

*James Stillman, 1888. His success as a capitalist and his understanding of the way corporate America was run was the equal of the Rockefeller family.*

*My maternal grandmother, Isabel Stillman Rockefeller.*
(COURTESY OF THE ROCKEFELLER ARCHIVE CENTER)

*The Percy Avery Rockefeller residence in Greenwich, Connecticut, "Owenoke Farm" (Hiss & Weeks architects). When James Stillman built a magnificent townhouse in New York City the Rockefellers sought parity.* (COURTESY OF THE ROCKEFELLER ARCHIVE CENTER)

*Percy Rockefeller. Mother always kept this photo on her desk.*
(CREDIT: MONTAUK PHOTO CONCERN)

*Isabel Rockefeller. My mother's coming out picture.*

*Mrs. Frederick W. Lincoln, Junior. This wedding of Miss Isabel Rockefeller to Mr. Lincoln, a son of Mr. and Mrs. Frederic W. Lincoln, senior, of New York and Greenwich, Connecticut, was solemnized in Christ Church, Greenwich. The wedding ceremony was followed by a large reception at "Owenoke Farm," the country estate of the bride's parents, Mr. and Mrs. Percy Rockefeller. Mr. and Mrs. Lincoln will spend the greater part of their honeymoon in South America. A great-niece of John D. Rockefeller, Mrs. Lincoln is one of the important heiresses of American society. (A newspaper caption of mother's wedding, September 26, 1925.)*

*When my mother married Frederick W. Lincoln, Jr. a notable gathering bid them* bon voyage *on their honeymoon on the "SS Essequito Pacific." (Left to right: Mrs. R. G. Coombe, the former Hope Lincoln, sister of the bridegroom; Mr. George Piper; Mr. Thomas McCarter; Mrs. Frederick Lincoln, mother of the groom; Mr. and Mrs. F. Lincoln, Jr.; Mrs. Percy Rockefeller, mother of the bride; Miss Winifred Rockefeller; and Betty Griggs.)* (CREDIT: FOTOGRAMS)

*My mother was merely doing her Christmas shopping, but the press headlined this photograph: SOCIETY FOLK SNAPPED DURING XMAS SHOPPING.* (CREDIT: © KEYSTONE VIEW CO.)

*Croatan, the gracious mansion my Grandmother Rockefeller built in
Overhills, North Carolina.*

*"The Cabin" at Upper Saranac Lake, N.Y., 1929, where Grover Cleveland spent his honeymoon. It was a favorite of my parents.*

*My parents' house in Greenwich. Built in 1938, it was used as our summer and weekend home.*

*Easter Sunday, 1938. My father and Mother with Cal and me and cousin Hopie Wonham (my father's twin sister's child).*

*Out West. Lee and me, August 1938 at the "S⋈" (2 Quarter) ranch, Cody, Wyoming.*

Wyoming was a place the family would vacation many times in our lives. Here are Cal, Posy, my father, my mother, Percy, and me, in 1948. We are at the Deer Creek Ranch in Cody, Wyoming. (CREDIT: STAN KERSHAW)

My parents in 1953.

*The author, about one year old.* (CREDIT: CLAYPOOLE)

"Then you'd better check your mail, dear," she said calmly. "Two or three letters have come that might interest you." He did, and they did. Three like-minded friends who had already joined up had written him, each urging him to join their particular branch of the service. My father weighed them all and decided on the Naval Air Corps. Though no one ever said so, I suspect he secretly hoped he might become a carrier pilot. But at forty-three, he was overage; in fact, he was too old to be called at all, especially with five dependents. But my father loved his country too much to sit it out, and he had never gotten over his parents thwarting his sailing with his cavalry unit in 1915.

So the Naval Air Corps it was, and they had an assignment that exactly suited him. Possessing a rare blend of wisdom and compassion, my father all his life had people coming to him for advice, and now the Navy needed such a person to counsel young, would-be aviators down in Pensacola, Florida. They offered him a lieutenant's commission, and by December, he was just waiting on the results of his final physical before heading south.

That first Sunday in December, I was in Greenwich for the weekend, at my cousin Hopie Wonham's. We had all finished a big Sunday lunch, and Hopie and I, having completed our homework, were sprawled on the living room carpet, poring over the funnies. Aunt Polly, my father's twin sister, was on the sofa, knitting and remarking that she hoped the berries that had just come out on their twin holly trees would last long enough to use as Christmas decorations. Out on the sun porch, Uncle Stapely, who had been one of my father's closest friends at Princeton, was gently snoring, his face covered by the sports section.

His snooze was interrupted by the jangling of the telephone on an end table next to his head. He grumphed and turned over but it kept ringing, and since he was the closest, he finally groped for the receiver and answered in a tone that indicated how thoughtless it was of anyone to call anyone else on a Sunday afternoon.

His tone abruptly changed. "Polly!" he shouted. "Turn on the radio!" Getting up so quickly that her ball of wool rolled in the floor, Aunt Polly went to the big Stromberg-Carlson and switched it on. There was news on every station: "We have just received word that, shortly after dawn, the naval base at Pearl Harbor was attacked by Japanese aircraft. Several capital ships have been sunk, including the U.S.S. *Arizona*. . . ."

The announcer's voice betrayed the horror he was feeling as he read the bulletins being handed to him, and in the Wonham living room, none of us could breathe. Uncle Stape had hung up the phone and stood in the doorway, transfixed. The phone rang again. It was my father, calling to see if we had heard the news, and to tell them that he was coming up to fetch me. Normally, I would have ridden into New York on the early train with Uncle Stape, who would drop me off at school on his way to work, but my father apparently wanted his family close about him at this time.

The next morning Cal and I went off to school as usual, but the student body was called immediately to the assembly hall, where we all listened to a broadcast in which President Roosevelt declared war on Japan. Germany and Italy were quick to side with Japan, and suddenly America was involved in a second world war, only this time we were within the enemy's reach. He could hurt us badly, as he had demonstrated with his opening blow.

New York was obviously a prime target, and so our school, like all the others in the city, had air raid practice, during which we all ran down to the furnace room in the basement. There they instructed us how to sit with our knees tucked up and our arms protecting our heads. Up to that moment the war had been thrilling. But I had seen the newsreels at the Trans-Lux, showing the bombing of London, with the fires and ambulances and stretcher-bearers. It wasn't thrilling any longer; it was real, and it was frightening.

That afternoon, my mother came to pick me up. She had been buying heavy black cloth to cover the windows, and that night we listened to the whistles of the air raid wardens in the streets, as they checked for uncovered lights. We kept the radio on constantly, and the news kept coming. All over America, men were enlisting. The devastation at Pearl Harbor had been horrendous, but by the grace of God, the carriers stationed there happened to be out at sea when the attack came. They were still between us and the main Japanese fleet.

Almost overnight, everything had changed, and so had my father's orders. What the Naval Air Corps needed most now was officer-candidates for flight school, as many top-caliber ones as they could find, and *fast*—before the enemy turned the far Pacific into a Japanese lake. My father was put in charge of officer-candidate procurement in the Philadelphia area, and my mother went with him, to find a place for us to live. Miss Taylor had already gone off to work in a factory, nurse Mina had, of all things, gotten married, and except for nurse

Nana, who looked after Percy, four, and Posy, two, only Oscar, our family retainer, was left. He was in his seventies now, but still active and still in charge of the staff, and my mother relied heavily on him. On weekends, when he had the time, he loved to take Cal and me to the American Museum of Natural History or the Planetarium. But for the most part, we, who had not even been allowed to ride the Madison Avenue bus alone, were now—at twelve and fourteen —left to fend for ourselves.

This heady freedom was heartily welcomed by us, and the same sort of thing was happening in the households of our school friends; indeed, a number of us, on our own for the first time in our lives, would go over to Broadway in our bobby sox and saddle shoes and hang around the theaters there, hoping to get into one of the shows where Frank Sinatra was singing. How grown-up and mature I felt—until the next air raid drill at school would reduce me to a frightened little girl again. All the younger children got to wear plastic disks around their necks with their name and telephone numbers on them, and I wondered what would happen if I were killed in an air raid; would anyone know who I was?

As always, my fears were worse at night, and I would get up and check on Percy and Posy. They had Nana, of course, but when my parents left for Philadelphia, I assumed responsibility for them in my heart. Somebody had to, I thought, not realizing how much I resented my mother for abandoning us in this way. She, who could be so smotheringly protective, at other times would appear completely oblivious of us. And so, unconsciously, I took her place, trying to give my little sisters what she wasn't giving them, and in the end bossing them around so much that they could hardly stand me.

The war was a kaleidoscope of memories, a montage of snapshots in a young teenager's album. There was Eastertime 1942, when we took our one and only family vacation, in Atlantic City. We went with the Coombes, who were still mourning the death of Lee less than a year before. Our hotel room looked out on a grey and dreary ocean, where we saw endless convoys of ships, steaming over the horizon for England. One afternoon, Cal and I went exploring up on the hotel's roof—and were startled to find Marines with submachine guns, keeping a lookout for an invasion fleet and guarding that high place against reconnoitering saboteurs.

In June, we children joined my parents in Philadelphia, where they had rented a small but comfortable brick house in Ardmore. I was astonished to find how happy they were! My father, ever charming and persuasive, looked especially dashing in his navy blue uniform—how could anyone choose the *Army* Air Corps, after seeing him? He was busy visiting campuses and signing up whole squadrons of bright young men, eager to join the fight in the Pacific. My mother had started working full time in Dr. Harriet Felton's lab, where they were developing the vaccination for whooping cough with which children all over the world would one day be inoculated. After work, she would don her smart-looking, navy blue uniform and serve as an Emergency Aid volunteer in one of the service canteens, staffed by wives and daughters of navy officers.

It did not dawn on me then, but this was the first time in years that my father had been fully challenged, and neither of them had ever worked that hard to help others, rather than themselves. No wonder they were happy! I should have been glad for them—but I was not. They were so busy and having so much fun, they seemed to have no time for me. True or not, that was the way I perceived it, for all my life up until then, I had been special to someone—first Mina, then Grandma Rockefeller, and then Lee. Now I was special to no one, and I resented it.

I particularly blamed my mother. In her newfound independence and sense of self-worth, she was happier than I had ever seen her. But as that happiness did not derive from being with me, I subconsciously punished her for it. One night, when my father was down in Washington on temporary duty, my mother called Oscar and told him that she was with some former school chums and would not be home until late. Dutifully, Oscar passed this information on to Miss Bellita, as the oldest Lincoln present, and I thanked him and waited for her return. When she had not come home by three o'clock, I called my father in Washington. As I had anticipated, he was furious, and the more so, because there was nothing he could do about it.

When my mother finally did come home, she explained that they had run out of gas and out of ration coupons, and she had stayed with her friends. I let her know by my expression what a lame excuse I thought that was, and I looked forward to when my father would get home, and she would get it. But it was not the last time she went off alone, without telling me where she was going. With all her new independence, she was behaving like an irresponsible teenager. (It would be forty years before I realized that I had become the mother, and she, the daughter.)

There were other things I held against her, not the least of which was making me go to dancing school. Socially, my mother and father had a surprisingly easy time of it, even though Main Line Philadelphia society was far crustier than New York and almost as crusty as Boston. For they made a very attractive couple, having a warmth that drew people to them. Soon, much to their eldest daughter's consternation, they were receiving more social invitations than they could accept. And because they were both involved in commendable, patriotic work, their new friends and their wives adopted my parents and made them their "war effort," doing everything they could for them, including getting me into the most exclusive dancing school in Philadelphia.

Dancing school was bad enough in New York, but at least there I had lots of girlfriends, plus some boys that I could count on to dance with me. Here, I had no one. That first Friday evening, I stood in my pale purple chiffon long dress with the other girls on the right side of the room, dreading what was coming next. If they did it like New York, any moment now the boys would be directed to cross the floor and invite girls for the next dance. "Cattle call" was what we used to call it back home; the boys were supposed to behave like young gentlemen, but what they usually did was stampede across the hall like cowboys, to get to their favorite filly first.

And so I waited, heart pounding, among girls who were twittering on both sides of me and paying no attention to me whatsoever. How wretchedly self-centered of them, I thought, it never occurring to me that I would have done exactly the same, had one of them come to New York. Someone blew a whistle, and looking around, I saw that it was the dancing school teacher, in a flamboyant red velvet gown with lots of blond curls piled on top of her head. "Young men," she announced in her most cultured voice, "will you now please rise and cross the floor *slowly* and select your partner for the next dance?"

Immediately, there was a roar, as the boys tore across the room toward us. My heart sank: just like home. Oh, please, *please*, let somebody pick me! But no one did, and all of a sudden I was standing alone against the wall, while everyone else got ready to practice the tango. Eventually, the dancing school teacher went over to a clutch of extra boys and hauled one over to dance with me. He mumbled hello, and I replied, and we labored through the step-step-step-slide-close.

As soon as the dance was over, I excused myself and fled to the powder room. There I spent the rest of the evening, but it was almost as bad as being out on the ballroom floor. Girls would come in, laughing and chatting with their friends about their respective partners, touching up their lipstick and rouge—and not even saying hello. And then, just as I was about to perish from loneliness, someone said "Why, Bel Lincoln, is that you?" It was Carol Blagden, whom I had met one summer up in the Adirondacks. Never was I so glad to see another human being, and she, bless her soul, saved the evening—and all the other Friday evenings that stretched before me—from being an unbearable nightmare.

My mother, of course, had no idea what dancing school was really like, or how I felt about it—because I never told her. Still, if she were a proper mother, I reasoned, she would have sensed it without having to be told.

That was the worst thing about Philadelphia during the war; the best thing was being sent away to finishing school. I wasn't sure I would like Westover, situated in the little hamlet of Middlebury, Connecticut, but I wound up loving it. I made friends easily, lots of them. The school was divided into two teams, the Wests and the Overs, and in my junior year I was elected junior captain of the Wests. And my group of special friends—Lambie, Lucia, Joanie, Ginger, Sala, and Eyre—all assured me that I was certain to be elected vice president of our senior class.

In the meantime, I found my courses interesting and challenging, especially biology and chemistry, for I had not given up my goal of one day working in cancer research. I also particularly appreciated the morning and evening chapel services. Having had almost no religious exposure, I found these Episcopal services of morning and evening prayer comforting. I looked forward to them, and as time passed, I began to sense that there might be a God. I entered confirmation class my first year and was confirmed by the bishop in the spring. My parents didn't know quite what to make of that, but Aunt Win, my godmother, was delighted. She wrote me a beautiful letter and sent me a pearl cross, which I began to wear on the outside of my dress. Inside, of course, I wore the silver locket Lee had given me.

At one of those dreadful Friday evening ordeals in Philadelphia, I had met a boy named Tom Sargent, who was 6'4" and shared my passion for science. Tom went to St. Paul's School, and while we started writing each other a lot, we never got serious. Still, though there were other boys during this period, Tom was the one I wanted to spend my time with when we were home on vacations, and it lasted until he joined the Navy in '45.

In the spring of my junior year, our class held its elections for class officers for senior year. Lambie, Lucia, Joanie, Ginger, Sala, and Eyre were wrong; I did *not* get elected vice president. I was dumbfounded. So sure was I that it would happen, that I half believed that it already *had* happened. But the voting process continued over several days; perhaps I would at least be elected secretary or treasurer. Meanwhile, how could I face my friends? I couldn't, and spent a lot of time hiding in the large walk-in closet in the room I shared with two other girls. There, comforted by the darkness, I said my first prayer: "Please, God, let me have a position!"

But if He heard, He didn't answer. I was not elected treasurer or secretary. I was not elected *anything*. I wished I were dead. How could I face my parents? My friends seemed as friendly as always, but I could imagine what they were saying: "Isn't it too bad about poor Bel? And such a shock—to find out people didn't really like her as much as she thought."

I was crushed. My friends continued to include me in all their activities, just as if nothing had ever happened, and perhaps in their eyes it hadn't. But in mine, the world had ended. I was still captain of the basketball team, which was more of a position than most girls had. But for me, it was not enough; compared to being president or vice president, it was nothing. (Looking back, I can see that if it meant that much to me, my anxiety—and the extreme control I always went into, when I was fearful—must have been stifling to those around me. No wonder I wasn't elected!) All I could see then was that I had been rejected and counted as worthless. And there was no one I could talk to.

One rainy spring afternoon, I received a call to report immediately to the headmistress's office. What had I done now? My mind racing, I knocked on Miss Dillingham's door. But her voice sounded friendly, even cheerful, as she called out, "Come in." Slowly, I opened the door—and there was my mother!

With a sob, I ran to her, and she reached out her arms to me and held me in a firm embrace, as I cried and cried. No one said anything; my mother just held me, until at last my weeping subsided. Finally,

Miss Dillingham said gently, "Your mother has come to take you to your uncle's for the weekend, Bel. Now you just go and have a good time; relax and share everything with your mother."

We went down to Uncle Avery's in Greenwich, an hour and a half away. It rained all weekend, but I didn't care. I slept and read and ate delicious home-cooked food, and even went out in the warm spring rain and let it run down my face, making me feel clean and new and refreshed. For the first time since Lee's death, I felt I really had my mother's attention. We never did talk about my problems at school, but it was one of the closest times we ever had, and it would always remain with me.

I returned to school a much happier girl, and in retrospect I marvel at the wisdom of Miss Dillingham, in sensing what was wrong with me and knowing exactly what I needed. But only in recent years have I come to see the depth of my mother's true love for me. She responded the instant Miss Dillingham called, leaving her work and the rest of the family in Philadelphia and coming at once by train to the school, which meant traveling all day long and changing trains three times. When I needed her, *really* needed her, she was there. And that was always true. But my demand for her attention was voracious; I wanted it *all* the time. And even if I had gotten it, it would not have been been enough.

That weekend should have been the end of my problem, but it wasn't; I began to experience increasing pain in my right wrist and forearm. By the time I returned home for the summer, I could hardly move my hand at all. My parents, with Lee's illness fresh in their memory, were deeply concerned and took me to a Philadelphia specialist, who did a lot of tests, finally putting my whole lower arm in a cast.. His best guess: I might have undulant fever, as a result of drinking unpasteurized milk out West. When there was no improvement, they thought that perhaps it was an infection in my impacted wisdom teeth, and so I had them out at a Navy clinic. But instead of getting better, the arm got worse, and now the pain and the stiffness went into my back.

In desperation, my mother took me to a top arthritis specialist in New York, Dr. Ralph Boots, and after many more tests, including one for sedimentation rate, he discovered that I had a severe case of arthritis. Having had my arm immobilized in a cast for four months had been the worst possible treatment for it. He put me on massive doses of aspirin and recommended daily sun lamp treatments. In

September, not long after my seventeenth birthday, I went back to school a semi-invalid, unable to take part in basketball or any of the sports I loved. Each week, I would take the bus to Waterbury and the train to New York, to be tested again. Sometimes, my mother would meet me there; more often I went alone.

As fall turned into winter, there had been some improvement, but not very much. And there I would sit, in Dr. Boots's waiting room with his other patients, the only non-septuagenarian in the bunch. Finally, one day he called me into his conference room and said sternly: "If you do not show a marked improvement in the next month, I'm going to have to send you to Arizona and arrange for you to receive injections of gold."

That ominous news frightened me so much that I started to improve immediately. It would be another six months before the last symptoms disappeared, never to return, but there was no question that the road to recovery began the moment he spoke those words to me. How much of that arthritis was a subconscious, psychosomatic play for my mother's attention, I'll never know. But given the combined strength of my imagination and my will, I could venture a guess. And I suspect that Dr. Boots ventured one also.

As it happened, I was in New York to see the good doctor in May 1945, when the news suddenly came that the Germans had surrendered. Joyous crowds poured into the streets, and I joined them, going over to Times Square to watch the news flashing in lights across the Times Tower. Victory in Europe! The war was almost over! Everyone was so excited, but I felt lonely and out of place in that boisterous, beer-swilling crowd. Pushing through them, I made my way back to Grand Central, to wait for the train that would take me back to school.

I was not at all happy about the coming end of the war. In fact, as I stood there alone on the platform, I realized that I actually felt threatened by it. For the war had become a way of life for my family— a challenging, maturing way of life, which had pulled us together in a new and more honest way. So many others had lost so much, but none of my family had really suffered very much, and now I sensed that my parents would never feel so happy or fulfilled again.

# 1 0

IN JUNE OF '44, my father was transferred to Washington, D. C., and once again the Lincoln family packed up all their belongings and moved to a rented house in the nation's capital. Anyone who has ever been in Washington in July knows how debilitating the heat and humidity can be. And those were the days before air conditioning, so there was no relief when you got inside, or when you got in your car (if you had the wartime ration coupons for gas). But the worst was at night; you lay on top of your sheets and sweltered and yearned for a breath of cool, dry air.

Thanks to my parents' yen for camping and their memory of the screened sleeping porches at Overhills, we fared better than most. Out in our tiny backyard, my father erected a wooden-floored "wickiup"— a large tent with plenty of screening in the walls. To this wondrous structure each evening the Lincoln family would repair—Percy and Posy first, as soon as it was dark enough for them to sleep. Then came Poppy in his blue bathrobe, then Mummy, and last, Cal and I. Our neighbors—and it was a friendly, old-fashioned, caring neighborhood, drawn even closer by the exigencies of wartime—delighted in this nightly diversion.

Unable to sleep themselves, they would hang out of their windows and offer our procession loud, positive encouragement.

I loved that neighborhood; Cal and I explored everywhere on foot and by bus, and six young girls who worked for the government, and roomed in a wooden frame house next door, adopted my father. They even brought him a blue birthday cake on Father's Day! My parents' happiness continued in Washington: my father, a full commander now, was assigned to BuPers (the Navy's Bureau of Personnel), and my mother was able to find challenging lab work in a nearby hospital.

THE WAR MAY HAVE BEEN in its final stages, but my war with my mother continued unabated. I had graduated from Westover and was in the process of making up my mind which college I would go to. I knew how much my mother wanted me to go Vassar, where she herself had yearned to go, before her father declared that she had had enough schooling. But my young friends at Westover and I had decided that we would have nothing to do with "society" colleges like Vassar and Smith. I would go to Barnard, which was affiliated with Columbia, as Radcliffe was with Harvard. And I had an ace in the hole: I knew my father would prefer to have me living at home, when we moved back to New York after the war. If I had to, in order to get my own way, I would set him against my mother; it would not be the first time.

It never occurred to me to tell them how I felt and what I wanted, and to talk things out with them. Our family simply did not do that— any more than my parents had talked with their parents, or my grand-parents with theirs. Always, the older generation had imposed its will on the younger, who had meekly submitted—and then done the same thing to children of their own.

But the war had changed all of that—women were filling men's jobs in factories, and anyone, man or woman, who demonstrated that they could handle responsibility, was given it. As for the children, they learned to get along with far less parental supervision, and it gave them an early taste for independence. The truth was, I didn't *want* to talk things over with my parents, for with the collective wisdom of five times as many years on this earth as I had, they would undoubtedly have persuaded me to see it their way.

And one day, when I came home from volunteer hospital work and discovered that the acceptance from Vassar had arrived, I took radical and immediate action: I called Western Union. I had never sent a tele-gram before, but I was going to now; I had to decline that acceptance before my mother got home! It wasn't so hard: the woman typing on the other end helped me and showed me how to keep it as short as possible.

I was shaking when I hung up, but I was not done yet. I hurried up to Cal's and my room, got out the Barnard application, filled it in, put it in an envelope, stamped it, ran to the nearest mailbox, and mailed it. There! Let her try and change *that*, if she could! And I sat in the living room and waited for her to come home, enjoying the prospect of her impotent rage. I had won, and there was nothing she could do about it!

The front door finally opened, but it was my father, not my mother. He was hot and tired and anxious to get upstairs and take a shower. I said nothing. And then at last my mother came home. "Hi, Mummy," I said cheerily. "Did you have a nice day at the hospital?"

She nodded; like my father, she was too hot and tired to carry on much of a conversation, until she got bathed and changed. "Oh, by the way," I said casually, "I got accepted by Vassar."

She stopped on the stairs, her eyes brightening. "Darling, that's wonderful! Have you told your father yet? He'll be so—"

"I turned them down," I interrupted her, "sent them a telegram," and I watched the joy on her face turn to stunned dismay—just as I had imagined it would.

"You did *what*?"

"I turned them down, Mummy," I said patiently, as if explaining it to a child. "I sent my application in to Barnard, instead. That's where *I* want to go." I smiled and waited for her attack.

Suddenly, my mother looked crushed, much smaller and thinner than I had ever seen her. "Oh, well," she sighed, her voice breaking, "if that's what you want." And she turned away and went slow-ly upstairs.

All at once, it wasn't what I wanted at all! What had I done? The taste of victory turned to ashes. I *loved* her, and look what I'd done to her! Smashed one of her fondest hopes and dreams. What difference did it make what college I went to? Everything in me wanted to run upstairs after her, and cry and ask her forgiveness, and get it all right again. But our family never did that, either. So I went to Barnard, and my mother supported me and encouraged me through all my years there. And never once did she mention her disappointment.


WITH THE SURRENDER OF JAPAN in September 1945, and the mustering out of my father, we moved back to New York City, to an apartment on Fifth Avenue at 87th Street. Much smaller than the one we had had before the war, it was also much more attractive and

homey. And it was only twenty minutes by crosstown and uptown bus
to Barnard. From the beginning, I took as many science courses as I
could. Science was a tougher field than the humanities, and at Barnard, the top-ranked women's college academically, it was very tough
indeed. Putting in long hours in the afternoon labs, I struggled to
maintain a B average, and by the courses I was taking and the effort I
was putting into them, everyone assumed that I was a premed student.
My only on-campus diversion was basketball, to which I apparently
brought the right blend of skill and intensity; I made the varsity my
freshman year. But in junior year, as I commenced my zoology major,
even this had to go. At times I got so discouraged I was ready to give
up, but then I would remember Lee and my vow to join the cancer
research team at the Sloan-Kettering Institute.

On weekends, as soon as I finished my homework, I became a completely different person—a debutante. Here was the other battlefield,
and here my mother's will won out over mine. For my mother was determined that I would come out in society, as she had. I hated the whole
process, and for the life of me, I could not figure out *why* acceptance by
the top level of society was so important to my mother, for I assumed
that the Rockefeller name, and the tremendous amount of press attention she herself received as a debutante, had assured that for her.

It was only years later that I came to understand that press coverage
did not guarantee social position, that, on the contrary, those in the
uppermost echelon, whose families had always been there, shunned
publicity—and looked down their noses at those who received it. Wise,
shrewd Aunt Elsie had known that, she who had had no illusions about
the Rockefellers. She knew that they were exactly what the grande
dames of society were calling them, as they whispered behind their
fans: nouveaux riches social climbers. No matter, let the old money call
the new money whatever it pleased. If she played her cards right, in
another generation the distinction would be sufficiently blurred that by
the following generation—mine—it would be obliterated; our position
in society would be secure.

Aunt Elsie was aware that the Rockefeller men cared little, one way
or the other, about their social standing. Their arena was the business
world, and in it they excelled, achieving a record unparalleled in the
history of the country. There was no man on earth to whom they
needed to tip their hat. But the women's arena was society, and for
them it was still an uphill battle.

So Aunt Elsie had planned my mother's coming out—the first

Rockefeller of her generation to make her debut—with all the skill and cunning of a Prussian field marshal, mapping out a military campaign. Plan for every contingency, pay attention to the minutest detail, leave nothing to chance—and you will achieve what you set out to accomplish. New York society was impressed with London society? Very well, Isabel would be presented at the Court of St. James's. Let the local matrons make snide comments—and then watch them move heaven and earth to have *their* daughters and nieces presented at court!

Aunt Elsie's campaign was successful: my mother *was* accepted—far more than she herself realized. For although she had learned a great deal from her aunt, she did not have the serene confidence that if you did A and B and C, then D and E and F were bound to follow. Instead of being proud of all that her grandfather William and his brother John D. had accomplished, she was embarrassed. Nor did she count her own popularity, leadership, and administrative skills in charitable organizations, to say nothing of her laboratory research, as factors worthy of consideration; in this one area her normally clear vision was flawed. For she feared that the ladies with the fans were still whispering, and that at any moment, they might decide to deny her daughters a place in their society.

That was why my attending the right dancing school was so important, and being invited to the right teas and, later, tea dances, and making the list for all the coming-out parties in my debutante year. Most vital of all was that I make my formal debut at the Junior Assembly, the most exclusive of debutante balls. The Junior League and the Grosvenor were right up there, but it was the Junior Assembly that got mentioned, when the New York *Times* and the *Herald Tribune* announced one's engagement.

To a freshman at Barnard, who had read and discussed Kant and Kierkegaard and was formulating a rather modern philosophy for herself, all of this emphasis on social standing was repugnant. Aside from the stupidity and superficiality of it, and the quantities of time it wasted, I hated its underlying implication: that certain people, by accident of birth or money or worldly success, or a combination of same, were somehow better than others. It seemed antidemocratic to me, and vaguely un-American—wasn't it exactly the sort of thing that we had gone to war to rid the world of? America was supposed to be the country where anyone could be elected President, indeed where anyone with enough grit and gumption could achieve whatever he set out to. Where even an ordinary schoolgirl, if she worked hard enough, might one day discover a cure for cancer.

None of these arguments impressed my mother. If society had any function, it was to ensure that the right sort of girl met the right sort of boy. It was just as easy to fall in love with one's own sort as with a total stranger, and in the long run, the marriage had a much better chance of succeeding. Besides, she would not have me undoing what had taken such a long time to achieve; if for no other reason than for the sake of my sisters who would follow me, and whose future I could not be allowed to ruin, I must do my part and do it cheerfully.

And so I came out. And in all honesty, once I had resigned myself to the inevitable, it was fun. Actually, it was like being in a movie—a musical comedy, where all the men wore white tie and tails, and all the girls were beautiful (or for a few hours could forget that they weren't, for even the plainest of us were ensured of constant dancing partners, thanks to the tradition of inviting twice as many escorts as debutantes), where money was no object, and all the endings were happy. It was a fantasy of elegant dinners and limousines and grand balls that whirled on and on, to the fast, upbeat music of Lester Lanin, who was awfully good, or Meyer Davis, who was tops.

The Junior Assembly would take place just before Christmas, and the girls making their debut at it would be honored at small formal dinner parties beforehand. I would share one in our apartment with Judy Felton, who was also coming out at the Assembly, although, needless to say, neither of us had any input as to who was invited. Mother and Mrs. Felton decided that, drawing up the list of eight debutantes, sending the engraved invitations, and requesting the names of the two boys who would escort each girl to the ball, so that they could be invited, too.

One afternoon, I came home from college, to find my mother at her desk, working through a stack of responses. She looked up and smiled. "One of the boys your cousin Kate from Long Island is bringing is Basil Beebe Elmer, Jr. Now how's that for a name?" She chuckled, thumbing through the *Social Register*, to see who his family was, and where he went to school. "Oh, he's a cadet at West Point," she said with satisfaction. "That should be interesting. Hmm—went to St. Mark's before that, and—oh, look at this! His mother was in your Aunt Polly's class at Farmington. That rings a bell; I think her people were in admiralty law, and her husband is a partner on the floor of the

Stock Exchange for Eastman Dillon.'' But I could not work up much
enthusiasm for a boy whose first name was Basil and whose middle
name sounded like his first two initials; with a name like that, he
had to be a bit odd.

By Christmas vacation, the debutante season was in full swing, and
throughout the city there was a festive spirit in the air. The long war
was at last over, and it seemed that all New York was ready to
celebrate. For the debutantes, luncheons at posh restaurants were
followed by tea dances, followed by dinner parties and culminating in
magnificent balls. We would dance until three in the morning, then go
down to Greenwich Village to hear jazz, and get to bed about an hour
before dawn. Then, shortly before noon, we would drag ourselves out
of bed and struggle to get ready for the next luncheon.

Finally, the evening of the Junior Assembly arrived. My father
looked so handsome in his tails, my mother wore her new blue ball
gown, and Oscar, dressed in a tuxedo, manned the front door. Promptly
at eight, the guests began to arrive. All the girls glowed in expensive,
voluminous white ball gowns, while the boys were dressed either
in white tie, or in dress uniform, as it was still so soon after the war.
Judy and I stood in the living room between our parents and were
formally introduced to our guests—which was a bit strange for we
already knew all the girls and most of the boys. One in uniform caught
my eye—the West Pointer, and I decided to chat with him, as soon as
the receiving line was over.

Now where *was* he? We were standing around, sipping cocktails in
our large living room, although my glass held ginger ale. (I couldn't
stand the taste or smell of alcohol; it reminded me of something that
had been left standing too long in a lab beaker.) *There* he was, over by
the window—talking with my mother, of course. I went over and
joined them, and on closer inspection decided that his was the most
gorgeous uniform I had ever seen! The jacket was a fitted grey tunic
with three rows of brass buttons, surrounded by coils of embroidered
gold, and cut away to form tails behind, with trousers of grey flannel
pressed to a sharp crease. On his sleeve, he wore a gold-edged chevron,
indicating that he was a cadet officer. At 5 '9 ", he was only a little taller
than I was, but standing so erect, he seemed at least six feet tall, with
the brightest blue eyes I had ever seen, and an infectious grin to match.

''This is Cadet Elmer,'' my mother said, smiling. ''We've been
having a most interesting conversation.''

"How do you do, Cadet Elmer," I said with mock formality, as my mother discreetly excused herself to go look after the other guests. "Do you ever call each other by your first names up there?"

He smiled. "My friends at the Point call me Beebe, which is actually my middle name, but my old friends call me Buzz."

"I like Buzz better," I replied, adding, "I'm Bel, short for Isabel." All at once I started to laugh. "Good grief, Buzz and Bel—isn't that awful, we sound like an amusement arcade!"

We both laughed, and as we chatted for a few more minutes before it was time to go in to dinner, I felt completely at ease, as if I had known him for ages.

After dinner, we put on our wraps and went down to the hired limousines waiting to take us to the St. Regis Hotel, the site of the Ball. When we got there, my heart was pounding, and my throat was so dry I could barely talk. Slowly, we mounted the broad, sweeping stairway that led to the Grand Ballroom, with my parents just ahead of me, and my two escorts right behind. At the top of the stairs was the receiving line of the ball's patronesses and their husbands. And now we were announced by a gentleman with an impeccable English accent: "Mr. and Mrs. Frederic Walker Lincoln, and their daughter Isabel."

Down the line we went, and before each patroness I made a deep curtsy, as if they were royalty. That was hard enough, but what was even harder was filling the brief pauses in between, with the utterly inane chitchat one reserved for the perfect strangers in receiving lines. All at once my heart went out to the husbands, these stalwart, goodhearted men, many of whom customarily got up about the time we would be going to bed, and who were usually fast asleep by now. But their wives had insisted that they endure this annual ordeal, making the smallest of small talk and wondering how many more hours would pass before they could put the pearl studs away for another year and get into something a whole lot more comfortable, like bed.

Before I knew it, we were through the line, and that was it: I had officially come out. All those tea dances for that? I shook my head and smiled to myself, as my escort led me out onto to the floor, to Meyer Davis leading the band in "Deep Purple." The rest of the evening was a swirling, magic fairy tale, in which among others Cadet Elmer distinguished himself with gallantry and joined my list of favorite boys.

WITH THE COMING OF SUMMER, I was able to take another step toward my life's goal: I became a volunteer at Sloan-Kettering. I was so glad to be there, I happily did anything they asked me to, from taking case histories of new patients to looking after pathetic children whose small frames were ravaged by cancer.

In the meantime, the strange dichotomy in my life continued. That summer, my parents decided to give me a debutante dinner-dance at our home in Greenwich. There would be a reception tent in our backyard, large enough to contain a dance floor, buffet tables, and the musicians of Meyer Davis. As the United Nations had just come into being, my mother thought that would be the perfect motif for the party. From somewhere, she arranged to rent large flags of all the nations, and with these she had the tent decorated. The girls were asked to come in red or white or blue dresses, and each young man who arrived would be given a tiny flag as a souvenir.

The evening itself was all that anyone could have hoped. Among the guests was a newly commissioned second lieutenant, looking as hand-some as ever. As it happened, Buzz Elmer and several of his St. Mark's cronies each received little Greek flags, and they made it a game to endeavor to capture the large Greek flag, hanging among the others high in the tent.

To do so would require my cooperation, as I knew where the ladder and the house power switches were, and Buzz made it his own game to attempt to persuade me to become a fifth columnist at my own party. He did not succeed, but we laughed most of the evening, as he tried. From that time on, I looked forward to seeing him at parties, until in 1947 he was posted to West Germany.

With September, my life changed again, as I returned to Barnard and once more became absorbed in zoology. I continued to date throughout my college years, but my parents, perhaps recalling the chaos of my mother's numerous "engagements," made clear their strong desire that none of their daughters would consider marrying before the age of twenty-three. As my main interest was in pursuing a career at Sloan-Kettering, I had no difficulty agreeing with them, and actually it provided a way of discouraging several young men who were more in love with love than with me.

And then along came Rossie's nephew. Rossie had joined our family as Aunt Glad's special trained nurse and had become my grand-mother's friend and companion. Out of the blue one day, my parents received a call from her nephew, a doctor, over from England for six weeks of study in New York on a special research grant. They invited him to dinner, and as I expected him to be their contemporary, I ate early with my younger sisters, whose dinner hour at six fit in much better with my college schedule than my parents' customary eight-fifteen.

But I did answer the door when Adrian arrived—and was astonished to greet a strikingly attractive young man who turned out to be the doctor. From the moment I met him, we talked shop, and needless to say, six weeks never passed so quickly. When he returned to England, he took my heart with him, and we corresponded voluminously. I was due to graduate from Barnard that summer, and as a graduation present, my parents were giving me a trip to Europe, with three girlfriends who were going, too. Naturally, the high point of my trip would be the four days we were scheduled to spend in London, where Adrian was, after which my parents and Cal were coming over to London for an additional two weeks.

During my preparation for final exams, I also received a letter from Buzz, inviting me to let him know if I ever came to Europe. It was a long and interesting letter, and I put it in my desk to answer, as soon as exams were over. But before I knew it, there was graduation, and we were embarking for Europe, and I never did answer it.

By the time my parents and Cal reached London, I was convinced that I wanted nothing more than to spend the rest of my life as Adrian's wife. My parents were very gracious to him, yet I could sense that they were not entirely comfortable with him or convinced that we would be happy together. Just before we were due to sail for home, my parents and I had a long private talk. It was one of the few times we had ever talked, and the first time they had ever treated me as a full-fledged adult.

"Bel," my mother said, "what about Sloan-Kettering? For years, you've been telling us that working there was your one ambition."

"Yes, Mum, and Adrian and I have talked about that. He thinks I could get a job in a research lab over here, doing the same sort of work."

"But you also spoke of going back to school, to get a master's degree in zoology—I don't know if you would be able to do that here."

"Yes, I know, but over here, they put more emphasis on learning as you work."

I was arguing with her, only we weren't really arguing, not the way we used to; it was truly more discussion than argument. I sensed that for once she was not pushing to impose her will on me; she genuinely wanted to know how I felt and what I wanted to do. Had I sensed the least bit of pressure from her, I would have responded with equal resistance, and it would have become another contest of wills—one that I would have won, because it was my life, and I was prepared to follow my heart, whatever it cost, and wherever it led me.

Perhaps my mother intuitively knew that; perhaps she had set her will *not* to pressure me. Whatever the reason, all I felt from her was loving concern—and it took me by surprise. For I was well familiar with the saga of Isabel Stillman and Percy Rockefeller, and the five years of enforced separation that they'd had to endure, like some evil curse in a medieval fairy tale. That was the family pattern, but with me that pattern was going to be broken, once and for all.

And now here they were, being so darned decent and understanding. I had never loved them so much as at that moment.

At last, my father spoke. "I'll tell you what—come home and start your job at Sloan-Kettering. Give it three months, and if you still feel as strongly, and can line up a similar job over here and a proper place to stay, then not only can you come back with our blessing, but we'll help with your expenses." He smiled and looked at me. "One more thing: wait a full year before you get engaged. You've got to be absolutely certain that he's the man for you." He paused. "And also that England is the country for you. That's more important than you might suspect. Right now, your feelings have blinded you to the differences. I've worked with the Brits for years, and some of them are close friends, but believe me, the differences are there. For some people, they're not important, but you may find that you're more American than you realize."

I looked over at my mother, who nodded and smiled and said nothing. And I marveled at that, too; usually she had more to say than my father. Indeed, I could not remember my father ever having had so much to say to me all at once.

I agreed, and went back with them to start at Sloan-Kettering. Three months later, I felt just as strongly about Adrian and had lined up a lab position in the Chester Beatty Institute, which was connected with the Royal Cancer Hospital. I was to come as a working student, which meant that they would pay for my room and board and living expenses. As for a place to stay, my old friend Judy Felton was in London, studying to be a concert pianist, and she was able to get a room for me in the same proper boarding house where she was staying.

With all my parents' conditions met, on the day after Christmas 1949, they drove me to Idlewild, where I had a berth on board one of Pan American's new transoceanic airliners. On the way to the airport and waiting for the flight, they remained steadfastly cheerful and supportive, as they had been all through the holidays. Only many years later would I learn that it had all been an act. Inside, they were heartbroken, and regarded that Christmas as the saddest of their married lives.

ENGLAND! It was no surprise to me that I loved everything about the country and the life there, especially those places where it was different from home; I took to it like a duck to water. And the same was true of my work, which grew ever more fascinating and absorbing. Alas, the same was not true of my relationship with Adrian, and that *did* surprise me. But it seemed that I was far more the modern American woman— independent, democratic, career-oriented, outspoken, and hard-headed—than either of us had realized. My father, in his patient wisdom, had been right. As much as I loved England, and Adrian, so far as fundamental attitudes were concerned, we were an ocean apart.

After six months, I returned home. And now I knew that it *was* home, and for me would always be home. My parents met the plane. I never talked to them about it; I just hugged them.

# 11

---

ONCE BACK IN NEW YORK, that summer of 1950, I threw myself into my job at Sloan-Kettering. The hours were long and irregular, and we had to work every other weekend—but I didn't mind a bit. I'd had enough of romance and was determined to get on with my career. And I loved my work. I was assigned to the Chemotherapy Division, where we tested different chemical compounds, to see if they had any effect on cancerous tissue. It was careful, painstaking work that demanded sustained concentration—one slip could destroy weeks of work. And patience: literally hundreds of tests might be negative, before one compound that showed promise. But that one positive result made it all worthwhile!

We were encouraged to do independent research, and on Wednesday afternoons we would attend lectures given by resident and visiting experts; everything possible was done to motivate us in our search. Feeling very much at home with the other young women in Chemotherapy, and content to spend the rest of my life in the search for a cure for cancer, I now began to give serious consideration to the graduate work I would need to do if I was going to concentrate on independent research.

I was well aware of the effort it would entail, but my work was my life—and I didn't want it any other way.

As for living accommodations, there was a change there, too. In England, I had developed a taste for living on my own, so when Laura, a friend of my cousin Nancy, asked if I wanted to share an apartment with her and three other girls, I accepted. I anticipated some resistance on my parents' part, but to my relief they thought it was an excellent arrangement. After all, I was almost twenty-three, and this was 1950.

One Thursday evening I got in from work about six, which was early for me. Hanging up my lab coat, I kicked off the white shoes, wriggled my toes, and absently sorted through the mail. There was nothing— only a couple of bills. As I put them on the edge of my bureau, I noticed a cocktail party invitation that I had left there sometime before. It was for that same evening and was being given by a Barnard girl who had interesting friends. The green silk dress from Lord & Taylor's was just back from the cleaner's; if I took a fast shower and threw it on, I might just catch the end of that party. Well, why not?

I could tell that it was a good party, as soon as the door opened, because there were so many people still there. Dull parties were usually dead on their feet long before their scheduled end, as guests would leave early, using dinner as an excuse. But from the crowd and the happy din, guests were postponing their dinner plans to linger at this one. Joining a group of Barnard friends, I kept an eye out for a passing waiter, taking drink orders. A tall ginger ale with lots of ice would go just perfectly right now—

All at once, a man's voice behind me quietly inquired: "By any chance have you seen a large Greek flag around here?"

"Buzz Elmer!" I exclaimed, whirling around. "I thought you were in Germany!"

"I was, until a few months ago."

My, he looked good! He seemed older and more mature than when I had last seen him. He was deeply tanned now, with a flashing smile, and his blue eyes seemed brighter than ever.

"Hey," he said, "how come you didn't answer my letter?"

"I meant to," I said lamely, "but—" How could I tell him about Adrian?

"Never mind," he smiled.

"Well," I beamed back, relieved to be off the hook that easily, "what do they have you doing now?"

"I'm out of the army and working on Wall Street," he said, and then he told me what had happened since I had last seen him.

When he had been graduated and commissioned, he had gone into the Signal Corps, then the only way for a regular Army officer to get into military intelligence, which was the field he wanted to specialize in. He suffered through Signal Corps school and finally, after three years of trying, obtained assignment to the Russian intelligence school in Oberammergau, where he became fluent in Russian, and learned all aspects of Russian life, culture, and military operations. Upon graduation, he was about to be assigned to the U.S. Embassy in Moscow as Signal Liaison Officer, when someone noticed that he was a graduate of West Point.

"Who told you that you could go to Intelligence School?" demanded the general in charge of the Signal Corps in Germany. "Don't you know that regular Army officers are now under a new, twenty-year career plan, and that Intelligence isn't in that plan?" Buzz shook his head. "Who signed your orders, anyway?"

"You did, sir," Buzz replied quietly.

The general was nonplussed—but only for a moment. "Well, it's out of the question! You need to be in the field, my boy, gaining experience in command! Leave the cloak-and-dagger stuff to the civilian soldiers!"

"But, sir, if I could just explain—"

"No explanation necessary; you can't go, and that's all there is to it."

Buzz submitted his resignation the next day, and as they were trying to reduce the number of regular Army officers at that time, it was accepted. When he had gotten home, he had taken a job as a trainee at the First Boston Corporation, one of the largest underwriting firms in the country.

I must have been a good listener, because all at once he exclaimed: "Hey, why don't we go out for dinner somewhere? It's really fun seeing you again, and we have so much to catch up on." I laughed; he had done all the talking, which was fine with me. I doubted that I could make London and Adrian sound as interesting as he had made Germany— nor, in fact, had I any desire to go into all of that. He had the sort of perceptive, inquisitive mind that would want to know *why* I went to England, and *why* I came home. As much as I was loving his company, I would not enjoy rehashing that—and fortunately I didn't have to.

"Oh, Buzz, I'd love to, but my father's away on business, and I promised my mother that I would come home and have dinner with her."

"I remember your mother from your dinner party; she's fun."

"Say—why don't you come home and have dinner with us? I'm sure she wouldn't mind." The words were out of my mouth before I realized what I was saying, but my parents had always been extremely good about my bringing friends home without warning, and their apartment was still home to me. Buzz nodded, and I went and called my mother, who said it would be just fine. I told her we would be home right away, but the party was so much fun that we lingered awhile, arriving home about half an hour later.

My mother usually had a couple of cocktails with my father before dinner. This evening, perhaps because she was alone and because we were so late, she had a third. It didn't show, but when we sat down to dinner, the first question she asked, as we began the first course (cream of asparagus soup), was: "Buzz, what would you do if you had a daughter, and she had holey underwear?"

Choking on my soup, I threw my mother a horrified glance, but she was in her Katharine Hepburn mode and blithely ignored me, chattering on to Buzz: "I mean, the other day I happened to be looking through the laundry, and every piece of Bel's underwear had holes in it."

Speaking of holes, I fervently wished a great one would suddenly open beneath my chair and swallow me forever. In all my life, I could not remember being so mortified. The worst of it was, it was true. I knew my underwear was a bit rundown, but I was simply too busy to bother replacing it. I was not about to waste one of my rare Saturday afternoons off, shopping for underwear! Besides, even though I brought my dirty laundry with me on the occasional evenings that I slept at my parents' place, I never dreamed that my mother would see it! And it was beyond my wildest nightmare that, having seen it, she would discuss it with one of my beaux!

And Buzz, who I thought was my friend, was loving it. "Mrs. Lincoln," he exclaimed, with an enthralled look on his face, "that's an interesting question. What did *you* do?"

My mother, delighted that he was entering into the spirit of the game, now strove for new heights. "You know, it really was a bit of a shock." She frowned at the recollection. "I mean, once it was really very nice underwear—from Saks and some from Bonwit's. But then, gradually, imperceptibly, the holes must have started. Little ones, at first, not enough to worry about"—and she squinted, as with thumb and forefinger she made a tiny circle. "But then, once you get used to wearing holey underwear, I suppose you just don't notice those little holes getting larger and larger. Why, some of them were this big around!'' and she made a large circle with thumb and forefinger, and I would have liked to die.

"*No!*" gasped Buzz. "Really?"

"*Yes!*" exclaimed my mother, "*that* big," and she paused for the enormity of the hole to sink in.

Buzz was speechless. So was I. There was a tiny sprig of parsley, garnishing the pat of butter on my butter plate. I launched it into my soup and studied it.

Mother, alas, was not speechless. Far from it. "The reason, Buzz, that this concerns me is that we brought up Bel well. And part of that upbringing was to be presentable at all times, in any eventuality. One must wear clean, unholey underwear at all times, because—what if one were in a train wreck?"

Buzz's eyes widened, as he contemplated the possible ramifications. My mother was contemplating them, too: "Why, just last week," my mother went on brightly, "there was an accident on the Third Avenue E1. No one was seriously hurt, but the *Daily Mirror* had pictures of people being lowered to safety," she paused. "I mean, can you imagine, if Bel—?"

"It doesn't bear thinking about," interrupted Buzz, closing his eyes and slowly shaking his head.

I closed my own eyes and slowly shook my head. Was this ever going to end?

At last, the endless dinner ended. We had after-dinner coffee in the living room, where I sat in stony silence, as they happily carried on their conversation. Finally, Buzz looked at his watch, apologized for staying so late, and got up to go. Mortified at the prospect of his seeing me home to my apartment—in fact, determining that I would not see him alone again ever—I informed him that I had decided to stay at my parents' apartment that night. And as I would be getting up quite early in the morning, I bade him good night, as graciously as I could manage.

"Hey," he said, "aren't you going to at least see me to the elevator?"

Not seeing any way to refuse, I went out in the hall with him and pushed the button. And wondered why it seemed to take much longer than usual to reach our floor; where was that blasted elevator?

"I had a good time tonight." Buzz chuckled. "Your mother is a riot." Then he turned to me and said seriously and tenderly, "You know, she loves you very much."

I nodded, but at the moment I was finding that just a bit hard to believe. I smiled, then—not at him or what he had said, but because at last I heard the ancient elevator groaning and clanking its way upward. In another few moments he would be gone, hopefully forever.

"Bel," he said rapidly, as the door opened, "could I take you to a square dance next Tuesday at Hans Jaeger's Brauhaus? It's up at 85th and Lexington, and they've got a dance hall on the second floor that some friends and I have hired for every other Tuesday evening. It's great fun; what do you say?" He put his foot out, to block the door from closing.

I almost looked around, to make sure he was talking to me. To think that he really wanted to see me again, after—

"Yes," I stammered. "I'd love to." So we made a date, the door slid shut, and I walked dazedly back inside.

He was to pick me up at my apartment at seven-fifteen the following Tuesday. At seven the phone rang, and Laura answered it. "Bel, it's for you," she called. "Buzz Elmer."

I put down my hairbrush and went to the phone. Well, so the underwear proved too much for him after all; he's calling to cancel. "Bel?" he said. "I've gotten held up at the office." Here it comes, I thought, bracing myself. "So I'm going to be a few minutes late."

"That's fine; take your time." I couldn't believe it; no one called if they were only going to be a few minutes late.

At seven-twenty the downstairs buzzer rang; it was Buzz. A few moments later he was at our door, and I was on his arm. His politeness continued, as he opened first one door and then another for me, and quickly assumed the gentleman's place on the outside, as we emerged onto the sidewalk. I was impressed; I had assumed such manners went out with the war.

To my surprise, I knew a lot of the people at Hans Jaeger's; apparently, our crowd had decided that square dancing was the thing to do, and this was the place to do it. The large dance hall radiated conviviality—what the Germans called *gemutlichkeit*. I was a little self-conscious at first, but this vanished as soon as we joined the first set. The caller was superb; if you listened carefully, you didn't have to know that much about square dancing, and by the end of the evening I felt very much at home.

Two Tuesdays later, we were back, and again two Tuesdays after that. We became friends, and although I still saw other boys, and he other girls, he would often call me on evenings when we were both home.

Things stayed at that level for some time, and I was perfectly happy for them to stay there. But then came Christmas, and could New Year's Eve, with its dread midnight tradition, be far behind? (It seems astonishing today, that a kiss could make such a difference, but thirty-six years ago, it could, and it did.)

Sure enough, the day after Christmas, Buzz called. He, and the two boys he shared an apartment with, were each asking a girl to a home-cooked dinner, after which they would go over to join the crowd at Times Square, to watch the ball atop the Times Tower go down, signaling the birth of the New Year.

"I'm sorry, I can't," I told him. "I took Christmas Eve and Christmas Day off from work, to be with my family. So now I'm on duty New Year's Eve and New Year's Day."

But he was not going to give up. "I'll bet that if you check with the girls you work with, you'll find someone who doesn't have plans for New Year's Eve, and will be just as happy to swap with you. In fact, it will probably be a relief for her to have work to do, to keep her mind off the fact that she doesn't have a date."

"You're impossible!" I scolded him, "but I'll see what I can do." He was right; I had little trouble getting a sub.

The three boys prepared a surprisingly good dinner for their dates, after which we helped with the dishes and played some fiercely competitive Monopoly, and then, at eleven, wandered over to Times Square. I had never been there to see the New Year in, and had no desire ever to repeat the experience. There was a mob of people with champagne bottles and noisemakers and confetti, and since they all apparently felt that they were supposed to be having a screaming good time, they screamed. Midnight came, the ball went down, the shrieking gave me a headache, and Buzz gave me a chaste kiss on the cheek. I told him that I had had a wonderful evening, which was true, but I had to be in the lab at eight the next morning, which was also true. He nodded and started to lead the way through the crowd, with me close behind him.

The next morning, he called me at work, to see how I was doing. For some reason I couldn't explain, I didn't feel the least bit tired. "Good," said Buzz. "Then, since I don't have to feel guilty, how about seeing a movie with me next Friday?" Slowly, our dates began to get closer and closer together. I found myself beginning to worry about what to wear on these occasions, and then I would remind myself that it didn't matter; Buzz was just a friend. And then one evening, toward the end of January, as he was saying goodnight after a cheeseburger date, he gave me a friendly, nonthreatening kiss. It became a tradition, and each time a little more feeling crept in.

Meanwhile, my work at Sloan-Kettering went on. It came first, and with the exception of New Year's Eve, Buzz never complained about the fact that I worked every other weekend. In so doing, I was accumulating extra days off, and in the middle of February, when I had seven days stored up, my parents suggested that I accompany them to Cuba for a week at the beautiful resort complex of Varadero Beach. It was their favorite winter vacation spot, and I was touched that they wanted me to share it with them.

The night before we were due to leave, I stayed at their apartment. Buzz had come for dinner, and I noted that my father seemed to be as taken with Buzz as my mother had been, ever since the dinner that we now all joked about. After Buzz left, I had a serious talk with my mother. "Mum, I'm worried about Buzz."

"What's wrong?"

"Well, you know, we're just friends. We have a good time together, and I don't feel a bit awkward with him. But I still want to get another degree—maybe even my doctorate."

"So?"

"I think Buzz is getting a bit too interested. I don't mean to lead him on, and I certainly don't want to get married—to him, or anyone else —for a long, long time. I don't know what to do."

"Well," she said with a smile, "I wouldn't worry too much about it. Why don't you just go on the way you're going. I'm sure it will all take care of itself."

"Thanks, Mum," I sighed, relieved. I hadn't wanted to break off with Buzz. I just wasn't ready to think about marriage.

We flew down to Cuba, and though it was every bit as beautiful as my parents had said, I found myself spending a lot of time thinking about Buzz. Apparently, he was doing the same, for there were several letters from him. Then one day there was one from Cal, who was at Vassar, and who mentioned that she had seen Buzz on campus the previous weekend, at their winter festival.

Well, that was nice, I thought; I'm glad he got out of New York and had some fun. It made no difference to me; after all, we were just friends. Then why was I—furious, wondering who he was with? Well,

I certainly hope he enjoyed her company! I mean, I was only going to be gone a week! Well, that'll be the end of dear old Buzz.

But of course it wasn't; he met us at the airport with his Plymouth, to offer us a ride home. Though my parents' greeting to him was as warm as mine was cool, my father shooed me off to ride with him, claiming that his and my mother's luggage would take up too much room, and they were going to take a taxi, as planned. "Pop, you and Mum only brought two suitcases; they'll fit," I pleaded. But he just smiled as if he hadn't heard me, and waved for a cab.

"Well, did you have a good time?" asked Buzz cheerfully, as he negotiated the car out of the terminal parking area.

"Yes, thanks."

"How was the beach?"

"Very nice."

"Do much shopping?"

"Not much."

And with that, bewildered by my sullenness, he gave up. We drove toward the city in silence, the only noise the *whish-click* of the windshield wipers, as they coped with a sudden snowfall.

At length my curiosity got the better of me. "Well, did you have a good time at Vassar?"

"*What?* How did you—"

"Who was your date? Anyone I know?"

"She was a blind date. It was one of those last-minute deals; the guys I room with were going up, and they asked me to come, and I didn't have anything else to do—"

"So you went, and there was this poor girl whose winter carnival date had canceled out on her, and suddenly there you were."

"That's about right, but—"

I turned away from him.

"Look, Bel," he said, not smiling any longer, "if you really want to know, I had a terrible time. The weekend was a complete dud."

Suddenly, I wasn't upset anymore. I moved over closer to him and nestled my head on his shoulder. We drove on in silence again—but it was a very different silence from before.

The following week the snow melted, and we had a pre-spring thaw. On Saturday, to celebrate the unusually warm weather, I fixed a fancy picnic for us, and we drove out to Greenwich. A little dismayed to find snow still on the ground out there, even though little purple and yellow crocuses were poking their heads through here and there, I suggested we have our picnic at my parents' place. Technically, the house was closed, Elsa the housekeeper being off in Florida visiting relatives, so we would have the place to ourselves. We built a big fire in the living room, spread our blanket, and feasted on roast beef sandwiches, German potato salad, deviled eggs, and chocolate cake.

When Buzz begged that he could not eat another morsel, I suggested that we work off some of the lunch by walking down to Aunt Win's, which was less than a mile away. Having talked to her just a few days before, I was sure she was home. As we set off, the sun came out, making everything sparkle, and even though there was still snow on the ground, it was suddenly easier to believe the promise of the crocuses. I laughed and took his hand, proud of the fact that he was wearing the wool gloves that I had made for him, the most ambitious knitting project I had ever attempted.

Along the way, Buzz asked me to tell him about Aunt Win. There wasn't a whole lot to tell, I explained, most of it sad. On one of the family vacations, spent up in Vermont, she had met a man named Brooks Emeny. He had paid attention to her—the first man who ever had—and after three dates she had agreed to marry him, which she proceeded to do very quickly, presumably before Grandma and Grandpa could talk her out of it. It was not a good marriage. Brooks Emeny fancied himself an intellectual, and above the rest of us. He wanted a job in the State Department, and so my family obtained one for him. After that, he traveled quite a bit, seeming to spend as little time at home as possible, not even returning when his daughter Betty Brooks was so tragically ill.

When he was home, the family was polite enough to him, but privately they all considered him a rather sad joke. One Saturday evening, my father had gotten into an argument with him. Brooks was insisting that my father's distrust of the Japanese, which was typical of a growing number of informed businessmen in America, was totally misplaced. He, Brooks, had spent a great deal of time in Tokyo, where he had had long consultations with their top officials, and thus understood these things far better than any of us. He could assure us unequivocally that the Japanese wanted only to be our friends, and that they were hurt by our suspicion. My father wryly observed that friends did not build fleets of carriers, capable of carrying bombers five thousand miles across the Pacific. At that, Brooks had lost his temper, shouting that they were only to protect the home waters of their Great East Co-Prosperity sphere. That Saturday evening was December 6, 1941.

Most of the time, Aunt Win lived alone with her three daughters, the oldest of which was about four years younger than I. Even down at Overhills, she was withdrawn and restless, often getting up at five in the morning to do her laundry. In fact, it eventually got on Uncle Avery's nerves to the point where he built her a home of her own, just 50 yards from Croatan. But she loved to ride with me, and the two of us would spend many hours together on the bridle paths that wound their way through the Southern pine.

Aunt Win, a homebody, loved to putter about in her garden in Greenwich, where she lived in a large stone house that she had made quite appealing. But lately her moods had been growing worse. Aunt Win had always been subject to bouts of deep melancholy and despair, of which the grown-ups simply said, "She takes after the Stillman side of the family." Now those times of shadow were enhanced by her increasingly unhappy marriage—to the point where she had sought professional help, when psychotherapy had not yet become commonplace. People did not go to psychiatrists, unless the need was urgent.

On this afternoon in February, I admitted to Buzz that I wanted to try to cheer her up. I felt so good that I had more than enough cheer to share, and besides she had done so much for me in the past. I told him of the cross she had given me, when I was confirmed, and how she had written often when I was at Westover, even phoning occasionally, just to see how I was doing. What I didn't tell him was that Aunt Win always had tea at four o'clock, with real English scones. If we were lucky, we would arrive just in time.

But when we got there, no one answered the door. We walked around the house, and there was no one home. What was eerie was that the shades were all pulled down. If she had just gone out to run an errand, she would not have done such a thing. And where was her housekeeper? At last we gave up and walked back to my parents' home. The sun was gone now. A chill wind came up, and I could not shake the sense of premonition that seemed to hang over me.

# 1 2

_____

As FEBRUARY turned into March, I continued to see much of Buzz, and as we almost always ate out, I was delighted when the four girls with whom I shared the apartment decided to have a dinner party. Each of us would invite a date, and I made sure that on that day I would be able to get out of the lab early.

And so, on Thursday afternoon, the 15th, I got home early enough to help with the cooking—a frantic, comic-opera process that would have been laughable, had our guests not been arriving in a scant two hours. For all of us had been brought up in homes where cooks and housekeepers managed everything. So the five of us stood around, arguing about what the directions in the cookbook meant. We may not have known what we were doing, but that did not keep us from having strong opinions—if broth had been on the menu, we surely would have spoiled it.

But there was not too much you could do to ruin a steak, beyond overcooking it, and Caesar salad was tasty *and* simple, and French bread lightly buttered and garlicked was manageable, as long as you didn't burn it. There would undoubtedly be some botches, but we were counting on Renée's *crème brûlée*, a fabulous dessert recipe learned from her grandmother's French cook, to save the day. Give them a sensational ending, and that would be the taste and the memory they would take away with them.

Promptly at seven-thirty, the buzzer signaled that our guests had arrived. We pressed the button that would release the lock on the front door downstairs, and waited. I glanced around, but there was nothing to straighten. The apartment had never looked neater; there were even fresh-cut flowers on the coffee table.

The steak came out of the broiler almost exactly medium rare, as we had hoped, and everything else went so smoothly that we girls finally began to relax. Soon we were having such a good time that we almost forgot to eat. But in the back of my mind I looked forward to the *pièce de résistance* that we would be serving for dessert, and that would make this an evening to remember.

And then I began to be troubled. It had nothing to do with the party; I just felt increasingly uneasy and suddenly had an overwhelming urge to go home. I tried to push it down or reason it through—if there was anything wrong, my parents would have called me—but it was no use, and soon Buzz leaned over and whispered, "Is something wrong?"

I nodded. "I've got to go home—*now*," and I got up from the table.

"I'll take you," said Buzz, telling me, not asking me, and he got up and got his coat.

As we hurried up the seven short blocks and two long ones, Buzz asked me, "Can you tell me what it is?"

"I don't know," I said, fighting back panic. "I've just got to get home."

I threw a greeting to the doorman and almost ran to the elevator. And then, of course, it wouldn't come. I must have punched the button half a dozen times, while Buzz alternately tried to find out what the matter was and to calm me down. At last it came, and we rode up to my parents' floor. I pushed the front door open (in those days, my parents didn't lock their front door) and ran into the living room—to find my parents contentedly sipping their after-dinner coffee.

They looked up, surprised but delighted to see us. "Come in, come in!" my father said, rising from his easy chair. "It's good to see you two!" He was wearing his blue velvet smoking jacket, and I thought how handsome he was, so young and healthy-looking for fifty-three.

"Would you like some coffee?" my mother asked. We nodded, and she rang a little bell. She was curled up at her favorite end of the sofa, and she, too, looked terrific in a rose-colored, full-length tea gown—not formal enough to go out in, but just perfect for dressing up at home. My parents always changed for dinner, a tradition I never appreciated as much as right now.

Oscar came in, and soon reappeared with a tray containing two gold-rimmed demitasse cups, and a silver creamer and sugar bowl, and an elegant little silver coffeepot with a bone handle. My mother poured coffee into the cups, which Oscar now passed to us, and as I used the tiny silver sugar tongs to put a half cube into my cup, I began to feel a bit foolish. Everything seemed perfectly peaceful here; what on earth had I been so upset about? And obviously I still was, for I could not keep my cup from rattling in its saucer. Noting this, my mother raised an eyebrow, but said nothing, waiting until I was ready to volunteer an explanation.

And then the phone rang. It was answered in the kitchen, apparently by Oscar, who now appeared at the living room entry. "It's Mr. Avery on the phone," he said in his usual dry tone. "He wants to speak to both Mr. and Mrs. Lincoln." And then his tone changed. "He says it's urgent."

Alarmed, my mother got up from the sofa and went quickly to their bedroom, while my father entered the library. Buzz and I looked at one another, speechless. Minutes passed as we listened to the ticking of the mantel clock. I strained to hear my father's side of the conversation, for the library was next door. But there was precious little to hear: "Yes. . . yes . . . Oh, good Lord! . . . Yes, I understand." The ominous silence pressed in on me, so that I could hardly breathe.

Finally, my mother came back into the living room, reaching for a chair to support herself. Looking at me, her eyes filled. "Oh, Bel, I'm so sorry that you have to go through this . . ." her voice trailed off, and she broke into sobs. In times of crisis, concern for her children's suffering always came before her own. *What* had happened? I wanted to scream the question, but couldn't speak.

My father came in, crossed to the antique harvest table that served as a bar, and poured himself and my mother stiff Scotches. Never in my life had I seen him do that—or either of them drink after dinner, for that matter.

Now my mother pulled herself together, and maintaining tight control of her emotions, said: "It's Aunt Win. She's tried to kill herself— in the garage with the cars running. The police and the fire department are there now, trying to revive her, but it looks like it's too late. And the worst is, she took Wendy and Jo-Jo with her." Here, in spite of her control, her voice broke and she could not go on.

My father finished. "She gave the cook-housekeeper and the maid the day off, the same way she did that day you two walked over there, and she had taken the girls for an all-day drive. She had stuffed towels at the bottom of the garage doors, to make it airtight, and apparently had given the girls sleeping pills. Jo-Jo was found in the back seat of one of the cars, but Wendy was found beside the garage door. Apparently, she had woken up and tried to get out." And now my father's composure broke as well. Stopping, he squeezed his eyes shut, as if to keep from seeing the image that was forming in his mind. When he continued, he could barely talk. "They've got oxygen there, but they're not responding."

He took a drink, walked over to the window, and looked out at the night. No one else said anything, and I stared at the carpet between my feet. At length, my father completed the explanation. The children's nurse, feeling uneasy, had come back early from her day off. She had found the house completely dark, and sensing that something was very wrong, without even entering, she had gone to the next-door neighbors and called Uncle Avery, who came right over. As soon as they went in the house, they smelled the car exhaust fumes. Going to the garage, they discovered the tragedy and called the police, throwing the doors open and dragging the bodies out into the fresh air.

"It's murder," my mother said quietly, "not only suicide, but murder." I sensed that she could have forgiven her sister for taking her own life, but not for taking her children's, too. Later, my parents would learn that Aunt Win had seen her psychiatrist that very morning, and he had written an optimistic report, for at last she seemed to be showing some signs of improving. What he could not have known was that she had finally made up her mind to end her torment.

Sometime after midnight, the final word came: all three were dead. Earlier, my parents had asked Buzz if he would like to leave, and I was glad when he replied, "If it's all right, I'd like to stay." But now, as there was nothing more that could be said or done, he said good night. I saw him to the elevator and thanked him for staying. He started to speak and reached in his coat pocket, but just then the elevator door opened, and he thought better of it, and was gone.

Five minutes later, our doorbell rang. I was still in the living room and answered it; it was Buzz.

"Here," he said, "I want you to have this." He thrust a battered envelope into my hand, turned, and left (later I would learn that he had been carrying it around in his pocket for ten days).

It's funny the way tragedy and joy in real life are often inextricably combined. The envelope contained a letter, in which for the first time Buzz spoke of his love for me. He concluded by saying that one day when he knew that I felt as he did, he was going to ask me to be his wife.

THE NEXT MORNING I went to work. I didn't know what else to do, and I thought that perhaps I could get my mind off the horrendous events of the night before. That week it was my turn to cope with our department's paperwork, and I went right at it, but there was no respite—and no escape either.

Somehow I had thought that no one at Sloan-Kettering knew of my family background. But now, with the front pages of all the papers blaring the news of the Rockefeller double murder and suicide, I discovered how much I had deluded myself. In the lab, in the elevator, in the ladies' room, everywhere I went, people told me how sorry they were. Even Dr. Stock, the head of our department, stopped me in the hall to express his condolences. Everyone was being very kind, but as one person after another spoke to me, the tears welled up. I started to cry and soon was silently sobbing.

Finally, my immediate boss, Dr. Buckley, came into the office and closed the door. "Bel," she said, "go home. Your mother must need you now. And don't come back until you feel that it's right."

I nodded, tremendously grateful to her, and hurried home. My poor mother! I'd been so wrapped up in my own thoughts and feelings, I had lost sight of how devastating this was for her. As broken up as I was, I resolved to be strong enough to be a support to her.

At home things were grim. My mother had contacted the minister of Christ Church in Greenwich, which Aunt Win had attended, and where Wendy and Jo-Jo had gone to Sunday school.

"No!" the minister had exclaimed. "It was suicide and murder. I'll have nothing to do with it!"

"But the children," my mother had pleaded, "surely you'll do something for them?"

"There will be no service," the minister had replied. "Not in my church," and he hung up.

Eventually, an arrangement was arrived at, however; Aunt Win and her children would be cremated at the Ferncliff Crematorium, and a private memorial service would take place at Christ Church. But the hurt had already been done, and my mother, feeling betrayed and rebuffed by her church, refused to have anything to do with Christ Church for the rest of her life.

Aunt Win and the children were scheduled to be cremated on Saturday—the same Saturday that Buzz and I had been planning for weeks to go up to West Point. I had never been there, and he was looking forward to showing me the place that had played such a prominent role in his life.

"Shall we go, Mum?" I had asked. "I don't want to leave you, if you need me."

My mother looked at me with great compassion, knowing even better than I did how much I wanted to escape. She was extremely fond of Buzz and did not want this dark cloud to obliterate what she saw budding between us.

"Of course," she smiled. "Go up to the Point and have a lovely day. Only do be back for dinner."

"I will, Mum!" I exclaimed, unable to keep the joy out of my voice, and I gave her an impulsive kiss on the cheek.

Buzz pointed the long hood of the black Plymouth north, and the city and all its problems receded rapidly behind us. This was the first I'd seen him since I had read his letter, and I smiled contentedly at the memory of it. The sun was shining, the sky was crystal blue, and here there was no snow at all on the ground—yes, spring was definitely coming, I thought, and curled up to enjoy the rest of our drive up the Hudson.

When we got there, Buzz checked his watch and then took me to the bleachers overlooking "the Plain," as the parade ground was called. we weren't sitting there very long before we heard and then saw the marching band. Behind them came "the long grey line" of rank upon rank of cadets, so proud and erect, their brass buttons gleaming in the sun. I knew now why Buzz had been anxious for me to see this. After the drill, we walked through the ivy-covered portals, gazed up at the tall chapel tower that had tolled its blessing over the river valley for one hundred and fifty years, and looked in at the field house, which had seen the graduation of so many famous Americans. At that moment, one was being sought as a Presidential candidate by both parties, and another, commanding the U. N. forces in Korea, had just taken the offensive.

Buzz had saved the best for last, for there was one sight that every girl who visited West Point wanted to see—the famous trysting-place, known as Flirtation Walk. As the ground was just thawing, we had to pick our way carefully, but at the appropriate spot, where so many cadets had declared their love to their sweethearts, we joined that hallowed tradition. It was a moment out of time—a moment I would never forget.

My mother had encouraged me to have a lovely day, and it had been—the loveliest I could remember in a long, long time. It was dark by the time we started for home, so we stopped and had supper at an inn on the way, arriving back at my parents' apartment a little after ten.

To my surprise, my father was at the door, as we opened it. To my shock, he was furious! *"Where have you been?"* he thundered at me. "Your mother and I have been beside ourselves! You said you'd be home for dinner, but you never even called! For all we knew, you'd been in an accident!"

My eyes widened, as I realized the enormity of what I'd done. Here I had determined to be a support to them, especially Mum, in this time of grief and unrelieved stress, and I had gotten so wrapped up in what we were doing that I'd forgotten all about them. I felt even worse, after my father had calmed down, when he explained to us what *their* day had been like at the crematorium. "Your mother could have used your help," my father said reprovingly, "and then, when you didn't come home, we began to worry."

Tearfully, I told him I was sorry, but the guilt would stay with me for many years.

Two days later, I was by my mother's side on a cold, raw afternoon up in Tarrytown, huddling against the wind as Aunt Win's ashes as well as Wendy and Jo-Jo's were buried in a family plot in the shadow of Great-grandfather William's mausoleum. Above the capitals of that imposing, Greek-columned edifice were carved the words of St. Augustine: "Thou hast made us for Thyself, and our heart shall never be at rest until at last it rests in Thee."

But there was little thought of God on that mournful afternoon. As we stood shivering there, we were joined in our grief by the John D. side of the family, and I was touched that they would share our times of sorrow, as well as our times of joy. The bond between the two brothers clearly extended down through the generations.

But the support of family and loved ones was not enough; looking down at the empty grave, I was suddenly overwhelmed with a sense of hopelessness. Gone were the recent promises of spring—the pussy willows, the forsythia, the robins chirping. There was only a gaping hole, waiting to receive our earthly remains—all of us. *What was the point of life?*

I put it out of my mind, but in future years the question—and the memory of that cold, black hole in the ground—would come back to haunt me.

# 13

---

THE DAY AFTER THE FUNERAL, my parents went down to Overhills for a week, and I went back to work. No one said anything, for which I was profoundly grateful, but at our mid-morning coffee break, the ten girls in our department brought in an especially nice coffee cake, which I sensed was their way of welcoming me. I was glad to be back, and now I truly *was* able to pour myself into my work, to forget about the tragedy for a while.

One evening, because of a splitting headache, I interrupted our date and asked Buzz to take me home—not to my apartment, where we had three out-of-town girlfriends visiting, but to my parents', where it would be quiet. When we got to the front door downstairs, I tried to say goodnight there, instead of having him see me to the apartment door, as he usually did. "Oh," he said, "I'd hoped to come in for a few minutes."

"Oh, well, all right, but please, Buzz, only a minute or two; my head is killing me, and I feel a migraine coming on."

Oscar came to the door, my parents not being due back until the next day. "Would you like something to drink, Miss Bel?"

Before I could decline, Buzz piped up, "I'd love a Coke." Great! All I could think of was laying my head down on that cool, crisp pillow that I knew was waiting for me in Cal's and my room.

"Miss Bel?"

"Oh, uh, nothing for me, Oscar. I'm too tired," and as if to underscore my obvious implication, the mantel clock chimed ten-thirty. I yawned and didn't try to hide it. I knew I was being rude, but it was rude of *him* not to have a little more consideration.

As petulant as my mood was, Buzz was apparently oblivious to it. His eyes sparkled, and for some reason he was grinning.

"Good grief!" I exclaimed, irked that he could feel so good when I felt so bad. "What on earth is the matter with you?"

"I want to get married!"

"*What?* To who?" I demanded, my headache forgotten.

"To you, silly!"

I just stood there, gaping at him. And then I was in his arms.

"Well, what do you say?" he said, pulling back to look at me.

"I say *yes!*" And suddenly, the oddest thought crossed my mind: God was pleased. I smiled to myself and thought of those wonderful old words *That which God hath joined together* . . .

"What is it?" he asked, catching my smile.

"Oh, I'll tell you, sometime."

We talked for a long time, trusting one another with deep feelings, and I realized that, by sharing our recent tragedy, Buzz had grown closer to me and my parents than he might otherwise have in months. All at once, the mantel clock was chiming again. No, it couldn't be! It was one o'clock in the morning.

My parents returned from Overhills late the next day, and early the following morning, hearing them talking in their bedroom, I took a deep breath and knocked on their door. They invited me in, and I found them having Sunday breakfast in bed—just as Grandma and Grandpa used to, many years before. I was relieved at how tanned and rested they looked, and I asked them how it had gone. Very nice, they told me, and we continued chatting, while all of us waited for me to get my courage up. Finally, I blurted it out: "Pop, Buzz would like to talk to you—today, if possible." There, I'd said it! My heart was pounding; I couldn't believe what was happening.

Mum and Pop looked at one another. "That will be fine," my father said, without expression.

"Why don't you do it after church?" my mother said to him. "That way, we can all have lunch together afterward."

My parents hardly ever went to church, except during times of great stress, and certainly the tragedy of the past week qualified on that score. All at once, it struck me that the events which I had just set in motion would mean the end of such cozy moments as this one. No longer would there be just the three of us, like this—and I found a lump rising in my throat. I loved Buzz, and looked forward to becoming his wife. But I also loved my parents; in fact, I could not remember loving them more than I did just now. I was an adult of twenty-three, but part of me wanted to remain a little girl—*their* little girl.

While my parents were at St. James's, the great gothic Episcopal church that towered over Madison Avenue at 71st Street, Buzz and I went for a walk in Central Park, holding hands and smiling back at strangers who turned and smiled. Pretty obvious what we have here, I thought; two young people goofy in love. Fat pigeons waddled the path in front of us, girls were skipping rope, and everywhere grass and leaves were turning green. As the noon hour approached, I could feel Buzz getting nervous, but I could not imagine anything going wrong and did my best to cheer him up.

We arrived at my parents' apartment just moments after they had returned from church. "Buzz, why don't we go into the library," my father said affably, putting his arm around Buzz's shoulders, for he was noticeably nervous. It didn't help.

The door closed behind them, and my mother and I sat and watched it, nervously chatting. In those days, we both smoked, and one by one the pile of stubbed-out cigarette butts in the ashtray grew. What was taking them so *long*? I mean, how much time did it take for Buzz to declare his intentions, and for my father to give his blessing? Were they going over Buzz's life history, or what? My mother and I gave up making small talk and just stared at the library door.

Finally, just as my mother got to her feet, murmuring, "This is taking too long," and headed for the library door, it opened, and Buzz and Pop emerged, beaming. "Well," my father announced, "I've given my consent for Buzz to marry Bel."

My mother came over and gave me a hug and then one for Buzz, and I was deeply touched, for in all my life I could count the times she had hugged me on the fingers of one hand. We were all laughing now, and Mum rang for Oscar and asked him to bring us the sherry. As he returned with the antique decanter and its delicate little glasses, he said, "May I presume that congratulations are in order?"

"You may, Oscar," I exclaimed. "Isn't it wonderful?"

"Yes, it is!" he heartily affirmed, and I was reminded that he had been looking after our household and that of my grandparents since before I was born. Pouring us each a glass, my father proposed a toast: "To Bel and Buzz, and a long and happy life together."

After that, we went in to lunch, and my mother asked, "When would you two like to get married?"

"Um, would September be too soon?" I asked. Buzz and I had talked it over in the park and figured that was the earliest we'd dare hope for.

"September?" my mother replied. "What's wrong with June?"

My jaw dropped, and so did my spoon—back into my soup, making a colorful pattern of cream of tomato specks on the white linen tablecloth. I looked over at Buzz, who was equally nonplussed.

"June would be great, Mrs. Lincoln," he managed, as soon as he could talk.

"I think, under the circumstances, you might call me something a little less formal. How about Aunt Iz?"

"And you can just call me Pop," my father chimed in. "Everyone in this household does."

I couldn't believe the whole thing; everything was going so *fast*! June was less than three months away!

"I'm afraid we won't be able to have it on a Saturday," my mother mused. "All the June Saturdays have undoubtedly been taken at St. James's months ago. But a Monday would be nice—"

"And it would mean my business friends wouldn't have to make a special trip into the city," my father added, "since they would already be in for work."

"Uh, Mum, I'd like to get married at Christ Church," I said, thinking of the big church in Greenwich where she had been married.

For the first time all day, a cloud passed over my mother's face. "Absolutely not!" she snapped. "I won't have anything to do with that man, or his church!"

"But Mum, it's *my* wedding—" My voice trailed off, as I noted the set of her jaw. I was so happy, I didn't have the heart for an Isabel-to-Isabel confrontation. I looked over at Buzz, who ever so slightly shook his head, and I realized that we ought to be grateful that we were getting married three months earlier than we'd dared hope. A Monday it would be.

After lunch, Buzz and I made plans of our own—who our bridesmaids and ushers would be, where we would go on our wedding trip, where we would live when we got back—and then Buzz began to get nervous again. For there was still one more hurdle to cross: telling *his* parents.

During the past year, I had, of course, met his parents a number of times, most recently the week before, when they took us to Easter dinner at the Union Club. His mother was a classic beauty. When she was a young girl, she had had any number of suitors, and now besides the beautiful white hair that softly framed her face, her most prominent features were a Roman nose and green eyes. Her clothes she wore with a casual flair that came from years of being able to afford the nicest things. Her father had been a top international shipping lawyer, and she had grown up in an atmosphere of wealth and privilege.

Buzz's father, Basil Beebe Elmer, was a tall, husky, good-humored man, with a grey moustache, wavy grey hair, and bright blue eyes. He had grown up in Ithaca, New York, the son of a Classics professor at Cornell, where he himself earned his degree. During the World War I, he had fought in Europe as a captain in the famed Rainbow Division, after which he returned to his peacetime job with the Bank of Manhattan Company.

For the Elmers, the Depression had brought an endless succession of dark days, as it had to so many of their friends. Buzz's father, with considerable help from his father-in-law, had bought a seat on the New York Stock Exchange, only to see the plunging market and subsequent years of doldrums virtually wipe him out. Throughout these hard times, his mother had remained steadfastly cheerful, despite the fact that they suddenly had hardly any money at all. But the pressure grew greater, and she came down with an incurable circulatory disease, causing her to hemorrhage and clot at the same time. The disease particularly attacked her legs and required frequent hospitalization.

With the advent of World War II, Buzz's father rejoined the Army, being stationed this time on Governor's Island. But he retained his seat on the Exchange and his partnership with the prestigious Wall Street firm of Eastman, Dillon & Company, and eventually his perseverance was rewarded in the years of postwar prosperity.

At Easter dinner, the week before, the Union Club's French chefs had prepared a magnificent buffet, and while we filled our plates, Buzz's father asked me if I liked the huge chocolate bunny that graced the center of the long and splendid spread.

"Oh, yes," I'd replied, not knowing what else to say, "it's lovely."

"I'll get it for you," he said abruptly, and before I could object, he went to persuade the maitre d'hotel to part with it. The maitre d' did not want to part with it; it would spoil the overall effect of the buffet for the rest of the members and their guests. But when Buzz's father set his mind to something, he could be extremely persistent and persuasive, and their tightly smiling discussion continued. Before the end the of the meal, I was presented with a huge box with the chocolate bunny inside of it.

Having told my parents our news, Buzz went that evening to his parents' apartment on 86th Street, just off East End Avenue. "Guess what!" he started, as soon as he'd gotten his coat off. "I'm engaged to the most wonderful girl in the world!"

"You're *what*?" demanded his father, his face contorting. "Who is she?"

"It's Bel, of course," Buzz stammered, startled at his reaction. "Bel Lincoln."

"What do you know about her," thundered his father, "and about her family?"

Now his mother came to the rescue: "I went to Farmington with her aunt, Polly Lincoln. She was an awfully nice girl, and they're a nice family."

"Nice, shmice," his father muttered, and still livid, he went over to the bookshelves and pulled out the familiar black-bound *Social Register* with the small orange lettering on the cover. On finding the Lincolns therein and discovering my background, he noticeably relaxed. By the end of the evening he was almost pleasant, and the next day he went to the bank and removed from their safe deposit box the 2½-carat diamond ring that Buzz's maternal grandmother had left to him.

Soon after that, my parents had Buzz's parents to dinner, and everything went as smoothly as all hoped it would—until my mother, who could be breathtakingly candid at the most inopportune times, broached the subject of Aunt Win. It was obvious that she wanted to put her cards on the table, and as soon as the roast turkey, new potatoes, and string beans had been passed, she laid them all down, every last one. As I sat there, listening to gruesome details I had never heard before, I wondered if I would ever breathe again.

As soon as my mother finished, Buzz's mother leaned over and put her hand on my mother's arm. "Isabel," she said quietly, "I understand. My youngest brother, Mark, decided one day that life was too much for him. So he just walked out into the sea and never came back.'' She paused. ''Our family, too, has had its tragedies.'' My mother breathed a visible sigh of relief, and from that moment on, I liked Buzz's mother very much.

It was decided that our engagement would be announced on April 23rd, which happened to be the wedding date of my Rockefeller grandparents, and also of my christening. And what joy that announcement brought! Suddenly, my mother's family, which had been so long immersed in the gloom of Aunt Win's death, had something to be happy about—very happy! Indeed, at our engagement party in my parents' apartment, they were positively giddy. The Lincoln side of the family and my parents' close friends were delighted to join in, for they, too, had felt awkward over the tragedy. Everyone was grateful to have cause for celebration, and Buzz and I were showered with gifts and feted with parties and dinners. In later years, it would occur to me that my mother may have sensed an urgency to dispel the awful pall hanging over the family, and for that reason had suggested that the wedding be in June, instead of September.

As the agreed-upon date of June 25th approached, the tempo and pressure of preparation increased. The reception would be at the Colony Club, an exclusive ladies' club to which my mother belonged. One morning I accompanied her there to arrange the catering details, and dutifully nodded my agreement, as she dealt with each item on her list. In New York society thirty-five years ago, such details were considered too important to be entrusted into the hands of the young couple getting married; their mothers would plan everything, with most of the burden resting on the mother of the bride. The one decision I made that morning was that the tiny boxes used for souvenir pieces of the wedding cake would be pink, instead of the traditional white.

The invitation lists were drawn up and double-checked, the engraved invitations were ordered from Tiffany's, Ben Cutler and his band were booked for the reception (we would have needed a year's notice to get Meyer Davis), limousines to transport the wedding party from the church to the club were arranged for, and all the complicated floral arrangements were made.

My mother coped with all of these myriad details—and then collapsed. On top of the prolonged strain of Aunt Win's death, it was just too much for her. She had held herself together as long as she could, but now her doctor, gravely concerned for her health, ordered her into Doctors' Hospital for a complete rest. She was to see only her husband and children—and we were strictly admonished not to bring her problems that would reinvolve her in the planning of the wedding.

I should have been understanding; I should have been grateful for the enormous amount she had already done and for the love she had shown in doing it. But I was young and selfish; I felt abandoned in my hour of greatest need—exactly as she had felt when her mother had thrown up her hands and taken her sisters to Europe, leaving all her own wedding plans in Aunt Elsie's lap. But I had no Aunt Elsie—how could my mother do this to me?

Very well, I would show her I could get along without her just fine. I needed a wedding dress? This time we would do without all the elaborate handwork and fittings that had gone into my coming-out gown. This time I would get one off the rack, and I found a perfectly nice one at Lord & Taylor's for $70. It was Buzz's mother who told my mother what I'd done. As my will was obviously set, and my mother was in no condition to contest it, damage control was the best they could hope for. The cheap lace that made up the bodice of the dress was replaced with real Belgian lace that had been in the Elmer and Lincoln families, some of it for four generations. Add to that a cathedral-length, rose-point veil, which had come down through the Stillman side of our family, and the overall effect was all that anyone could ask for. My petty vindictiveness was not allowed to spoil the wedding.

I did not see it that way, of course, and thought they were making much ado about nothing. For I had convinced myself that my sole motivation had been to get a dress that any of the girls I worked with could have afforded. Part of me was still ashamed that my family could afford a handmade dress, and still wanted to be no different than anybody else.

A few weeks before the wedding, we had a talk with the minister who would be marrying us, Arthur Lee Kinsolving, rector of St. James's. He was an old friend of my parents', having married Mary Blagden, whose family had been close to my mother's family in the Adirondacks. A deeply spiritual man, he was at the same time an intriguing combination of strength and gentleness, and we all called him by his nickname, Touie. He and Mary had asked my mother to be godmother to their third son, and he had been a great comfort to her during the recent tragedy.

He had also come to know Buzz's mother quite well, having called on her when she was in the hospital. As for me personally, his wedding up in Saranac had been the first I had ever attended, and he and Mary were always special to me. . . . Then why, as we waited to see him, was my hand trembling on the arm of this stupid chair?

"Dr. Kinsolving will see you now," said his secretary, smiling as she showed us into his wood-paneled office.

"Hello, Bel, Buzz," he greeted us warmly, shaking hands and indicating that we should sit in the two leather-backed visitors' chairs. His voice was deep and reassuring, and instantly all my nervousness vanished. We chatted awhile, telling him how we had met and eventually fallen in love, and then Buzz said, "You know, Touie, Bel and I don't understand it, but in addition to loving each other, we both feel that God wants us to marry."

Touie looked at us, and for a long time he said nothing. In the stillness, my hand on the arm of the chair began to tremble again. Finally, he spoke. "Nothing you could have said could have pleased me more. That's the way Mary and I felt, too." He paused, then added, "We did something that perhaps you might want to do, too. As a symbol of how you both feel, would you like to learn your marriage vows by heart, instead of repeating them after me?" Without looking at one another, we both nodded in deep appreciation.

June 25th, 1951, dawned cool, clear, and sparkling, and stayed that way all day. I was exhausted but of course didn't know it, running on the same nervous energy that had kept me going through the nonstop merry-go-round of the past several weeks.

THERE WAS THE HAIRDRESSER, the bridesmaids' bouquets, and a million other things—and then, after my mother and three sisters and all the bridesmaids had departed for the church, and the apartment was silent for the first time in what seemed like months, I put on my gown. There was no one home but my father, who would take me to the church, and Oscar. I struggled into the white satin, and then called to my father to button me up, because we were running out of time. Fumbling a bit, he did up the long row of satin-covered buttons that I could not reach, and then adjusted my veil.

When he finished, we both looked in the full-length mirror. I was stunned; that couldn't be me! My father, apparently, was similarly affected. "Bel, I —" His voice broke, and he whispered the last, "you're beautiful."

"Oh, Poppy!" I exclaimed, seeing him in the mirror with his eyes brimming, and I turned and gave him a hug.

We hurried down to the waiting limousine, and got to the church just in time. As my father helped me out, my heart sank: the broad steps in front of St. James's were covered with reporters and photographers from all the papers, and after the tabloid coverage of Aunt Win, I never wanted to see another newspaperman again. We hurried up the steps through them, ignoring their shouted questions. Momentarily blinded by the barrage of flashbulbs in my face, I could not at first see the dark interior of the church. But when I could, I was again speechless. White bouquets and satin bows adorned the end of each pew down the center aisle, and waiting for us were some seven hundred guests. A buzzer signaled our arrival, and as the distant organ began the traditional wedding march from *Lohengrin,* the first of the bridesmaids in white organdy started down the aisle.

My hand on my father's left arm started to tremble, and the closer our turn came, the worse it got. Now Cal, my maid of honor, went, and it was our turn next. All at once, my father, so handsome in his morning coat and grey cravat, leaned over and whispered, "I'm proud of you! And very happy for you." I was nonplussed; in all my life, I could not remember him saying such a thing. And now he had done it twice in the same day! But he wasn't finished; winking, he added, "Now let's go down that aisle and wow them all!"

With a laugh, I got off on the right foot with him, and as we approached the altar rail, there was Buzz, standing as straight as the day I'd first set eyes on him in his cadet uniform. He couldn't help grinning when he saw me, and his blue eyes were shining. I just wanted to kiss him and run away with him!

Gracefully, my father transferred my hand to Buzz's arm, and Buzz and I now looked up at Touie, who smiled down upon us and began the familiar words, "Dearly beloved, we are gathered together here in the sight of God and in the face of this company, to join together this man and this woman in holy matrimony—" And all at once, he choked up and could not continue. Looking at us, he was so happy for us and for our parents that his eyes filled with tears—and his emotion swept through the congregation. Practically everyone present was overcome, including the bride and groom.

At length, Touie regained his composure and continued with the ceremony. When the betrothal was completed, we proceeded up to the high altar. Cal adjusted my train as the organ played "Love Divine All Loves Excelling." I handed my bouquet to her, and we began the wedding vows, which we had learned by heart. Buzz went first. Holding my right hand, he solemnly declared, "I, Basil, take thee, Isabel, to my wedded husband . . ." He did not realize what he, in his nervousness, had said, and so was bewildered at the wave of suppressed mirth that now spread through the congregation behind us. But I just smiled; it was the perfect antidote for the deep emotion which had gone before, and Touie nodded at him, encouraging him to continue.

Suddenly, we were man and wife! Buzz gave me a kiss, and we started out of the church, to the joyous strains of Mendelssohn. There were the photographers again, as we ducked into the limousine and headed for the Colony Club. All the way there, Buzz and I just grinned; we were married!

And then I did something very strange: I took off the wedding band that Buzz had placed on my finger just a few moments before. "What are you doing?" he asked.

"I don't want to ever be as superstitious about wearing any piece of jewelry, as I was with Lee's locket. I wore that for years after I should have taken it off. I don't want to do that again, not even with this ring."

"Well," said Buzz, ever practical, "let me put it back on you now, before you lose it. As far as I'm concerned"—he smiled, pushing it back on—"it's on for keeps now, even if you do take it off."

"Yes, sir," I said, squeezing the arm of the man I had just vowed to love, honor, and obey.

The reception was dazzling. Once again, there was that "gracious gauntlet," the receiving line—down which hundreds of guests would now come and pay their respects. There followed the first waltz with my new husband, and the dancing and the cutting of the cake and the changing into going-away clothes, and the throwing of the bridal bouquet.

To Cal's surprise, I threw it directly to her. Serves her right, I thought with a grin. Cal and I had grown very close over the years. While I was more outgoing than she, and she was more calm and secure than I, we confided in one another more and more, as we grew up. Gradually, she had filled much of the void left by Lee, and so I was hurt, when she had begun being dreary about how the coming wedding would break up the closeness of our family.

A popular senior at Vassar now, the last thing she expected was to become interested in any of Buzz's ushers—but that is exactly what happened, as Henry Harder, Buzz's friend from St. Mark's, took quite a shine to her. "I wonder if they're falling in love," I whispered to Buzz, as we had danced past them. "Do you think they'll get married?"

"Ridiculous!" Buzz guffawed. "They've only just met."

But I threw the bouquet her way anyway, and she caught it, and time would tell.

After changing, Buzz and I raced out of the Colony Club, under a shower of rice from all sides, and jumped into the waiting limousine. Taking a last look back at the club entrance, I saw my father there, with his arm around my mother, who had tears streaming down her cheeks, but was smiling and waving.

I waved back, profoundly aware that one life had ended, and another was about to begin.

# 14

AS THE SUPER CONSTELLATION banked sharply to the right and settled into the glide path for its final approach, I had my nose pressed to the window, like a kid in front of F.A.O. Schwarz. "Buzz!" I gasped, "the water is so *blue*!" He looked over my shoulder, as we passed over the end of the runway, flashed past the long, low white terminal building, and came to a stop. Ground attendants pushed stairs up to the side of the plane, and we started to disembark.

Stepping out the plane's door, we felt the breeze through the scraggly palms at the edge of the tarmac; it was hot and dry, and carried with it the faint aroma of oleanders and hibiscus. In the distance, over the entry to the customs shed toward which the first passengers were now walking, weatherbeaten cedar letters spelled out: B E R M U D A. I clutched Buzz's arm and hugged it; our honeymoon had begun!

Once we had cleared customs and gone outside, it seemed as if every taxi on the island had gathered at the airport to meet the plane from America. Buzz started toward a sensible black Hillman, but I pleaded with him to take one of the open cabs, which had a big gaily colored umbrella in place of a roof. He smiled indulgently, and we piled on board, and in a few miles he admitted that he was glad we were in an open car, because there was so much too see—and to *smell*; with jasmine and bougainvillaea growing in wild profusion on both sides of the narrow roads, we seemed to be driving through a greenhouse.

The scenery was lush and breathtaking, with every available field green with fruit trees or vegetables. The houses were small and quaint, made out of Bermuda limestone, and every one was either white or pale pastel with a white stepped roof glistening in the sun. Except for the taxis, there was very little four-wheeled traffic. Tourists and locals alike either pedaled or rode motor-assisted bikes or walked. We passed a school, where boys wearing white caps were playing cricket.

"Oh, Buzz, I *love* Bermuda! Let's always come back here for our vacations!"

"Hey, let's enjoy this one first, before we start thinking about coming back."

We were staying at a charming cottage colony hotel known as Cambridge Beaches, in the parish of Somerset, at the opposite end of the long, narrow island. Our cottage sat on the side of a hill, with a fabulous view of the ocean and of a small beach, its coral sand glowing pale pink in the setting sun. No place in paradise could be more beautiful, I thought, and I was so happy I could have burst.

We spent our days swimming and sunning, and exploring the island on bicycles, which had little motors on the front wheel to help climb the many hills of Bermuda. Buzz grew more and more tan, till his blue eyes seemed to shine out from his bronzed face. At night we would dine on the hotel terrace, where each evening I felt a twinge of delight as the hostess said, "Good evening, Mrs. Elmer," and showed us to our table. Sometimes we would go dancing; sometimes we would watch the incredible gyrations of limbo dancers, as they slithered under impossibly low bars without touching them or the floor. Again, we might enjoy the music of the Talbot Brothers, a local calypso group that would soon gain a loyal Ivy League following. Everything we did was fun; we were in love.

And then one day, on that clear and vivid blue horizon with the dazzling sun and the pink sands and the delicately perfumed breezes, a tiny cloud appeared, no bigger than a man's hand. Buzz and I had been pedaling our bikes for several hours when we saw an inviting wayside restaurant coming up ahead. "Hey, Bel," my husband called out, "what say we stop for something tall and cool?"

"No, we've only got a little farther to go. We can have it at our cottage."

"Oh, come on, Bellita bug," Buzz coaxed. "Just think of a lemon Coke in a frosty glass with mint and ice—"

"You asked me, and I said no, and no means *no!*" I heard myself shout, and both of us were startled at the force with which it came out. I was not chagrined; I was furious and impulsively spurted ahead, pedaling as hard as I could past the restaurant and leaving Buzz no choice but to pedal after me.

When we reached Cambridge Beaches, we entered the little cottage in stony silence, the Cokes long forgotten. I pulled off my sneakers, plopped down on my side of the bed, and put my head in the crook of my arm, feigning sleep. Buzz sank down on his side of the bed, turned his back to me, and was soon fast asleep.

For a long time I lay there, fuming. Why couldn't he have just done what I wanted? But finally, as he slept on, my anger subsided. After all, what difference would it have made if we had stopped, instead of coming straight back? We were hot and tired; perhaps it would have made sense to stop. Perhaps, just perhaps, I was wrong.

"Buzz?" I poked him. "Are you awake?"

"I am now."

"I'm sorry I got so cross. We should have stopped. I shouldn't have wanted my way so badly," and I started to cry.

Buzz put his arms around me. "Hey, I'm sorry, too. I was pretty angry myself." He held me and kissed my tears, and it was as if it had never happened.

In my relief, I believed it would never happen again. But neither one of us had any notion of the depth of our buried anger, or the strength of our wills.


WE SAILED HOME ON THE CRUISE SHIP *Queen of Bermuda*, extending the silvery illusion of our make-believe honeymoon world to the last possible moment, when we docked at Pier 47. Down the gangplank we went—smack into reality. Buzz had to go straight to work at the First Boston Corporation, and I had to go home to my mother. The tiny apartment we had found in Dobbs Ferry on the Hudson would not be ready for another week, and my parents had invited us to stay with them at their place in Greenwich. In those days, wives did not pursue independent careers, so I had resigned from Sloan-Kettering. I had mixed feelings about that; I felt I was losing a part of me—a part that was really *me*, and not an extension of my parents or a fulfillment of society's life plan for young ladies, or a younger version of my mother (although she, too, had loved lab work, and given the opportunity, she would gladly have carried on in medicine). But the prevailing wisdom of the day was that newly married wives would have their hands full, learning to be competent homemakers and mothers, and in my case, since I could do little more than boil water (lab procedure 14a), that was wisdom indeed.

As glad as I was to see my parents and two little sisters, it was still a shock to walk in the door and be greeted by Oscar. It was almost as if I had never left. Although I was hardly conscious of it, there was a tug-of-war going on within me, between Miss Bellita and Mrs. Elmer. All day long, I kept looking at my watch and wishing I could make the hands go around faster, until it would be time for me to drive to the station and pick up my new husband from his first day back at work.

At last it was time to make the two-mile trip down to the station. Borrowing my parents' green Chevrolet, I set off—and soon asked myself why I was driving so fast. I had plenty of time, and it wouldn't make the train come any sooner. But I couldn't help it; I was so anxious to see him. I had put on the pink-and-white linen dress that he liked so much, splashing on Chanel Number 5. I used my mother's brand of perfume, not daring to try anything else.

And so I spent almost half an hour sitting in the car in the parking lot, waiting for the the six-fifteen. Finally, on schedule for a change, we could hear it down the line, and the other waiting wives and I got out of our cars and went to the platform, to meet our husbands. Some had little children in tow; one had a Labrador, whose leash kept getting wrapped around her. I was so excited to be a part of this domestic scene, I imagined what it would be like to be meeting Buzz a few years from now, with a little boy or girl in tow, and a dog on a leash.

The train creaked and groaned to a stop, and hot, damp, and tired businessmen dismounted. Most of them looked quite similar in their seersucker suits and attaché cases—but none of them looked like Buzz. Where *was* he? I hurried up and down the platform from one cluster of people to another, and then studied the receding backs of the older, two-car-family men, who were heading for their own cars in the station parking lot. Soon, there was no one on the platform but me, and as the six-fifteen lurched into motion and rolled out of the station, two large tears started to roll down my cheeks.

Completely panicked, I walked up the platform, then down it. What was I to do? My mother would know. I found a phone and a dime and called home. Thank heaven, she answered and not Oscar! "Mummy, Mummy!" I wailed. "I've lost Buzz! He's not on the train!"

"Now, Bel," my mother replied in tones that indicated she did not consider this nearly the catastrophe that I did, "he probably just missed the train. Maybe he was working late and didn't allow enough time to get to the station. Now just calm down and call back in ten minutes. Everything's going to be fine."

How could she be so sure? I thought, reluctantly hanging up the receiver. My husband of three weeks was missing and unaccounted for, and all she could say was: call back in ten minutes. Those next ten minutes passed more slowly than the previous ten hours, but at last they did, and I called again.

"Bel, it's all right; he just called. He slept through the station and didn't wake up until Cos Cob. He's waiting for you there." Cos Cob was the next station up the line, and my mother gave me directions on how to get there, repeating them to make sure I had them.

As I got behind the wheel and pulled out of the parking lot, my relief began to give way to indignation. How could he fall asleep, when here I had spent the entire day waiting for him? Wasn't he as anxious to see me as I was to see him? By the time I reached the Cos Cob station, I was miserable, and so angry I was shaking.

When Buzz saw me, he waved and grinned sheepishly. I jumped out of the car and ran toward him. As soon as I was within earshot, he pointed up to the old station's rafters. "See that nest up there? There are four baby swallows up there, and I've been watching their mother flying back and forth to feed them."

I didn't look up; I looked at Buzz. He smiled and said nothing, and then, eyebrows raised, he silently pointed again toward the roof, inviting me to look up and forgive and forget. I felt a smile tugging at the corners of my mouth and decided to let it come. Shaking my head, I went to him and we embraced. Wrung out by the emotions of the day, I forgave and forgot. (Thirty years later, at Boston's Leahy Clinic we would discover that Buzz was a narcoleptic, which meant that he could be overcome by sleep in almost any situation, including behind the wheel. The doctors said it was a result of dead brain cells, caused either by a blow to the head or by a very high temperature shortly after birth. As an infant, Buzz had suffered both.)

OUR APARTMENT IN DOBBS FERRY was a two-story garden apartment, and getting it ready for us to move in now occupied all of my attention, as well as all of Buzz's time after work. Part of the reason we had picked it was because we did not want to live in New York, where our parents spent the winter, or in Greenwich, where mine stayed in the summer, or in Rye where his did. We wanted to start our new life, as much as possible, on our own.

What fun we had, choosing wall colors, draperies, furniture, and rugs! Every decision seemed vitally important, and every one we made together, right down to where the wedding gifts would be placed. We were like children playing house, only this time it was for real. During the day, while Buzz was at work, I tried to learn how to cook. The kitchen was a complete mystery to me. I had done no cooking whatsoever before moving to my own apartment with the girls, and precious little there. Other than toast and orange juice and coffee in the morning, or a bowl of cold cereal for variety, I simply ate out. And when we had occasionally given a dinner party, I set the table and left the cooking to the others, who knew a few exotic recipes, like the *crème brûlée*. To my horror, I realized that I had never actually been inside a grocery store; in New York, whenever we needed anything, we just called the store and had a box boy deliver it.

Absolute disaster was narrowly averted by the gift of a little book entitled *Your First Hundred Meals*, which must have been written for young women just like me, because it assumed that you didn't know how to do *anything*. I took that book with me everywhere, including to the A & P at the foot of the hill on which we lived. And it, plus the friendly butcher behind the meat counter, got me through, although when the grocery store became a supermarket, I was cast adrift again.

Elsa, my mother's live-in Swedish housekeeper, was another godsend. Possessing her own car and an extremely independent spirit, she one day announced to my mother that she was going over to help me—she didn't ask her; she informed her—and like the 7th Cavalry, she arrived at the moment of greatest need. I was sitting in the living room, staring at a white water mark left by a glass on our new mahogany coffee table. I had rubbed and rubbed and rubbed it to no avail, and now I was in tears, convinced that it was ruined.

The doorbell rang, and wiping my eyes with the back of my hand, I answered it. There was Elsa, who said, "Would you like me to teach you how to clean?"

"Oh, Elsa, would I! Come in, come in!"

And so she taught me everything she knew, starting with the trick of mixing cigarette ashes with mayonnaise, to remove water stains from wood finishes. She did things her own way and in her own time, which often drove my mother to distraction. But she was meticulous and thorough—"For the kitchen floor, you get down on your hands and knees; no other way is thorough enough"—and I could not have had a better teacher. We had been in our new apartment for about a month, when I felt confident enough to have my parents over for dinner. I had shined and polished, until the apartment glowed. When we sat down to dinner, I came forth from the kitchen with my crowning achievement—a casserole! I caught my mother looking quizzically at my father, for we had never had a casserole at home, other than shepherd's pie. Would she like it? She took her first bite. "Mmm, Bel, this is delicious! What is it?"

"Tuna fish and potato chips in cream of mushroom soup!" I announced proudly. I had seen one of my friends prepare it and considered it the height of sophistication. They liked it and even had seconds, and the evening was regarded as a success by all.

Those first months were happy months. We were both blessed with parents who were delighted to see us, but never pulled on us, leaving us to grow and learn together on our own. We saw quite a bit of Henry Harder, and each time he had a new letter from Cal. It was beginning to look as if my prediction would come true, and while I was thrilled at the prospect, I also had some strange twinges, as he read us her letters. For it was obvious that she was coming more and more to trust him, indeed to regard him as her sole confidant, the most important person in her life—the position I had always held.

With the coming of Christmas came the biggest fight Buzz and I had yet experienced. It is surprising to me—and sad—that this season, which should be so full of joy, for many people brings out deep-seated fears and hurts, often leading to conflict. Over the years, I've spoken to enough young couples to know that this is a common, not an unusual, occurrence. With feelings extra-sensitive, minor disagreements can quickly escalate from a minorbrush fire to a major conflagration. Such was the case in our home, thirty-five Christmases ago.

How many of our deepest convictions and most inflexible opinions center around how to celebrate the Lord's birth? Perhaps it is because, to a young child, nothing in the year is more important than

Christmas, or more looked forward to. And the way each child first experiences it, and the family traditions with which he or she grows up, must be the right way. For a new husband with one set of traditions and a new wife with another...

One Saturday afternoon, a few days before the holidays, I had just come home after several hours spent buying stocking presents for Buzz. I had gotten my feet soaked and half frozen, but they were tucked under me now, as I sat on the floor before the fireplace in the living room, with his presents all around me. One by one I was wrapping them in white tissue paper, just as my family always had, and imagining how much each would either please him or make him laugh.

The front door opened, and in came Buzz, who had also been shopping. Hiding the few still-unwrapped presents under my skirt, I smiled and said, "Go away; I'm wrapping your stocking presents."

But instead of smiling and quickly exiting, Buzz frowned. "What do you mean?" he demanded, looking at the array of little white packages. "You couldn't be wrapping my presents just in tissue paper!"

I couldn't believe he was serious, let alone upset. "What do you mean, 'What do I mean'? Our family always wraps stocking stuffers this way!"

"It just shows how little you care!" he exploded. "If you really cared about me, you'd take the trouble to wrap them with Christmas paper and ribbons, just like real presents. That's the way *my* family does it! *My* family cares!"

That did it! I was on my feet and stomping off to the bedroom, slamming the door behind me. I hated him! I hated marriage! I wanted to be home with my family, where the stocking presents would be wrapped in tissue paper! My head ached, and my stomach churned, but gradually I calmed down. Then I would think how cruel and insensitive he was, after I had practically gotten pneumonia out there, picking out his stocking presents, and it would start up all over again.

After about an hour, I began to wonder if he might not have had a point. I mean, there was no question that my family's way was the right way and the best way—but perhaps someone outside my family might not have been able to see that . . . But he had no business overreacting the way he did! And once again, my indignation would come to a boil.

Finally, I decided that, in the interests of avoiding a wretched Christmas, I would compromise. I would offer to wrap half his stocking presents with individual ribbons and bows—but only half; to wrap any more would be a tacit admission of wrongness, instead of a gallant gesture of magnanimity.

I came out of the bedroom and found him sitting in a chair, utterly dejected. "Buzz," I announced, "I will wrap half of your stocking presents your way, and half my way."

But if I expected this beau geste to be greeted with an ovation, I was mistaken. "Okay," sighed Buzz, still miserable, "if that's the way you want it, that's fine with me," and he went into the bedroom and went to sleep.

Had we had a third party to talk to, a professional counselor or a wise friend, we might have learned much from this encounter. As it was, the open hostility ended, but the hurt on both sides went unhealed. We did the only thing we knew how to do: we stuffed it deep down inside and forgot about it. But it did not heal, and as other hurts joined it, over the years they would begin to fester.

The highlight of Christmas 1951 was the news that Cal and Henry Harder would be married on June 28th, almost a year from the day when she caught my bouquet. I was delighted for her. Henry Harder had been a fighter pilot during the war, and still had a bit of that dashing, white-scarf air about him. He worked for the insurance firm of Chubb & Sons, and was doing very well there, so well, in fact, that we kidded him that he was a sure bet to one day become its president.

As winter dragged into spring, homemaking no longer intimidated me; indeed, time began to hang heavy on my hands, to the extent that I took on some substitute teaching assignments in the Dobbs Ferry school system. Then one day Cal called, to see if I would be interested in a temporary assignment, teaching science at the Spence School in New York, where she was working as a kindergarten teacher.

"Would I? Oh, Cal, I can't wait!"

So, Buzz and I returned to the city for a few weeks, until the regular teacher got over a severe case of scarlet fever. We moved into the library of my parents' apartment, the room where less than a year before, Buzz had asked my father for permission to marry me. It was great fun being back home at first. But as the tempo of preparation for Cal's wedding began to accelerate, and Mum and Cal were involved in endless discussions about patterns of china and silver and crystal, I found myself— jealous. The dress from Bendel's, the Bachrach photograph, the guest lists, the reception—a year ago that had been *me* with Mum. . . .

What I was feeling inside was so rotten, I couldn't share it, even with Buzz. And it wasn't Mum and Cal's fault; they went out of their way to include me in every conversation, every shopping trip. But it was still going to be Cal's wedding next month, not mine. And then one night, I thought of a way, the perfect way, to regain center stage.

Buzz had been working late, and when he came in, I practically pounced on him. "I've been thinking," I whispered in his ear. "Let's have a baby!"

"Huh? I thought we'd agreed to wait awhile."

"Well, we had. But I think we're supposed to have one now, as soon as possible."

He frowned. "I don't know, Bel. I think we ought to stick with our original plan. I'm not making all that much, and we still have a lot of settling down to do—"

"Oh, come on, Buzz, just think of how cute little Basil Beebe Elmer III is going to look, grinning up at you out of his bassinette."

Buzz grinned at the thought, and two weeks before the wedding, my doctor confirmed that I was pregnant. I never confessed my true motive to Buzz, or that, whenever I thought of the first Lincoln grandchild, the picture that came to my mind was of the fifth Isabel.

What I hadn't counted on was morning sickness, only instead of occurring in the morning, my worst time came around five in the afternoon, just about the time that I would be standing in our little kitchen in Dobbs Ferry, starting to cook dinner. Three days before the wedding, we had temporarily moved back to my parents' apartment, to avoid having to drive in and out of the city for all the festivities. And now, with the wedding reception over, and the newlyweds departed in a cloud of rice, at last Buzz and I were having a cozy supper with just Mum and Pop. Cal was gone, never to live here again—

My reverie was interrupted by my mother. "I hope you're not planning on staying here with us," she said in her customary blunt manner. "Tomorrow, you and Buzz must go back to your own home in Dobbs Ferry."

I was crushed; that was exactly what I had been planning. I had decided, without consulting Buzz, that we would stay with them, until my morning sickness passed, and I felt better. I really didn't want to go back to the struggle of making Buzz dinner, when the very smell of food nauseated me. Having conveniently forgotten what a strain it could be to live with someone as tense and difficult as myself, I had even convinced myself that my mother would be delighted to have us settle back into the family home.

I looked at Buzz and found him beaming in agreement with her, and then at my father, who nodded his approval. Well, apparently everyone but me thought it was a capital idea that once again we would be forging ahead on our own. Immensely sorry for myself, I excused myself from the table, murmuring something about feeling sick. Years later, my mother would tell me of the lesson she had learned, when Aunt Elsie had commanded Freddy Lincoln to leave his mother at once and come home to his wife and child. It had saved their marriage, and it would be the making of ours.

So back we went to Dobbs Ferry, and sure enough, I felt too sick to fix Buzz supper; he would just have to fend for himself. That summer became an endless procession of miserable days. Only for a brief period during the middle of the day did I feel at all well, and then I would do the cleaning or the laundry or the food shopping. The rest of the time, I lay on my bed, suffering and steeped in self pity. My worst day began with a news bulletin on the radio: George VI had suddenly died, and his daughter Elizabeth was now Queen. She was only a year older than I, and I had always identified with her. Now, at the thought of her losing her father, I sobbed and sobbed, and the tears wouldn't stop—they came for Grandma and Grandpa, for Lee, and for all the others I had lost, as all my unresolved grief surfaced. Well, it was resolved that morning; I finally felt so completely drained that there was not another tear left in me.

Eventually, the daily nausea subsided, and I began to feel better— much better. I had always made a fetish of keeping extremely thin, despite the fact that my doctor and others would periodically urge me to put on some weight. But I just ignored them; after all, my mother never weighed more than 110, and she was 5'11". Only now, with the baby coming, I was gaining weight—and I felt *good*; in fact, better than I had in a long time.

We would soon need a larger apartment, of course, and we found one in Greenwich, a darling garage apartment on an old estate. There was an extra bedroom, and this we transformed into a nursery. To furnish it, my mother took me on a shopping expedition to Macy's, where we picked out a crib and bassinette and other things we would need. Talk about dreams coming true! There we were, just me and Mum, shopping and having lunch together at the Palm Court of the Plaza!

The dream went on. Just before the baby was due, Buzz and I moved into my parents' apartment, to be as near as possible to the LeRoy Sanitarium, a small women's hospital on East 61st Street.

One evening at dinner—just a cozy supper for the four of us—my mother said, "You know, I can't have favorites with my children, but I can with my grandchildren." The men chided her and said she couldn't there, either, but I knew what she meant. And I knew that nothing would persuade her otherwise. The realization made me at once proud and apprehensive. For the game of emotional leapfrog was about to take another jump. James Stillman, incapable of showing love to his daughter, Grandma Rockefeller, had poured out his affection on her daughter, Mum. And Grandma Rockefeller, cursed with the same affliction, had made up for it by focusing on her daughter's daughter, me. And now my mother was about to focus on my daughter, her as yet unborn namesake.

Early on the morning of February 12th, Lincoln's birthday, I was awakened with a dull but pronounced pain. Half asleep, I looked at the clock: three A.M. Another contraction came, and another, as Buzz scrambled to find his trusty Bulova. Finally, he timed them, and found they were five minutes apart. Buzz tugged on his bathrobe and ran down the hall to alert my parents, who got up and started dressing immediately.

By the time he returned to the room, I was almost ready to go, and sat on the bed calmly pointing out where his shoes were, and that he couldn't wear a brown tie with a blue suit.

But if Buzz was nervous, he was nothing compared to my father, who stuck his head in our room and yelled, "It's snowing! I've got to get a taxi!" He slammed out the front door, on the dead run. At last, we were all on our way, and riding in the taxi, I noticed my mother was all aglow. Her first grandchild was about to be born.

My father was not exactly glowing; he was leaning forward and urging the driver to go faster on the rain-slick streets, until finally my mother said, "Freddy, relax! It's a first baby; we'll get there on time."

And we did. As we all walked up to the reception desk, I felt a little like the star performer in a traveling circus troupe. I was whisked upstairs into a lovely corner room. After they had prepared me, Buzz and my mother came into my room and prepared for the long vigil.

After a while, Dr. Burns, my doctor, came in and asked my mother to wait downstairs in the waiting room or, better yet, to go home. Suddenly, I felt bereft! Buzz was still there, but *she* was the one I had always wanted when I was sick, and I wanted her now desperately. Tears welled up in my eyes, as she departed.

A while later, Dr. Burns returned, to see how things were going, and he said in a gentle voice, "I had to tell her to go, Bel. It is too difficult for mothers to see their daughters going through the pangs of childbirth. I did it for her sake, and you must respect my judgment." Looking at his kindly round face with the snowy hair and hazel eyes, I decided that I trusted him.

All was proceeding according to plan. Buzz sat holding my hand and reading to me excerpts from the *Reader's Digest* between pains, when all at once a violent pain shook my body. I screamed, and bit hard on Buzz's thumb. When the pain passed, Buzz rushed to find a nurse, who took one look at me and panicked! "Quick," she yelled, "bring the stretcher, call the delivery room, call Dr. Burns, quick, quick, quick!"

I was put on a stretcher table and propelled down the hall and into an elevator, just catching a last glimpse of Buzz, who looked worried and bewildered.

Scarcely five minutes after I arrived in the delivery room, my baby was born. "It's a girl," Dr. Burns said, as he smacked her bottom, "a wee bonnie girl." He washed her eyes out, wrapped her up in swaddling clothes, and gave her to me. I looked at the warm tiny bundle. She was beautiful! Her little features seemed perfectly formed, and her head was covered with blond fuzz, which surprised me, as all the babies I had seen before had had rather long, black hair.

Buzz, my parents, and Buzz's parents, were waiting for me, when I returned from the delivery room. They all seemed ecstatic, for they had seen the baby, and they, too, were impressed with her unusual beauty.

"Another Isabel," my mother said softly, her eyes glistening. "I am thrilled, just thrilled!" I knew then, without question, that nothing I had ever done had pleased my mother more.

*But*—she would not be called Isabel, at least not by us. For just as my mother had nicknamed me Bellita at birth, so we nicknamed our daughter. And I promised her, as she slept beside me, that she, unlike me, would never be made to renounce her name in favor of Isabel. We named her Tinker, after Tinker Bell, the fairy in *Peter Pan*. Grandma had always been partial to fairies, considering them and the other woodland folk benevolent little creatures, and so did I. Tinker would be her name, for as long as she wanted to keep it.

# 15

BUZZ AND MY MOTHER AND FATHER proudly brought me home to our little garage apartment and settled me in—whereupon Mum and Pop promptly departed for a long vacation at Overhills. I couldn't believe it! She'd done it again, deserting me when she knew I didn't know the first thing about caring for a baby! In desperation, we hired a practical nurse to take care of the baby and me and the house, but Buzz sent her packing after three days, when she steadfastly refused to let him hold his new daughter.

Too proud to admit my total ignorance about being a mother, I tried to handle things myself. But soon I was practically beside myself and driving the baby to hysterics with my fumbling. Buzz now took matters into his own hands and called Dr. Burns, who recommended a superb baby nurse, a young woman named Mimi, from Latvia. She stayed with us for a month, and in the process of getting things running smoothly, she gave me a crash course in taking care of baby that would stand me in good stead. Week by week, Tinker grew, and so did we, in the parental department, until we were thoroughly enjoying ourselves. We took her everywhere with us, and if for some reason we couldn't, we left her with my mother, who was delighted, pouring out her love to her.

Cal had a son just five months after Tinker's birth, but so enthralled was I with our daughter that I was not bothered by my usual jealousy, even though she had produced the first son and named him after Pop—Frederic Walker Lincoln Harder.

That summer of 1953, Buzz and I took our first vacation since our honeymoon—two weeks at Prout's Neck, Maine. Tinker had just been weaned and delivered to my mother, who had been able to hire Nana, the baby nurse who had helped her with Percy and Posy, when they were little. One afternoon as we were down by the rocky shore, trying to skip flat stones on the water, Buzz said out of the blue, "What do you say we have another baby?" The stone I had just launched, instead of skipping, sank like a rock. "There were two and a half years between me and my sister," he went on, "and that's too long. It would be nice if we had our children closer together."

We talked for a while, and finally I said, "Well, if that's what you want, I'm game."

Not long after we returned in Greenwich, I drove over to my parents' house one afternoon. As they were only four miles away and had tea at five o'clock, I would frequently drop in. Their tea was not so elaborate as my grandparents' at Owenoke had been, but as my parents didn't eat dinner until after eight, it was still pretty substantial, with little sandwiches and lots of cookies. On this particular afternoon, they were talking about their coming trip to a guest ranch out West with my two younger sisters, when all at once my father looked at me and said: "You know, Bel, you look so well now. Please don't do anything foolish, like having another baby right away. Enjoy the child you have for a while; you've got plenty of time to have a family."

All the while he was talking, my teacup was held suspended in mid-air, and it stayed there for a moment after he had finished. It was uncanny—and I could not wait to talk to Buzz. In fact, I left early to meet his train, and got to the station with Tinker fifteen minutes early, as if by some fluke that might make the train arrive sooner. It didn't.

As soon as Buzz got in the car, I told him, "I saw my parents this afternoon. Pop feels very strongly that we should not have another baby right away. What are we going to do?"

"We are going to go up there and tell him exactly what we are planning and why. We can't let them go out West, believing one thing, when we are planning to do just the opposite. After all, it's *our* family, not his!" The prospect of this confrontation frightened me, because I knew my father, and I knew my husband. In Buzz's family, he had never been allowed to make any decisions, and his opinions were routinely steamrollered by his father. As a result, he got furious when anyone tried to impose a decision or an opinion on him (like the right way to wrap stocking presents), and his reaction doubled if it came from someone his father's age—like my father.

We drove home in silence, and when we got there, Buzz said, "Call your parents and see if we can stop by their house for a drink."

"Do we have to see them, Buzz?" I pleaded. "I'm scared."

"We've got to. Now." He kept his eyes straight ahead on the road, so unswervingly that I knew there was no point in talking further. I called my mother; she was surprised but delighted. "Why don't you come for dinner, too? We can put Tinker down in her crib." My mother loved being a grandmother; as Grandma had for me, she had converted the guest room into a nursery, complete with crib, changing table, and even a little refrigerator for baby food. As it was a typical August day in Greenwich—hot and unbearably humid—we changed clothes before going over.

Pulling up at the front door, we walked around to the back of the house. My parents would be on the flagstone porch; if there was any breeze at all, it was best appreciated there. My father was especially affable as he greeted us. "Your mother will be right down. I'm just making daiquiris; would you like one?" We nodded and sat down. My mother appeared, and I gladly passed Tinker to her outstretched arms. My father distributed the frosty glasses and took a seat next to Buzz, saying to him, "You know, I was just telling Bel this afternoon how well she looked. I've been worried about her for a long time—I guess for years—because she was so terribly thin and tense. Now, for the first time since I can remember, she looks healthy." He smiled over at me. "I mean it; I've never seen you look better." Then, turning back to Buzz, he added, "You, as her husband, have a responsibility: you mustn't let her get too tired or rundown."

It didn't take much foresight to see what was coming, and I braced myself as my father got up and walked to the edge of the porch, where he peered out into the gathering dusk. "One more thing, Buzz," he said without turning. "Given that responsibility, I think that it would be cruel—and extremely selfish—for you to ask her to have another child at this point. Your primary concern should be to to care for and protect your wife."

I looked at my father in amazement. We hadn't told him why we were coming; he had picked it up entirely on his own. And now he was speaking with such patient wisdom and candor, it would be difficult to argue with him.

Buzz didn't try. There was a telltale glistening in his eyes, as he stood up and said, "I'm sorry, Pop; I wasn't thinking about it that way, of the physical and emotional strain it would put on Bel. The truth is, on vacation we decided at my suggestion to start trying to have another child. That's why we came over tonight, to tell you about it, because we didn't want anything hidden between us. But I see now how selfish I was, and how wrong. Thanks for being so honest."

My father went over to him and held out his hand, and Buzz shook it firmly. That night, back in our apartment, we were both profoundly grateful for my parents, and for the security we felt in their willingness to be honest with us, even when it went against what we might want.

Nevertheless, in January, to my complete surprise, I discovered I was again pregnant. Our initial reaction, after we had gotten over the shock, was joy. But after a few days, it became clear that this pregnancy was going to be far more difficult than the first. My nausea was worse, and this time there were other complications, so that, in order not to lose the baby, Dr. Burns confined me to bed for the first six weeks. Add to that a severe calcium deficiency, leg cramps, the emergence of varicose veins on my legs, high blood pressure, and constant acid indigestion, and I began to understand more than ever the wisdom of my father's advice.

On top of everything else came the realization that our apartment would not be large enough, and we were going to have to move again. But that turned out to be the one bright spot during the nine long months. For on Boxwood Lane, a tiny dirt road in Greenwich, we found our dream house, and with the help of a loan from my father and a hefty mortgage, we were able to get it. We moved in quickly. My parents gave us the money to redecorate a few rooms, and to buy custom-made draperies for the living and dining rooms.

What fun I had, fixing up that little house! And how we loved it, as we sat out on our own cool terrace, sipping iced fruit tea! I should have been happy, really happy, for in addition to a dream house and all the possessions that anyone could possibly need, I had a loving, considerate husband, a beautiful, contented one-year-old daughter, doting parents, and a pregnancy that had straightened out and was proceeding according to plan. And yet . . . and yet underneath I felt that something was missing, and then I would feel guilty for even having such a feeling.

I shrugged it off. I would feel better after I had the baby. Let my indigestion clear up, and my veins stop hurting . . . and of course, I was smoking way too much. But I had to sit down so often, and it helped to pass the time, to pull out a cigarette. Normally, I might have smoked half a pack a day; now I was smoking a full pack.

The dog days of July and August descended on Greenwich again, and my parents escaped to Europe with my sisters Percy and Posy. My mother, possibly feeling a bit guilty, gave us an air conditioner for our bedroom. Needless to say, reading in bed became a favorite evening activity. Toward the end of the month, Dr. Burns's assistant advised us to move back to New York, for it seemed to him there was a good chance the baby would be coming earlier than its September 13th due date. Dutifully, we packed up, left Tinker with my parents who were now back from Europe, and moved into their unused New York apartment.

On Sunday, September 5th, I woke up early, feeling decidedly unwell and very sorry for myself. Nobody, but nobody, spent Labor Day weekend trapped in steaming Manhattan, with nowhere to go and nothing to do. Buzz went out and got the huge Sunday paper, which we, like other trapped New Yorkers, desultorily worked our way through. Finally, it was lunchtime, but it seemed too much of an effort to cook anything, and for once Buzz was not even interested in eating.

And then I had a fleeting pain. It was not much of anything, and I ignored it. When another one came, I waited for a third. But nothing came, and I ignored the second, also. Then, haphazardly, there was another. "Buzz, I'm having occasional pains, but I don't know if they mean anything. Probably not. Certainly they're nothing to get alarmed about."

But Buzz chose to get alarmed, anyway—anything to dispel the boredom of this afternoon. He started timing the pains, but they were so sporadic, he finally gave up and got himself a Coke. He offered me half, but I couldn't bear the thought of it. Finally, about seven-thirty, Buzz called Dr. Burns to bring him up to date, after which Dr. Burns told him to get me immediately to the hospital.

"Buzz, I don't want to go. Are you sure we have to?"

"Yes," he said, in a tone that brooked no further challenge, "and right now." So we called our parents and got a taxi.

My mother was already at the hospital, when we arrived, and so was Dr. Burns. My mother said to Buzz, "You look hungry; why don't you go out and get a hamburger? It will be a while before they have her prepped, and from what you said about the pains, we'll all have a long wait."

"Good idea," said Buzz, who had not eaten since breakfast. He waved and disappeared, while I went up to my room and started getting out of my clothes.

All at once, I was engulfed in an enormous pain. Dr. Burns came in and checked me, and ordered the nurse to get me on a stretcher and into the delivery room as quickly as possible. Another pain doubled me over; it was worse, far worse, than anything I had experienced with Tinker. And it came again. I screamed. "Oh, God, help me! Oh, *aagghh!*" Another pain wracked me and scared me, because each one was worse than the pain before. If it kept on, the third or fourth would kill me. "Oh, God," I cried, "I don't want to die! Please, if you bring me through this, I promise I'll never have another baby again! Oh, God, help—" and my wind was choked off by the next pain. But I was on the stretcher table now, flying down the hall and through the swinging doors, into the delivery room, my last sight the nose cone of the anesthesiologist, coming down over my face . . .

*Smack!* The next sound I heard was the lusty response of seven-pound, fourteen-ounce Basil Beebe Elmer III, to the rude hand of Dr. Burns, applied to his tender bottom. Can there be a more glorious sound than the cry of one's own newborn baby? All memory of pain vanishes, all travail is forgotten. To hear the sound of *life!* Obstetricians must be the happiest doctors in the world! I grinned up at Dr. Burns and held out my arms for my son.

As they wheeled me back into my room, Buzz was there, holding a cheeseburger and a milkshake in his hands. "I have a son?" he was saying to my mother, "How could I? I've only been gone ten minutes!"

His parents, needless to say, were ecstatic at the news. I had always gotten along well with my father-in-law, but now I could do no wrong! As the first BBE gazed down at the third, he murmured, never taking his eyes off the baby, "You know, Bel, you've really done it! You've given me a grandson, and he's got my name! When I leave here, I'm going to buy a box of the finest Havana cigars to be had in New York. And tomorrow, every friend of mine on the floor of the Exchange is going to get one."

I didn't have the heart to tell him that we didn't particularly like the name we had given our son, and had done it only because he would have been so hurt if we hadn't. But like the fifth Isabel, the third Basil was going to have a nickname we *did* like. A month before, we had had a really terrific evening at the movies, seeing *Road to Morocco,* with Bing Crosby, Bob Hope, and Dorothy Lamour. After the show, having a hamburger at Neilson's, I jokingly said to Buzz, "You know, if we have a boy, we ought to nickname him Bing."

"Bing Elmer," Buzz said, frowning slightly and thinking, as if he were sampling a fine wine. "You know, it has a nice ring to it."

"Well, I was just kidding, but—"

Buzz laughed. "You know, if we did nickname him that, we'd be Buzz, Bel, Tinker, and Bing!"

"Oh, no!" I gasped, laughing. "It sounds like a vaudeville comedy routine!"

Buzz closed his eyes and started laughing so hard that his sides ached. "And now," he intoned, "fresh from a three-week engagement in the Adirondacks, the laughing, singing Elmers: Buzz, Bel—" He couldn't finish, he was laughing so hard.

"Stop it, Buzz," I whispered, my sides shaking, "or I'll have little Bing right here!" and we both rocked in helpless, speechless mirth.

And so to us our son's name would be Bing, for as long as he wanted to keep it.

AFTER SIX DAYS IN THE HOSPITAL, Bing and I went home to our little red house on Boxwood Lane, and Mimi came back to help us. But this time she was only able to stay a short time, because she was waiting to go to Germany, to help her husband emigrate to this country. Before we knew it, she was gone, and Buzz and I were on our own—with Bing, whose favorite crooning time was all night long. Very quickly, all three of us were exhausted.

Finally, the pediatrician put him on phenobarbitol, but instead of calming him down, it only made him more hyper. After Mimi, we went through a succession of unsatisfactory nurses, and I became more and more tense, smoked more and more, and grew thinner and thinner.

One day I burst into tears. "Oh, Buzz," I cried, "what are we going to do? I'm up all day with Tinker, and we're up all night with Bing. I never see any of my friends anymore; I feel housebound, inadequate, and alone. I never realized motherhood was going to be like this!''

Buzz just shook his head. "I don't know what to say. This is probably not the time to tell you this, but frankly I'm not too happy at work, either." Startled, I momentarily set aside my litany of woe and concentrated, as he told me of the frustrations of being a stock and bond salesman, of his feelings of inadequacy and rejection in that position, and how he really didn't feel cut out for it. He shook his head, thinking about it, and I could see that he was deeply discouraged. "And the worst part is, I don't know what stock is going up, or what is going down, but I have to act as though I do. I hate that.''

Alarmed at the despair in his voice, even more than what he was telling me, I asked, "How come you've never told me this before?''

He thought for a moment. "Because I didn't really realize myself, until just recently. But," he said, shaking his head, "it's not at all what I thought it would be.''

We pondered our predicament and decided to take some positive steps to remedy the situation, starting with entertaining more. Every other Saturday night, we would have two or three couples over for dinner, and we joined the Field Club, a country club that my grandfather Lincoln had founded. Faithfully, we attended their occasional dinner dances, though the magic of my dancing debutante years was definitely past. We took bridge lessons. And we started going to Christ Church, the very church my mother had refused to have anything to do with after Aunt Win's death. But times had changed, and so had the rector. The new man was named Bob Appleyard, and sensing our need, he suggested we come to his confirmation class. Buzz and I had already been confirmed, but neither of us had had any teaching, so we were interested in taking his class. Perhaps it might help us with our general malaise. And it did soothe us somewhat, but it did nothing to help the haunting loneliness deep inside each of us. Nothing helped with that.

The thing that seemed to help somewhat was to spend a great deal of time with various members of my family, including aunts and uncles and quite a few of my thirty-four first cousins and their spouses. There always seemed to be something going on—a birthday, a christening, an engagement, or a wedding. The premise with the Rockefellers and the Lincolns—and it's true of many clannish old families—is that if you huddle together enough, nothing on the outside can hurt you.

Inside the stronghold's walls, aberrations were winked at, and as young children, we quickly learned the rules. Ocassionally, when sins were committed of such magnitude that they could not be overlooked, the family nonetheless contrived to "not see" them, carrying on for all the world as if they had never happened. For they had no way of coping with them.

But underneath this studied serene exterior, all was not well. Deep hurts were buried and forgotten but never healed; bitter resentments, jealousies, and broken relationships were smoothed over with smiling good manners. The old adage, "Out of sight, out of mind," was never more true: if we weren't daily confronted with unpleasant reality, we could pretend it simply wasn't there.

But for the game to work, it was essential that everyone in the stronghold be a player. Therefore, politeness and good manners were not merely trademarks of one's class; they were crucial to the maintenance of the illusion that all *was* well. Well-modulated behavior was highly valued; public display of emotion was considered unseemly. Angry outbursts were to be expected from children—but only from the very young.

Within the family, it was impossible to talk about deep personal problems, because supposedly there weren't any. The family itself was the solution—and to a surprising degree, it actually worked. But that meant there was no one I could turn to with my low-level but persistent sense of emptiness in the midst of plenty, or to whom Buzz might confess his deep-seated fears and anxieties.

His family was much the same as mine. One day his mother invited me to lunch at the Junior League Club, and because she was so kind, I decided to risk it. "Aunt Alice," I suddenly blurted out, over the jellied madrilene, "I don't know how to help Buzz. He's so worried and miserable at his work. Can you help him, or tell me how to?"

"What do you mean, he's miserable? Why, First Boston is the finest underwriting firm on Wall Street! I'm so proud of him, and so is his father! What should you do? Why, of course, nothing, child. He couldn't be in a better place! He's just young and a little unsure of himself. Everything will be fine, you'll see. Now don't you worry about it and eat your madrilene."

But I did worry, not just about Buzz, but about everything—so much that my stomach was frequently tied in knots. Eventually, it got so bad that my doctor prescribed a battery of tests, which revealed that

I had a "pre-ulcerous condition," and from then on should be eating bland foods and drinking plenty of milk. The diet helped, and so did a charming mother's helper we found named Anne Robinson. A middle-aged Scot, she had had a very difficult life. She and her younger brothers and sister lost both their parents early, and Anne had had to raise the others herself. Then her fiancé had been killed during the war. But Anne Robinson, undaunted by adversity, remained steadfastly cheerful, and now she attached herself to our family, as if we were her own.

Anne brought a sense of peace and stability into our environment, and things began to look brighter to both of us; in fact, our outlook improved so that in January 1956 we began to talk of having another child. All memory of the terror of Bing's birth was forgotten, and scarcely had we mentioned the possibility than I was pregnant again. And this time it *was* different: there was no morning sickness, no discomfort; I breezed through the pregnancy. Indeed, things were so relaxed this time that I was at home in Greenwich, on the morning of October 10th, when the labor pains started. I called my parents, who seemed delighted to drive us into the hospital in New York City. It was a happy trip; the trees were at the height of their color, and we drove down the Merritt Parkway, through a fabulous display of autumn foliage.

When we arrived at the hospital, all labor stopped and I was mortified.

"Don't worry," said Dr. Burns, as he came in to check me, "I'm going to give you something to relax, and then we'll take you to the delivery room."

"The delivery room? I'm not even in labor!"

"Well, with your track record, that's where you're going," he said firmly, and nodded to the attending nurse to get the stretcher. When we arrived in the delivery room, I gazed around at the pristine white walls and the shining chromium sterilizer—I'd never had time to notice that room before. The nurses were all wearing white masks and no doubt wondering why I was there, while over at the sink Dr. Burns rolled up his sleeves and began rubbing his already clean hands with disinfectant.

"What are you scrubbing up for, Doctor?" asked a nurse, "She's not even in labor."

"You'll see," Dr. Burns murmured, hurriedly holding out his arms for rubber gloves.

At that moment, an overwhelming pain wracked my body, and a nurse cried, "Quick! The baby's coming *now!*"

As a second pain shook me, down came the nose cone, and out I went. The first thing I saw, when I came to, was the clock on the wall: ten minutes had elapsed.

"Well," said Dr. Burns, smiling, "you have a healthy, eight-pound daughter. We've cleaned her up and taken her down to the nursery, for your husband and parents to see."

I was wheeled back into my room, and was comfortably in my white bed, when my mother came in. "She's a scream," she exclaimed, laughing, "an absolute scream!"

What did she mean by that, making fun of my daughter! And where *was* my daughter, anyway? How come everyone has seen her but me?

Just then, a nurse came in with a little bundle wrapped in a pink blanket. She placed her in my eager arms, and I pulled away the flap of the blanket and looked at the little face inside. She had a shock of dark brown hair, and it was standing bolt upright. And down her forehead ran an ugly red mark, covering her nose and chin.

At that moment, Dr. Burns came in. "Don't worry, Bel; that's just a temporary birthmark. It's not permanent. It's from blood vessels that burst close to the surface of the skin, during your fast delivery. By the time she's a year old, you'll never notice them."

I looked at this poor little thing with the hair and the mark, and felt a flood of compassion for her. I had always felt so severely plain myself, it was like seeing me all over again in her. And how I resented my mother for laughing at her! I clutched her close and vowed that I would make it up to her.

We named her Lucy Lincoln Elmer, a name Buzz and I both cherished. And since it was the first name that we had truly chosen for ourselves, there was no need for a nickname. Lucy was an easy baby; like Tinker, we could take her everywhere with us. I had been a nervous new mother with Tinker, and a distraught one with Bing, but with Lucy I just relaxed and enjoyed taking care of her. I nursed her for eight months, continually drawing her closer and closer to me. Too close—for I became dependent on her, in a way I had not with my first two children, and in her I fostered a deep dependency on me.

Years later, I would come to see how much I had to repent for—projecting myself into her and then pouring out my love and affection for her in an attempt to make up to the small child in myself for the mother's attention I had never received.

As Dr. Burns had predicted, by the time Lucy was a year old, the red marks had all disappeared. She became an attractive child, and as she grew into a young woman, she radiated charm and beauty—the type of girl who could easily have been "America's sweetheart."

At last our family was complete. We were just beginning to feel more adjusted to our life, when all of a sudden our complacency was shattered. "Buzz," I whispered to him one night in bed. "I can't believe it, and I've been putting off telling you for days, hoping that I was wrong. But—I think I'm pregnant again."

# 16

---

"YOU CAN'T BE!" Buzz cried, jumping out of bed. "You just can't be pregnant again!" He shook his head in disbelief. Lucy was barely eight months old, and we both remembered my father's admonition. Buzz stared down at me; he didn't say any more, but I knew he considered it my fault.

"Look," I snapped back at him, "I'm not any happier about this than you are! In fact, I kept putting off saying anything, in the hope that I was just late. But I'm two weeks overdue, and I'm getting nauseated."

He slumped down on the side of the bed, and I started to cry. "Well," he sighed, shaking his head, "you might as well go and get tested tomorrow, and get it confirmed." I nodded, sobbing now, incapable of talking further.

The next morning, Buzz left for work, still shaking his head, and I made plans to be tested at a nearby clinic. Soon the lab technician called me at home: "Mrs. Elmer, good news!" she said cheerily. "You're going to have a baby!"

"Oh, no," I moaned under my breath, and then thanked her as warmly as I could. As soon as she hung up, I phoned Dr. Burns's office. When his nurse answered, I burst out, at the edge of hysteria, "Please get Dr. Burns; I've got to talk to him immediately! It's a crisis!"

In a few moments, I heard Dr. Burns's calm, reassuring voice on the other end of the line and began to cry again. "I'm pregnant!" I wailed. "I'm pregnant again!" and my sobs overcame me. Dr. Burns waited patiently, until my sobbing subsided, and then he asked me to tell him all about it. So I told him of the missed period and the positive test, and all my other symptoms.

"Bel, I want you to stop worrying now," he said soothingly. "Come see me first thing in the morning, and we'll talk about it." His matter-of-fact manner calmed me down, and when I finally hung up, I took a deep breath and felt better.

That afternoon I went about my regular household chores, and around five o'clock started to fix dinner. All of a sudden, standing at the stove, I started to bleed. I decided to pay no attention, and went on with what I was doing. Buzz arrived home at seven-twenty, and after putting the children to bed, we sat down to enjoy a drink and nibble on some cheese and crackers.

At last Buzz asked, "Have you heard from the lab?"

"Yes, I'm pregnant. But don't worry about it; I've begun bleeding."

"You've *what?*" Buzz roared, spilling his drink.

"I've started bleeding," I replied, shocked at his reaction; I thought he would be pleased.

He got up from his easy chair and came over to where I was curled up on the sofa. "You're going to bed right now!" he said, helping me to my feet and taking me upstairs. As soon as I was settled in our king-size bed, he thumbed through our well-worn address book for Dr. Burns's home number. "Dr. Burns," he cried, when he got through, "it's about Bel. She's bleeding, and we're afraid she's going to miscarry! What should we do?"

Again Dr. Burns waited patiently, and then asked: "Now what do you two *want?* Bel calls me this morning, in hysterics because she's pregnant. Now you're calling, because you're afraid she's about to miscarry." He paused. "Do you want another baby, or don't you?"

Buzz covered the receiver and looked at me. "Do you want the baby?"

"Yes, yes I do!" I said vehemently, without even thinking about it.

"So do I!" exclaimed Buzz, and he turned back to the phone. "Dr. Burns, we want the baby."

"Very well, have Bel stay in bed and keep quiet. But I am not going to prescribe any medication, because this may be nature's way of avoiding another baby so close to the last child's birth."

*Belle in 1941.*
(CREDIT: WALTER SCOTT SHINN)

*West Point Cadet Basil Beebe Elmer, Jr. (Buzz), became my husband.*

*My school yearbook photo. I'm wearing the locket which my cousin Lee gave me.* (CREDIT: SARONY, INC.)

*June 25, 1951. Mr. and Mrs. Basil Beebe Elmer, Jr. coming down the aisle in St. James Episcopal Church, New York City.*

*Buzz and I and a group of enthusiastic dinner companions enjoying ourselves at the Stork Club, circa 1953.*

*Tinker, 6; Lucy, 3; Bing, 5; becoming acquainted with Buzz's responsibilities at The First Boston on the company's family day, 1959.*

*A family portrait in our backyard of the Alpine Road house, in 1968 including ou fourth child, Vicky (second from right).* (CREDIT: CLAYPOOLE)

*The Stanwich Congregational Church.*

*Nate Adams, Pastor.*

Cay, Judy, and Buzz in Orleans, Massachusetts, cira 1970.

The Bethany-Chapel complex at the Community of Jesus today. "Rock Harbor Manor" is on the extreme left.

*"Rock Harbor Manor," 1970.*

*Isabel Lincoln Elmer in 1986.*

So I stayed in bed—until Buzz went downstairs to get me some milk. We were a family who seemed to save old prescriptions forever; a whole shelf in our medicine chest was taken up with little brown bottles, some of which had dates on them that stretched back for years. Now I slipped into the bathroom, and hurriedly rummaged through our collection. Incredibly, I found what I was looking for—the remnants of a prescription Dr. Burns had given me three years before, when I was having a similar problem at the beginning of my pregnancy with Bing. I took the prescribed dosage, quickly got back to bed, and was under the covers by the time Buzz returned.

I stayed in bed as much as possible, during the next few weeks, using up the remainder of the old prescription and trying to stay calm. It wasn't easy, for Anne Robinson left us; the prospect of a fourth child under six years old was too much for her. My mother sent her chambermaid to help with the house, while Buzz tried to find another mother's helper. Needless to say, I was frequently in tears, and felt generally worn-out and useless.

One hot and muggy morning in July, I was looking through the *Herald Tribune* and happened to notice an announcement of a Billy Graham Crusade, which was going on in the huge old Madison Square Garden, at 50th Street and Eighth Avenue. I'd never heard of Billy Graham, did not know what an evangelist was, and the word *crusade* sounded medieval to me. But the announcement said that it would change my life, and something inside of me stirred; I wanted to go.

When Buzz came home, I asked him, and to my surprise, he agreed to take me—if we could get tickets. For the six-week crusade had made the newspapers, and they said that the waiting lines were two or three blocks long. Obviously, there was no way in my condition that I could wait in line that long. But something urged me on, and that night I wrote to the organization, explained my physical predicament, and had Buzz mail the letter on his way to work.

Two days later, I received a reply and two tickets. Also included were directions on where we could park, with the incapacitated. So, on a hot and muggy evening later in July, in the back seat of our Chevy station wagon, I lay down with a pillow, while Buzz drove us into Manhattan. We had no trouble finding the parking area, and were soon ushered in to good seats, low down, and to the right of the speakers' platform, although still a fair distance from the podium.

I had been to the Garden before, of course, with my father and then

my husband, to see the Rangers play hockey, and with my mother to
see the Ringling Brothers Circus. But always before, there had been an
atmosphere of rowdy excitement, with vendors constantly in the aisles,
loudly hawking their wares—popcorn and hotdogs and programs.
There was excitement tonight, too, but it was different—quieter
somehow, with a sense of subdued anticipation.

Settling into my seat, I did the first thing I always did in a strange
situation: I fished a cigarette out of my pocketbook. I was just about
to look for my lighter, when I happened to look around—and noticed
that no one else seemed to be smoking. Not one glowing red cigarette
end could I see, nor for that matter the customary haze of cigarette
smoke above us, hanging around the floodlights. And of course,
that made me want a cigarette all the more. "Buzz, do you think
it's all right to smoke?"

He looked around and shook his head. "I wouldn't," he said. "It
feels like church in here."

Soon the 500-voice choir, dressed in white blouses and shirts, started
to sing old familiar hymns, and then gospel-type songs. I had never
heard so large a choir, and they were impressive. I noted also that quite
a few people in the audience were singing along with them. Then a tall,
handsome man called George Beverly Shea came to the podium and
sang "How Great Thou Art." His deep, resonant voice filled the
entire Garden, and inside I felt an emotion—a yearning—that I had
never felt before. Was Buzz feeling anything? I glanced at him, and
was astonished to see tears in his eyes. What was going on here! What
would my father say, if he could see us here?

I had just decided that I did not like this situation one bit, when Billy
Graham strode to the podium. We were too far away to see the details
of his face, but you could see the man, and the air of undeniable
authority about him. "Let's all bow our heads," he said, and then he
prayed for God's presence and inspiration, and dedicated his words to
His glory. It was short, direct, and to the point—and you could have
heard a pin drop, such was the hush in the Garden.

He preached about the reality of Jesus, a living Saviour, Who was
alive today, and Who could give new meaning and direction to our
lives, if we would let Him. He seemed to understand the emptiness I
had felt for so long, and the feelings that had haunted Buzz. Though
there was much that I didn't understand in my head and would have
liked him to stop and explain, my heart seemed to be having no such

problem. It seemed to be understanding perfectly and could have gone on listening forever.

Billy Graham spoke for about 45 minutes, and then he invited those who wanted to make a decision for Christ, to stand and come forward and gather at the foot of the platform. The choir began singing "Just As I Am," and people began coming down the aisles, just a few at first, and then more and more.

I sensed the presence of God in that vast arena. It was the first time I had ever felt anything like that—so powerful and majestic and unknowable—and it made goose bumps rise on my arms. Inside my chest, my heart was tugging me forward. I didn't know exactly what that entailed, but I now felt impelled to my feet.

I turned to Buzz, to ask if he minded my going forward, but before I could speak, he said, "Bel, would you mind if I went? I'll be back, just as soon as I can."

"I'm coming, too," I responded, and we walked hand in hand down the aisle, neither of us fully realizing the momentous step we were taking.

When we were all gathered, more than a thousand of us, Billy Graham led us in prayer: "Jesus, I give my life to You, just as it is. There is much that I've done that I'm ashamed of, and I ask Your forgiveness for these sins. I invite You into my heart, and from this moment forth, I declare that You are the Lord and Master of my life. In Your name, I pray. Amen."

After the prayer, a nice young girl named Judy, who seemed all of eighteen, invited me to accompany her downstairs, where she had something she wanted to give me. I followed her, down past where they used to have the sideshow in the circus, to where we used to feed the elephants peanuts, and where we laced up our skates, before going out on the ice. I thought of Lee, then, and of the time right after she had died, when I had stood almost in this very spot, my heart breaking, as my mother had pleaded with me to go on with my life and perform in the Junior Skating Club production which was part of the Ice Follies, then appearing in the Garden.

Judy was telling me about how my life would be different, and I realized that I wasn't paying attention. Concentrating now, I still couldn't understand very much of what she was saying, but she gave me a paperback Gospel of John, and four weekly studies to fill out and send in, and I thanked her and went to find Buzz.

When we got home, I went straight to bed—and more or less remained there, on Dr. Burns's orders, for most of the summer, spending more time now reading the Bible than the *Herald Tribune*. There was much that I didn't understand, but I kept at it for the first time in my adult life. Finally, as September approached, I began to get up more, and life began to return to normal.

ONE MORNING Betty Lou Bush called. I knew her and her husband Press from the Field Club, where they were part of a group that was a little older than ours. Press's father had been a Senator, and his brother George would one day be Vice President. Betty Lou asked me if Buzz and I wanted to join a Bible study group that she was organizing. At that time I had never heard of people getting together to study the Bible, but I was flattered to be asked, and I accepted, without bothering to check with Buzz. It never occurred to me to wonder why she would call us out of the blue, although I did think it an unusual coincidence so soon after our attending the Billy Graham crusade. Fortunately, Buzz liked the idea, and so, every Tuesday evening for more than five years, we met and pored over the heavily intellectual Interpreter's Bible.

Meanwhile, Bob Appleyard, our young rector at Christ Church, noticing that we were now coming to church every Sunday, asked if we would be willing to help out a little "back country" mission church named St. Barnabas, which was affiliated with Christ Church. We agreed, and Buzz was soon asked to teach Sunday School there, and then to be on the board. But somehow the presence of God, which I had sensed at the Billy Graham crusade, was not in our worship, nor did I sense His power guiding our lives.

With my due date approaching, and the prospect of our family enlarging again, there was no way our little house on Boxwood Lane would hold us all. We started looking for a new home, and finally found just the right one fifteen minutes out of town, on the edge of what was called "back country Greenwich." It was almost country, and for the first time in my life, I found out what it was like to live in a neighborhood, and become friends with the people next door. There were barbecue suppers and coffee klatches, and our children were delighted to have so many new friends to play with.

OUR BABY ARRIVED on April 1, 1958—healthy, bright, and perfect. "Oh, God," I breathed in wonder, "she's *beautiful!* Thank You, thank You! I don't deserve such a beautiful child." It was the first time I had ever given Him the credit for anything. And the first time I had a hint that perhaps I didn't always deserve the love and mercy He was showering down upon me. We named her Victoria Hoyt; the middle name was a surname from my mother-in-law's family, but Victoria simply expressed how we felt about her, as we gazed down at her delicate features and blue-grey eyes. Looking at her, we now knew that our family was truly complete.

As Vicky grew older, she proved to be a happy child—far happier than her mother. My stomach trouble had gotten so bad that I often had miserable heartburn, and would frequently have bouts of retching in the middle of the night that would last for hours and leave me limp on my bed for several days. I also had recurring migraine headaches, an ailment that Buzz, too, shared. My emotional health was on a par with my deteriorating physical condition; I was becoming increasingly insecure, so much that I would cry for hours, if Buzz forgot to kiss me goodbye when he went to work.

One mid-May afternoon in 1960, I dropped over to my parents' house, to have tea with my mother. She wasn't home when I arrived, but came in shortly afterward, and I was shocked to see her. Deathly pale and looking even thinner than usual, she looked old for the first time, and I had to remind myself that she was only fifty-eight.

We went out on the porch, and she poured us each a cup of tea, her hand shaking as she held the saucers. "Mum," I gasped, "what's the matter? You look as though you've just been to a funeral."

Startled, she stared at me a moment. Then in a low, weary voice she said, "I've been to see Aunt Faith in the hospital. She has breast cancer. She's known about it for two years and did nothing about it, and now the cancer is as big as a grapefruit."

I was stunned. My favorite aunt—

Her voice broke, as she continued: "She doesn't want to live! It's like Grandma all over again, after Grandpa died. The doctors told me she could have been healed, if she'd come to them, when she first knew. They say it's a form of suicide."

I went over to her, and put an arm around her slumping shoulders, to comfort her. I was the mother, and she, the daughter. I sensed that she had to talk, to get it out and let the grief come with it, so I said nothing and waited.

She cleared her throat and went on, about how Aunt Faith had never really been happy since she left school. Oh, she had lots of friends and lots of good works, but the right man had never come along. And then in 1941, when she was thirty-two, the wrong one did—a frightfully attractive Belgian named Jean, who had escaped from his country during the Nazi invasion. After a whirlwind romance, they married—and then came to realize that they had nothing in common. Aunt Faith was a simple, wholesome girl who loved outdoor activities, especially gardening. Jean, six years younger, loved night life and became a habitué of night clubs, his name often mentioned by the columnists who kept track of café society. They had three children, the youngest of whom had to be placed in a home for the severely retarded, and they grew further and further apart. In 1955, at the age of forty, Jean had contracted polio and died, but Aunt Faith had never emerged from her despair.

"Oh, Bel"—my mother broke down—"even with an operation, they've given her only two years to live! She wants me to send Bobby [Aunt Faith's oldest, who was seventeen] to Africa, so he won't see her suffer, and Cookie [her daughter] will stay on at the house. I'm supposed to care for her. But I can't; I'm just too old." And her voice trailed off, as she shook her head.

"We'll cope, Mum, somehow," I said, not knowing how.

Aunt Faith did not have two years; she lived barely six weeks after the mastectomy. I went to see her often during those final days, and watched her large frame rapidly waste away under the ravages of the disease. I would try to cheer her up, but the doctors were right; her death wish was too strong to be thwarted. First Grandma, then Aunt Win, and now Aunt Faith—so consumed by despondency that they could not bear to go on living. I wondered again: What was the point of life? Obviously, the three of them had seen no point to it. I had read somewhere that suicide was a trait that tended to run in families— would I be the first of my generation? I had not consciously considered it, but my own despair was more profound and unbroken now than it had ever been before . . .

On July 2nd, 1960, Aunt Faith, fifty-one, died of cancer. Three days later, the Rockefellers once again gathered around an open grave at the family burial plot in Tarrytown. And as before, John D.'s side of the family joined William's side in their mourning. Lawrence and Nelson had been especially fond of their cousin Faith, and her death affected them deeply. It seemed as if tragedy was stalking William's side of the family, and all of them were powerless to stop it. (And it would strike again—as three more William Rockefeller/James Stillman descendants would take their own lives.)

The final prayers were said, and the casket was lowered into the ground. There were tears—but only a few; we Rockefellers seldom let our emotions show. As the others began to file silently back to the waiting limousines, I paused to stare again up at the epitaph that William had had inscribed on his grand mausoleum: "Thou has made us for Thyself, and our heart shall never rest, until at last it rests in Thee." I hoped Aunt Faith's heart was at rest now. I wondered if mine would ever be.

The next day I became violently ill. The heartburn was so bad, I was doubled over in pain, as I dragged myself to the bathroom to retch. I called the doctor, and eventually he came and gave me a shot to stop the vomiting. A couple of days later, after I had recovered, I again went through a battery of tests, which again turned up nothing conclusive. Back I went on a bland diet, and my mother sent our family up to The Cabin in the Adirondacks, which was her universal panacea, but she and Buzz could not think of anything else to do for me.

But perhaps the immense peace of those ancient, fir-covered mountains and the tranquil ponds at the foot of burbling, rocky streams did have a soothing effect that science couldn't measure. For I did get better, and after a couple of weeks I was ready to resume our Greenwich life of cocktail parties, children's activities, bridge, and church— and only occasionally wondering what life was really all about. Buzz continued to be miserable at his job, but lacked the confidence to look for another, until one day he was stunned to learn that after having been there for ten years, First Boston was letting him go.

Buzz was badly shaken, and his parents were devastated; how could this have happened to *their* son? He tried to talk to them, but it was hopeless. He fared better with my parents, who were more compassionate, and he had several good talks with them. He had no trouble finding another job, at F. S. Smithers, selling securities in Europe. He enjoyed the glamor of that job, and the money he was making, but when the European institutions stopped buying U.S. securities a few years later, he again became discouraged and unhappy. My father had a friend at Loomis, Sayles & Company, an investment counseling firm, which sounded better suited to Buzz. They hired him, and before

long he was assigned to some of their most important accounts. They
made him a vice president, and once more the sun was shining—but
for how long?

We talked about our anxieties and our emptiness, but there didn't
seem to be any way of resolving such things. It never occurred to
us to get professional help or counseling; people in our walk of life
just didn't do that.

It was sometime after Christmas in 1962, that I first heard about the
Stanwich Congregational Church. I was at my Friday afternoon bridge
group, and it was a typical session—light on the bridge, heavy on the
conversation—only this time, one of the girls who couldn't be there
had arranged for a substitute, Pat Cooper, to take her place. I don't
know how the subject came up, but Pat started talking about this
wonderful church she belonged to, where the pastor really cared about
each member of the congregation. I'd never heard anyone talk about
their church that way, and it made me want to go. I told Buzz about it
that night, and the first Sunday we could, we bundled our four children
into the wagon and went.

The Stanwich Congregational Church was truly in the back country,
between Stamford and Greenwich, hence its name. As soon as I saw it,
I liked it. Its white steeple stood out against the trees that surrounded
it, and stepping inside the tall front doors was like stepping back into
the eighteenth century. The church still had its original pews and
windows, dating back some 250 years. Not since my Westover days
had I been inside a Congregational church, but the utter simplicity of
the sanctuary reminded me of the Middlebury Congregational Church
and was surprisingly soothing. I felt at home and welcome, even
though I didn't know anyone.

The minister was a tall, thin man with stooped shoulders and a broad
Down East accent, whom I guessed to be in his early forties. When he
preached, he spoke plainly and directly, from the heart, not the head.
Indeed, so clear and simple was it that I was surprised to learn later
that he had several earned doctorates. Whatever his homiletic method,
his heart was communicating to my heart, and the message was Jesus.
That was all he talked about the entire sermon—Jesus.

My heart leaped; this was the way I had felt, when Billy Graham was
preaching! This was what had been missing: Jesus! I was excited—we
would definitely be coming back.

After the service, a number of people warmly welcomed us and
hoped we would come back, and Buzz and I were nonplussed—this

was decidedly untypical of Greenwich, where Episcopalians lived up to their reputation as God's Frozen People. Comparing notes in the car on the way home, we discovered that the children felt the same way. They begged us to please go to this church, from now on. "We'll see" was our reply—the standard response of parents who were unable or unwilling to grant their children's request. But we *would* have to see—for obviously we had a number of ties and responsibilities to our present church.

On the weekend of Washington's birthday, we went on a family skiing outing to the nearest slope, Otis Ridge in Massachusetts. It was a clear, sunny, but very cold morning; on the big thermometer outside the lodge, the needle was well below zero. Buzz was just struggling with Tinker's bindings, when the public address system announced: "Basil Elmer, please come at once to the phone at the main desk."

When he returned, he was dazed. "My father just died!"

"What? Where?"

"Down in Florida, in the hospital at West Palm Beach. We've got to get down there; Mother's in a state of shock."

The children's skiis, which had gone on so slowly, came off in a flash and were stowed in the back of the car, along with the rest of our gear. We drove rapidly and silently to Greenwich, where we left the children at my parents', and caught the first flight out of Idlewild, landing in West Palm by seven P.M.

As we did our best to console Buzz's mother, we learned the sad story of his father's last year. For most of his business life, he had been the floor partner of Eastman, Dillon & Company, and for the past several years, the firm had been gently implying that at sixty-nine it might be time for him to consider retirement, although he had steadfastly refused to interpret it that way. We too had done our part, giving him books on hobbies, and suggesting some interesting trips that he and Buzz's mother could take.

But he was having none of it. The Stock Exchange was his life. Its energy was his energy, and it was his reason for living—all the reason anyone could ask for, as far as he was concerned. And so it came as a cruel blow when, shortly before his seventieth birthday, during a brief vacation in Florida, he received a telegram from Eastman, Dillon, saying that, as of March 1, his services would no longer be required.

It broke his heart. He had a miserable year, even going so far as to put an ad in the *Wall Street Journal*, for he still owned a seat on the Exchange and was sure he could be of use to some firm. But apparently no one agreed. So he and Buzz's mother had spent the winter in Florida, where he felt bored and useless and unwanted. He had picked up a slight case of pneumonia that should never have been fatal. But it proved to be so, because he had lost the will to live.

So there it was again: the eventual futility of life. Oh, God, was this really all there was to look forward to? (I did not mean it as a prayer, but it may have been taken that way, nonetheless.)

A couple of days after the funeral, there was a knock on our door in Greenwich. To my surprise, it was the minister from the Stanwich Congregational Church, Nate Adams. Having seen the obituary in the Greenwich *Times* (where we had put the death notice, because the New York papers were on strike), he wondered if Buzz and I needed help. Buzz wasn't there, and I had never been visited by a minister, but I did have some questions—a lot of them, as it turned out. I gave him a cup of tea and then proceeded to ask him about the meaning of life, the possibility of life after death, and why this cruel thing had happened to my father-in-law at the end of his life.

Through it all, Nate listened patiently, and then gently responded with the best answers he had. They seemed to help: I felt calmer than I had in days, and regarded him as a true friend, one who really cared.

When I told Buzz about his visit, we both agreed that as soon as he had fulfilled his obligations at St. Barnabas, we would switch churches. And so, in the fall of 1963, we started attending Stanwich Church and quickly got involved in its life. Buzz became a deacon, and eventually I was named deaconess.

I also decided to go back to work at Sloan-Kettering, when Vicky entered kindergarten. The Chemotherapy division, where I used to work, had moved to Rye, New York, less than half an hour's drive from us. I hoped that, even though I would be only a part-time volunteer, I would feel like I was once more making a contribution toward something of value, and that life would have more meaning.

But it didn't help; I was still plagued with heartburn and migraine, and was still desperately thin, extremely insecure, and tense and nervous all the time. I still had lots of friends, just as I had always had, in the vague hope that, if I had enough people around me, I wouldn't feel so insecure.

During the fall of '65, I started reading the Bible again, and though I found it tedious most of the time, something kept urging me on. One evening, as I was reading Colossians in the Phillips translation, I came across the statement: "Christ in you, the hope of glory." (Col. 1:27) I didn't know what it meant, but it seemed important enough to go downstairs to show Buzz, who was paying bills. He didn't know what it meant, either. But three months later, we began to find out.

Early in January 1966, Nate invited us to a Faith at Work conference in New York. Faith at Work was scheduled to hold a mission in our church in March, and he wanted to attend this conference, to check them out. We had never been to a religious conference before, and had no desire to start, but Nate was a friend, as well as our pastor, so Buzz told him that we would go with him, if he couldn't get anyone else.

Nate called two weeks later to say he'd been unsuccessful, so I managed to get a baby sitter for the whole weekend, and on Friday, January 28th, the three of us checked into the Statler Hilton, opposite Pennsylvania Station. It was an old traveling salesmen's hotel, oppressive and reeking of stale cigar smoke. I hated it.

The first meeting was in the main ballroom, where some 500 people had gathered. They droned on about bringing Christ into the office, and I grew bored and fidgety and wished I'd brought my knitting down from our room. I glanced at Buzz; he was asleep.

Back in our room after an endless evening, I said to him: "This is no fun. I don't know what they're talking about, and I'm bored. Let's go home."

"What about the baby sitter?" Buzz replied. "We've hired her for the whole weekend."

I thought for a moment. "Okay, why don't we leave tomorrow morning, and spend the rest of the weekend with my parents, at their apartment?"

Buzz smiled. "Now you're talking. Let's call them in the morning." But early next day, much earlier than I had planned to get up, Buzz bounced out of bed and started getting dressed. "What are you doing?" I asked sleepily.

"There's a session on healing scheduled for this morning; I thought I'd see what it was all about." I looked at him as though he were crazy, then shrugged and rolled over and went back to sleep.

When he returned, an hour and a half later, I was sufficiently awake to see that something had happened. He was glowing and grinning, and before I could ask him what it was, he exclaimed, "You should have seen it, Bel! People prayed for other people, and there really was healing. It was *amazing!*'' He paused. "Look, I really want to stay at this conference and find out more."

Blast! I wanted to go to my parents! "Buzz, do we have to stay?"

"Yeah, I think we should. I mean, you wouldn't believe what I saw!"

"Well, it sounds awfully kooky to me," I muttered, using an expression currently in vogue with our children. Reluctantly I got out of bed, got dressed, and prepared to spend a perfectly dreadful day. At least this time I would have my knitting with me, I thought, clutching it firmly, as I followed Buzz out the door. And sure enough, the day was every bit as depressing as I had anticipated. Sometimes we met in small groups; sometimes we all gathered in the ballroom. It didn't matter to me; all of it was ghastly.

Toward the end of the afternoon, I was in the ballroom, half listening to some young man go on and on. I dropped my wool on the floor, and as I bent to pick it up, something made me concentrate on the speaker, and what he was saying. He was of medium height and build, with coffee-colored skin and snapping dark eyes. His name was Bill Pannell, I would learn later, and what he had been saying before, I had no idea. But I heard very clearly what he said next: "I used to have a terrible time with the fact that I was a mulatto. I was angry at God: why couldn't He have made me black . . . or white, for that matter? Why did I have to be in between? Then one day I was on my way to school, kicking pebbles, when all at once I heard God speak to me. He said: *My son, I have made you as I have, for My purposes. I want you to be an intermediary between the blacks and the whites. This is the call I have given you for your life. Be obedient, and you will be blessed.*"

As I sat there, dumbfounded, all of a sudden I heard God speak to *me*. It was not an audible voice, but He spoke so clearly and distinctly in my heart that I had no doubt it was God. *Bel, I have called you for My purposes. I love you with an everlasting love. The money that you will have, I have entrusted to you, to accomplish My will. Be obedient, and the Kingdom of Heaven will be yours.*

I sat there, transfixed. The Lord had spoken to me! I felt as if an enormous burden had been lifted from my shoulders. And suddenly I realized what life was all about, what it had been about, since before I was born: God had created me for a purpose! It was not an aimless life; He had a plan for me. The wealth that had so often been an embarrassment to me, was to be given to me as a sacred trust. I felt as if I had just been born, or rather, born all over again. I had never heard the evangelical expression "born again," but when I finally did hear it, I knew exactly what it meant.

I spent the rest of the evening in a daze. Gert Behanna was the featured speaker. She, too, had come from a background of wealth and privilege, and as she spoke, I identified with her completely. I knew in my heart that the only reason I had not had her problem with alcohol was my enormous self-righteousness. When she finished, we drove home, for Nate had to be in the pulpit the following morning.

The drive took longer than usual, because we were feeling our way through a blinding snowstorm, but all the way home I kept repeating the first line of the children's Sunday school ditty—"Jesus loves me!" I had never really known that, until that night. Now the whole world was changed. I knew, beyond the shadow of a doubt, that Jesus loved *me* and had a purpose for my life, and that He had been waiting all my life for me to realize it.

THE NEXT TWO MONTHS were wonderful! Suddenly, the Bible was alive and made an awful lot of sense to me. I felt as if St. Paul's letters were love letters, written directly to me! As for praying—instead of a chore, it became a delight, for now I was praying to Someone, who heard my prayers, and answered them, and loved me!

One afternoon, some weeks later, I stopped in at Finch's Drug Store, where I had gotten so many prescriptions filled for my stomach. My grandmother had gone there, Aunt Glad had taken us there to purchase platinum nail polish, my mother went there, and we all felt a special rapport with the druggist, Mr. Macrudden. But now, as I brought my purchases to the counter, Mr. Macrudden didn't even say hello. He looked up—and then down again.

"Hi, Mr. Macrudden," I said, undaunted. "How are you?"

No answer. He filled out a charge slip, put my purchases in a bag, and turned his back, without speaking a word.

"Mr. Macrudden, is anything the matter?"

At first, he refused to turn around, then he did turn and say, "The matter? Yes, there is something the matter," he snapped. "After all these years, you've seen fit to change druggists!"

"*What?*" I cried. "I would never go anywhere but Finch's!"

"But," he stammered, "you haven't refilled your stomach prescription for more than two months."

My mouth dropped open—he was right! From the day I found out that Jesus loved me, I had not been sick once! No more heartburn, no more vomiting. I had been healed by a God Who I did not even know was still in the healing business today, just as He had always been.

What was more, He loved me, and He had a plan for what remained of my life. I couldn't wait to see what it was!

# 17

---

LATE IN MARCH 1966, the Faith at Work team came to our church. I was afraid that they were going to be kooky, but they seemed normal enough, albeit awfully enthusiastic about Jesus. The conference leader was a Congregational minister named Dave Emmons, who with his wife Mary ran a Congregational retreat center in Bristol, Connecticut. He was middle-aged and reassuringly calm, and I liked him.

It was suggested that we break into small groups, and I joined some of the women of our church in one. The leader, from Faith at Work, told us what Jesus had meant in her life, and in what areas she still felt very needy. She was absolutely candid, and her willingness to be transparent encouraged others of us to share our faith and feelings. Tentatively, hesitantly, several of us told what had been happening in our lives, and some of our problems, and how God seemed to be helping. Gradually, we realized that it was safe to do so—no one in the group was judging us for our weaknesses and foibles. An hour passed unnoticed, and then another, as we shared our joys and our sorrows, our successes and our failures, weeping with one another, and rejoicing with one another. When it was over, we who had been almost strangers at the outset, had become fast friends.

It was an extraordinary experience, unlike anything I had ever known. It turned out that we all felt that way, and wished that it could continue. Moreover, I sensed that God was pleased, and so I suggested

175

that we keep on meeting, offering our home as the locale, on a regular weekly basis. Not all of us were always able to come, and any of us who wanted to could bring a friend, so the makeup of the group was constantly changing. But the core group went on for years, and many lives were changed—all because at the outset one woman was willing to be totally open and honest.

Stanwich Congregational Church would never be the same after that. The church had come alive to the things of God, and for many of us, those things mattered more than anything else in our lives. Later, I would come to see that what had happened in our church was happening at the same time to churches of all denominations all over the country. It was the beginning of the Charismatic Renewal, though that phrase would have totally mystified me had anyone mentioned it back in 1966.

Nate's sermons also became vibrantly alive to me. I suspect that they always had been; it was just that I could *hear* them now. He would say things while preaching that I could take home and put into effect in my daily life. Before I knew it, going to church, which had once been something I did only for weddings and funerals, had become the most important activity of the week.

It was about this time that Nate told some of us about two unique women whom he had met the previous fall at a religious conference in Northfield, Massachusetts—Cay Andersen and Judy Sorensen. They ministered together as a team, and they had the gift of healing. I had no idea what "the gift of healing" was, but I certainly believed in divine healing—hadn't Jesus healed me? The more Nate told us about them, the more anxious I was to meet them, so when I heard that they would be at another Faith at Work conference, over in Swampscott, Massachusetts, on Memorial Day weekend, I wanted to go.

Buzz didn't. "Why should we drive four hours to another Faith at Work conference? They were just in our church for a mission, and it was only January that we went to the New York conference. Why on earth do you want to go to another one?"

"I don't know why; I just do. Can't we?"

He shook his head. "It would mean leaving the children for another weekend. And who would we get to baby-sit on a holiday weekend?"

"I don't know," I replied. "I just want to go so badly. Please, Buzz?"

He looked at me intently, and then, perhaps remembering that I had gone along with him when he had wanted to stay at the New York conference, he relented. "If it means that much to you, okay; let's tell Nate and start making plans."

We told Nate, who said that he couldn't go, but his wife Fran was eager to, so we made our plans with her. Buzz would fly from New York to Boston, where Fran and I would meet him, in time to drive to Swampscott for dinner.

When the three of us pulled into the driveway of an old wooden resort hotel, I felt we were going back to another era, of boardwalks and parasols, straw hats and panama suits, and wicker furniture on broad verandas. Once again, we encountered warm and friendly, expectant Christians, and this time we were one with them. As before, there were general meetings and small groups, but the only speakers I was interested in hearing were Cay and Judy. They were scheduled for the next afternoon, and I could just imagine what they would look like— tall and willowy, dressed in long white robes that flowed in the breeze...

I was more than a little disappointed, therefore, when they finally did appear, and turned out to be perfectly normal—nice-looking, fresh, and wholesome, with nothing glamorous or farfetched about them. Cay was in her early fifties with clear blue eyes and blond hair. Judy was younger, about my age. She had warm brown eyes and curly brunette hair. Both were of medium build, and they wore attractive knit suits whose colors complemented one another—Cay's, a soft beige, Judy's a medium brown. As they introduced themselves, I learned that they were both married and had children; Cay's adopted son was attending Trinity College in Hartford, and Judy had three boys and a girl, all about the same age as our own children. In short, there was nothing bizarre or mystical about them; they were just ordinary people.

When they started talking, their subject was pretty ordinary, too— the Way of the Cross, which they illustrated with little diagrams on a blackboard beside them. Now I was more than disappointed; I was annoyed. How could they be talking about something so mundane? I already knew about the Way of the Cross; I had read an article about it by Catherine Marshall in *Guideposts*. I didn't come all this way just to hear about it again; I wanted to hear about miracles!

I glanced over at Buzz and Fran, and was surprised to see that they both appeared to be interested. They couldn't be! They must be as bored as I am, I thought; they're just better at hiding it! The conference room was hot; I mopped my brow with a handkerchief. The old, folding wooden chairs could not have been more uncomfortable; I squirmed and jiggled my foot. Why hadn't I brought my knitting! I opened my voluminous, over-the-shoulder purse and rummaged about in it, in hopes of finding a Life Saver. It would take more than a Life Saver to save this afternoon—would they never get done?

And then they did finish, and asked if there were any questions. If we were going to leave, it would have to be now, before the question period began. "Let's go," I whispered to Buzz. "Let's get out of here. This is awful!"

"*Awful?*" said Buzz, astonished. "Why, it's the most exciting teaching I've ever heard! You can go, if you want, but I'm staying— as long as I can."

I was crushed. I turned to Fran, but she, too, loved it and wanted to stay until the bitter end. Fine! Let them! As I pushed back my hard wooden chair to leave, a splinter in it caught my stocking and made a run. I didn't care; I didn't care about anything, except getting out of that awful room and away from those two niggling women, and getting on with my own life.

Once outside the hotel, I breathed a deep sigh, only it was not one of relief, but of despair. I was forlorn. Having no idea what to do with myself, I started walking down the deserted streets of the old resort town. Swampscott might have been the height of fashion at the turn of the century, but now it appeared seedy and rundown and smelled of dead fish and dank salt air. Which matched my mood perfectly, for never had I been so depressed. I felt separated from God, a stranger on earth, whom no one understood, not even Buzz.

Where was the Jesus who loved me? He was gone. Everything was gone. I was all alone. I wanted to go home, but I knew that Buzz and Fran wouldn't agree. I felt forsaken.

For several hours I wandered aimlessly, until the fog rolled in, and I returned, chilled and hopeless, to our hotel room. Buzz was there and welcomed me warmly. I didn't even answer; I just threw myself on the bed and turned my face to the wall.

"Bel, what's the matter?" he asked gently.

I wouldn't reply. "Well, come on now," he finally said. "Let's go down to supper."

"Leave me alone!" I snapped. "I don't want to go anywhere. I want to go home. This is a dumb, stupid conference, and I hate it!"

He continued to plead with me, but nothing would move me. Finally, with a sigh, he left. But not for long; five minutes later he returned, knocking on the door, and calling to me. "Bel? I've just bumped into Dave Emmons; maybe he can help you."

I remembered Dave as the kindly leader of the Faith at Work team that had come to our church. I respected him. "Wait a minute," I said, "I'll come out." I pulled myself off the bed, went into the bathroom and threw some water on my face, ran a comb through my hair and put on some lipstick. I remembered that my stocking had a run in it, but I didn't change it; that would be going too far.

"What's the trouble?" Dave said, smiling, when I emerged.

"Those women," I retorted, "they're the trouble."

"Well, why not come downstairs? We can have supper together and talk about it, okay?"

Reluctantly, I agreed, leaving the security of our sparse room and going down to supper. I talked all the way through the meal about my anguished feelings of "betrayal" and my great disappointment over Cay and Judy. Dave didn't agree, or disagree; he just listened. Finally, I ran out of steam and wound down. I felt limp, but I did not feel forlorn. Someone had listened to me; someone cared.

After supper, Buzz and Fran went off to hear Cay and Judy again, who were going to teach on intercessory prayer. Not me; I was going to something safe—a workshop on family relationships. There, at least, everything in my life was fine, or so I thought. But as hard as I tried to listen to the leaders, I couldn't seem to focus on what they were saying. I felt uneasy. It must be the stuffiness of the room, I thought; they really ought to open more windows. But the uneasiness increased, until I hardly bear it. What *was* the matter with me?

Suddenly, I felt compelled to go join Buzz and Fran at the meeting with Cay and Judy. *No,* I said to myself, shaking off the urge; that's the last thing I want to do! But the feeling came back, even stronger than before. Again, I shoved it away; I would *not* go back there and hear them! Once more, the feeling came, this time so strong I thought I was going to explode!

"Excuse me, pardon me," I murmured, as I made my way out of the row I was sitting in. Reaching the long, drab hallway of the old hotel, I turned and headed toward the room where they were teaching. The hallway seemed a mile long, and as I walked, and my mouth was dry as toast. What am I *doing*? This is *crazy*! But for once my heart was in charge, not my head, and I kept walking, until I reached the room where they were.

*Don't go in,* came the thought; *you'll interrupt the meeting, and everyone will turn and look at you.* But I shook my head and quietly opened the door.

I took one step inside—and felt overwhelmed by the presence of God. *Holiness* was the word that came to mind, and I thought: Jesus is here. Fortunately, there was still a seat next to Buzz and Fran. I slipped into it, barely noticed by my husband, who was intent on what was being said. Cay and Judy were concluding their teaching on intercessory prayer, by inviting people to share with them the needs of others who needed prayer. As each request was made, they would lift that person's name up for prayer. Their own prayers were so simple and sincere, I sensed that they were going straight to the heart of God, and that He was already responding to them. I had never heard anything like it.

After they had finished praying for all the requests, they asked if anyone would like to come up and receive prayer for themselves, with the "laying on of hands." I had never heard that term used, although it sounded vaguely Biblical, but whatever it was, I knew I wanted it. Looking over at Buzz and Fran, it was obvious that they were going up, too. We walked up to the front, with perhaps a dozen others, and sat in chairs that had been vacated. I was third in line, and as I waited my turn, my heart was pounding so hard, I thought it would burst.

"Oh, Jesus, help me," I whispered, closing my eyes.

And then I sensed their presence in front of me, and I looked up and saw their smiling faces. "What do you want?" Judy gently asked me.

"I would like to be able to heal people, like you can," I stammered.

Then they calmly laid their hands on my head, and told me to just thank Jesus, as they prayed. They started to pray, so quietly that not even the person sitting next to me could hear them. Something—I can only describe it as like electricity—surged through my body. Everything inside of me seemed to sink to the floor, and then soar up into space. I burst into tears and started sobbing, not for sorrow, but for joy. I was filled with an exhilaration totally unknown to me, and I felt like shouting and laughing and crying all at once. I felt I had given everything to Jesus, and He was mine, and I was His, completely and forever.

After they were finished praying for me, they each gave me a hug and moved on to Buzz, who was on my left. I heard them ask what he wanted them to pray for, and he said, "a closer relationship with Jesus."

They nodded, and laying their hands on his head, quietly began to pray.

And then they did the same for Fran. After the meeting, the three of us were animatedly comparing notes, for something extraordinary had happened to them, too—similar, but not exactly the same, as if God's Spirit worked uniquely within each individual. And that was what it was, we would find out later: we had been immersed in His Spirit, a veritable baptism, as it were. Each of us sensed that we had crossed a threshold, and that nothing would ever be quite the same.

I found out immediately one thing that was different: as we talked, I instinctively took out my trusty pack of cigarettes, but as I started to light one, the thought came: *you have the power to stop smoking.* Instantly, I knew in my heart, it was true. And just as quickly, I knew I didn't want to stop. I knew they were bad for me; in fact, from my experience at Sloan-Kettering, I knew a lot better than most people did back then, just how bad they really were. But I *liked* cigarettes. I liked their taste, and the way they calmed me down and gave me a sense of security. Jesus had taken all of me—body, soul, and spirit—that much I was aware of. But nobody had asked me, if I had wanted to give Him all, and I was not sure that I did. In the meantime, I knew that I *did* want to have a cigarette, and so, defiantly, I lit the cigarette and inhaled deeply.

Just then, Dave Emmons walked by. "Dave," I called out, "it's all right now. I think that Cay and Judy are the two most terrific people I've ever met. They really know God."

"Yes, Bel," he said, giving me a big smile, "I know."

For the next six months I was floating on Cloud 9. Everything was new and wonderful: the grass was greener, the sky bluer, and the Bible was—thrilling. I read it avidly, concentrating on the Acts of the Apostles, a book I never knew existed. I was filled with joy to overflowing, and it stayed with me day after day.

That summer we began talking about taking a few days and driving up to Cape Cod, where Cay and Judy's families lived. I longed to see them again, and visit their retreat house, and I had written and found out that they held open meetings twice a week. Buzz thought he might be able to combine a visit to the Cape with a business trip to Martha's Vineyard and Nantucket. We were talking about it in general terms, without making specific plans, when Buzz's mother got sick again. She had been suffering from extremely severe varicose veins in her legs, and was frequently in the hospital.

We went to see her there, and were shocked at how pale and fragile she looked, lying there in the sterile white bed. "Mother," said Buzz timorously, "I've been reading in the Prayer Book, and there is a healing service in there called The Visitation of the Sick. Would you like some minister to come and hold that service for you? I could call Touie, and arrange something. It really might help you. Would you think about it?"

His mother started to shake her head, but then she looked at him and could see how much he wanted her to say yes, and she said, "I'll think about it; I really will."

The next evening she called us: "I don't want a minister to do it, but why can't you two pray for me?"

Buzz and I were startled; how could we? We didn't know how! Buzz cleared his throat. "Mother, I don't know if we can, but give us a few days, and we'll try."

When he hung up, he said, "You wanted to go to the Cape? Well, we're going, as quick as we can. We've got to see Cay and Judy; they'll tell us what to do."

Several days later, we called and made a reservation, packed up the car and our eight-year-old, Vicky, and drove to the Cape. Their guest house, Rock Harbor Manor, turned out to be a long, low, Dutch Colonial building, overlooking Cape Cod Bay, at Orleans. Not shown on most maps, Rock Harbor was a tiny fishing harbor at the mouth of a marsh creek, where charter fishing boats bobbed along the edge of the wharf. The manor was back up from the harbor, on a rise, and all around it were summer flowers, petunias and impatiens. There was a soft golden glow about it just now, as it was caught by the final hour of sunlight. The grounds looked immaculate and seemed exceptionally well cared for. As we pulled up at the front door, I noticed a rose garden over to the left, and for some reason it reminded me of Grandma—I smiled; this place had her kind of feel.

Getting out of the car, I started to tremble; were we doing the right thing? A young woman opened the door and warmly welcomed us. "Cay and Judy are so glad that you've come," she said. "They're busy at the moment, but they said to tell you that they will see you after the meeting tonight."

She showed us to our room, which had white and red rose-patterned wallpaper, with matching curtains. There were fresh roses in a crystal vase on the bureau, and a basket of fresh fruit on the night stand. I looked around and felt incredibly at home, in this little red room.

Tucking a sleepy Vicky into the cot they had provided for her, we showered and changed, and went down to the meeting. It was to be in the living room—a lovely gold and white room, with a picture window of the harbor and the bay, and enough regular and folding chairs to seat about fifty people. Self-conscious, we picked two at the back of the room.

Soon the room started to fill with people; it was impossible to categorize them. Some were old, but there were also teenagers. Some were simply dressed; others wore expensive clothes. One thing they had in common: there was a geniality about them, and a sense of expectancy.

Then Cay and Judy came in and warmly greeted us all, mentioning a number of the old-timers by name. We sang some hymns; then Judy opened the meeting with a prayer. She and Cay read to us from Galatians, and from Ephesians, and then they spoke about the gifts of the Holy Spirit and the fruit of the Spirit. I was entranced. What they said seemed to go straight from their mouths to my heart. Outside the picture window, the sun was setting now, firing the heavens with bank upon bank of crimson clouds. It was a gorgeous sunset, the sort which had made Rock Harbor famous, and for which tourists came from many miles to see. I was oblivious to it, so intent was I on what Cay and Judy were saying.

Halfway through the meeting, Vicky came creeping into the room in her seersucker nightgown, tears streaming down her little sunburned face.

"What's wrong?" Cay said smiling, as she stopped the meeting to talk to Vicky. "I'm afraid," sobbed Vicky. "I hear noises outside."

Judy laughed gently and said, "Oh, that must be the branch of that old elm tree near the window. That's all." Talking to her, as if that was all they had to do, they soon had her smiling, instead of crying, and she went over and climbed up on the lap of a motherly-looking woman, who turned out to be Catherine Marshall, the author of *A Man Called Peter*, and *Christy*, and several other books I had recently read.

After the meeting, Cay and Judy visited with their guests, until the last of them said goodbye, and then they invited us out on the adjacent sun porch. They listened intently, as we told them about Buzz's mother, and then encouraged us with some of their own experiences. "Imagine that you are a big empty funnel through which God is going to channel His power," said Cay.

"We'll pray for you," Judy added. "And we'll have our fellowship pray for you. Would you like us to pray for you now, with the laying on of hands, for this commission?"

Buzz nodded, but I declined; hadn't I already had that once? I would come to regret that decision very much, when I later realized that one could always receive more of God's anointing power.

The next day we drove home, jubilant, and went to see Buzz's mother as soon as possible. Guided by the service in the Book of Common Prayer, we prayed for her healing, gently resting our hands on her legs and on her head. Would God heal her phlebitis? I didn't know. But I knew He could, and I was willing to ask Him, believing that He would. Nothing dramatic happened then, but she seemed moved, and thanked us deeply, gladly accepting the New Testament that we left with her.

Sometime later, after she had been home from the hospital for a few days, she called us up early Saturday morning. We were surprised, for it was not even nine o'clock, and she never called that early. We were even more surprised, when she asked if she might come over—right away. Less than half an hour later, her car pulled up, and she hurried into the house, her green eyes shining. She sat down on our sofa, and raised the hem of her dress to just above her knees. My eyes widened: her legs, once mottled with bulging purple veins, were absolutely clear!

"Aunt Alice," I gasped. "What happened to your—?"

"Jesus healed me!"

Buzz and I just stared at one another, struck not only by the physical miracle but by the fact that she had never used the Lord's name before. "As soon as I get back to New York," his mother added, "I'm going to call my doctor—he'll never believe this!"

I tried to imagine Dr. Foley's reaction: would it be mystification? Consternation? Would he ascribe the sudden remission to the program of drugs and therapy he had prescribed? Or would he be forced to admit that there was no natural explanation, leaving open the possibility of a supernatural one?

Aunt Alice would live another half a year, before dying peacefully in her sleep—the happiest six months of her life. For as remarkable as the healing of phlebitis was, even more remarkable was the healing that had taken place in her heart. Where once she had been an extremely difficult person, now she had an abundance of love for all her family.

Her death took us by surprise, and we grieved for her. But it was not the numbing blow that all the other deaths of relatives and friends had been. For we were comforted by the knowledge that she had met Jesus the summer before, and was close to Him now. How grateful we were to Cay and Judy, for without their encouragement and example, we never would have prayed for her.

Two other milestones were passed that fall of 1966. No one had told me to give up smoking, not even God. But I grew more and more convinced that I ought to, and that He would be pleased, if I did. I fought it terribly—the more guilty I felt, the more I smoked, and the more I smoked, the more guilty I felt. It got so I wasn't enjoying it at all, because I knew the psychological hangover that it invariably triggered. But that just made me angry, and I would defiantly light up. I mean, whose lungs were they anyhow? And then I would cough and hate the blasted cigarette and stub it out, long before I was finished.

This went on, until I could stand it no longer. As I was obviously unwilling to give up smoking, I could not very well ask the Lord to make me willing; we were not puppets. He did not force His will on us, nor did He force our wills to align with His will for us. We had to *want* His will, and want it more than we wanted our own. As I thought and prayed about that, I saw that that was what Jesus had done for us at Gethsemane, when He begged His Father to let the cup which awaited Him at Calvary pass. But then He had added, "Nevertheless, not my will, but thine be done." And wasn't that what I prayed every morning, in the Lord's Prayer? "Thy will be done . . ."

So I asked Jesus to make me willing to *be* willing—to give up cigarettes. There was no magic wand, no instant deliverance; for weeks I prayed that prayer every morning in my quiet time. And then one morning, I realized that He had done it: I was willing. On Thanksgiving Day, I abstained. Buoyed by the encouragement of my family, I struggled all day and went to bed exhausted at 7 P.M.

The next morning, after Buzz had left for work, I crept down to the kitchen, fixed a cup of steaming coffee, turned to the crossword puzzle—and pulled out a cigarette. I had just lit a match and was anticipating that first delicious lungful, when I heard a voice, this one definitely audible.

"Mummy, Mummy! What are you doing?" It was Lucy in the doorway. "Haven't you given up smoking?"

Furious, I blew out the match and ran up to my bedroom, throwing myself on the bed and crying out, "Oh, Jesus, I can't do it! I can't give it up! You'll have to do it for me!"

And He did; I never smoked another cigarette. It was not easy;

there were many temptations, even months after I had quit. But each time I felt the urge, I simply murmured, "Jesus help me," and that was enough.

Where I had been flying high before in my newborn enthusiasm, now I was positively in orbit! Jesus could do *anything!* It was a honeymoon period for me with the Lord, and there was no reaching me. "When are you going to come down off that cloud?" asked Nate, chuckling, one Sunday after church. And then more seriously: "You know, you can't stay up there forever; you're not living in reality."

"I'm never coming down," I replied emphatically, little realizing the test that would soon come my way.

Toward the end of January, we learned that Cay and Judy were coming to Simsbury, for a whole day of teaching, on February 28. At first, I was ecstatic—and then I remembered that that was the date on which my parents were going to take us and Tinker to the theatre, as a special treat on her birthday. They had had the tickets for three months.

When Buzz came home, I told him the predicament, hoping that he would decide for us. But he wouldn't. "They're your parents," he said. "You'll have to decide."

"Thanks a lot, Buzz!" I grumped at him. "I'm going to call Nate." I did, and as soon as I explained the situation, Nate said the same thing.

For a week I agonized, crying out to the Lord, for Him to help me. But He, too, seemed to be saying that it was my decision.

My parents, or Cay and Judy's teaching—which? What made it even harder was the knowledge that they wouldn't understand and would be hurt. I loved my parents, and the last thing I wanted to do was hurt them. But deep down inside of me, I also knew how I wanted—and needed—to hear more about the Lord. And I also sensed that despite the spiritual high I had been on, all was not right within me, and I needed help.

Back and forth I went on it, until one day, in desperation, I decided to open the Bible blindly and just put my finger on a page, and claim that whatever was under my finger was God speaking to me. I closed my eyes, opened the Bible, and lowered my finger onto a spot. Fearfully, I opened my eyes and read:

> Do not think that I have come to bring peace on earth; I have come
> not to bring peace, but a sword. For I have come to set a man against
> his father, and a daughter against her mother, and a daughter-in-law

against her mother-in-law; and a man's foes will be those of his own household. He who loves father or mother more than me is not worthy of me; and he who loves son or daughter more than me is not worthy of me; and he who does not take his cross and follow me is not worthy of me. He who finds his life will lose it, and he who loses his life for my sake will find it. (MATTHEW 10:34-39)

The word could not have been clearer. It was a hard truth, but it was as surely from the Lord as any guidance I had ever received.

I called up my mother and told her we couldn't come. My path was set. I had made the first of many hard decisions to follow Jesus, and the two servants of His that He had put in my life, to feed and nurture me.

# 18

---

"I HATE YOU!" I screamed, as I ran downstairs and tore out the front door, slamming it behind me so hard the house shook. I got in the car and roared out of the driveway, headed for—I didn't know where.

Buzz and I had just had another one of our horrendous fights, accusing each other of the most dreadful things. Something terrible was happening to our marriage. I was off Cloud 9, all right; I had hit rock bottom. We who had been such good friends had become enemies, and the sewer lid under which for years I had stuffed down all the anxiety, jealousy, envy, and even hate, had now blown off. And it was all spewing out at Buzz!

Temper tantrums had lately become a way of life for me, as I continually demanded to have my own way. Our arguments would start in the morning, and I would keep them simmering on the back burner all day long, until they boiled over, as soon as Buzz came in the front door in the evening, exhausted from work. I had become secretive and vindictive, and after sixteen years of marriage, I knew quite well exactly how to hurt him the most. And because I was home with the children all day, I had ample opportunity to pull each of them, one by one, to my side, and turn them against their father.

I, who had always been tense and nervous, became even more so. It seemed as if the so-called "Baptism in the Holy Spirit," which had released so much that was good inside of me, had also unleashed all the darkness as well. For now, whenever I had my will crossed, or did not get my own way, I would behave like a maniac. Often, as our children huddled fearfully together in one of their rooms, Buzz would have to call Nate, even at night, to come over and calm me down, and bring some sense of peace into our house. Afterward, Nate would shake his head, not knowing how to permanently help us. With Buzz a deacon and me a deaconess, he had considered us an "ideal" family, and he was perplexed as the intensity of our flare-ups escalated.

We continued seeing Cay and Judy during this dreadful time, but I would not humble myself to ask for help. There was nothing really the matter with me that a little peace and a little consideration on Buzz's part wouldn't cure. One time Cay and Judy stayed for a weekend in our home, while they held a mission at the Stanwich Church. I took advantage of this opportunity to ask for help—not for myself but for Bing, who was being picked on by six boys at his school. They spoke with him for fifteen or twenty minutes and suggested that he pray for those six boys every morning and every night. His whole attitude toward them and his outlook on school changed, and within two weeks the six boys were his best friends.

Faced with such dramatic results of their counsel, it seems incredible that I did not avail myself of their wisdom. But that was the extent of my pride and self-righteousness—asking for help was not only a sign of weakness; it was tantamount to admitting that one might be wrong. I did like to hear them teach, however, and once a month Buzz and I would drive more than two hours to the Presbyterian church in Simsbury, where they had been invited to hold monthly teaching missions. I would listen to them raptly, determined to live my life differently—and then come home again and have another no-holds-barred fight with Buzz, whose anger, when he lost his temper, was a match for my own.

I was well aware of the hypocrisy in my life, and it only depressed me further but also made me feel more guilty. While I read the Bible and spoke of Jesus constantly, my heart was hardened to forgiveness, filled with vindictiveness and deceit. For I would do or say *anything* to be right and to get my own way. Indeed, I was so totally self-deceived that I firmly believed that what I wanted to be true, *was* true. And if Buzz or anyone else had doubts, I would rise up in furious indignation that they dared challenge my veracity.

In August 1967 we were looking forward to joining my parents on one of their summer vacations at a Western ranch, bringing along our four children. We enjoyed my parents' company and liked vacationing with them, whether at Overhills or out West, especially since they were not the sort of vacations we could afford on our own. My parents' generosity was spontaneous and often breathtaking—but it had to be their initiative; I would never dream of going to them and asking them to give us such a trip on our own. In keeping with the Rockefeller tradition, even now, eighteen years after I had married Buzz, the sum total of money that I could call my own was an allowance, given to me by my mother, of $200 a month. On this trip, Buzz and I were particularly glad that they would be there, for we knew that their presence would keep us on our best behavior and not let us get into one of those awful showdowns.

But as the time for departure approached, my father's health began to fail. He was sixty-eight, and suffering from hardening of the arteries, especially those in his neck and around his heart. Today, bypass surgery would have solved much of the problem, but that procedure was unknown twenty years ago. With the blood flow to his brain constricted, my father would black out for several minutes at a time, and not remember who he was, or where he was going. In June, he had a heart incident and spent a week in the hospital, after which his doctor advised him to give up any notion of going out West, and of course, my mother stayed home with him.

So Buzz and I and the children went out to the ranch in Montana alone. And sure enough, a few days after we got there, when the novelty of riding and campfires and exploring had worn off, Buzz and I got into the worst fight we had ever had, screaming and screaming at each other, with me finally ripping a shoe off and throwing it at him.

Sometime later, when we finally decided to speak to one another again, we found that we were both badly shaken by the severity of the episode. "We've got to get some help," Buzz said, his voice trembling. "We're going to kill ourselves, if we go on this way. I'm going to write Cay and Judy, and ask if we can come and see them."

I nodded, too exhausted and depressed to do anything but agree. What was happening to us? Where was all the joy I had felt when I first knew Jesus? We were worse off—much worse off—than we had been before, and I had no explanation.

As soon as we could, after we got home, we drove up to the Cape to see them. We asked if they could see us individually, and they agreed, talking to Buzz first. When it was my turn, instead of asking for help, I discussed different problems that my Christian friends were having. There was no point in bringing up my problem; they had just finished talking to him.

In spite of my attitude, that visit did relieve the tension between us—which was a good thing, because now not only was my father ill, but my mother was facing a radical mastectomy. I thanked God that unlike her sister Faith she wanted to live, although she absolutely refused chemotherapy afterward, for she had heard that it made one sick to one's stomach. Then in February my father had an attack so severe that his doctor worked on him all day long, trying to save him. I discovered this when I came by their apartment in the afternoon to see him. Not knowing what else to do, I went into the deserted living room, and prayed as I never had before.

"Lord, I am of my father's flesh and blood. I don't know whether he knows You, but on his behalf, I accept You as Lord and Saviour. Please Jesus, forgive him his sins, and grant him eternal life." I asked His forgiveness for everything I had done, known or unknown, which had hurt my father. Then I asked Him to remind me of any places where I still held resentments against my father, and as each came to mind, I would confess it and ask Jesus' forgiveness. On and on I prayed, as the Holy Spirit gave me thought after thought.

About four in the afternoon, my mother came into the living room, pale and drawn. "He's going to pull through," she managed, "but the doctor says he'll be an invalid for the rest of his life." She looked at me pleadingly for some word of encouragement, but I had none.

Buzz came in after work and joined us for supper, then we took the train home to Greenwich. I dragged upstairs into our large bedroom, and happened to notice on my bureau the little box of cards with quotations from scripture on them, which our son had given me for Christmas. Closing my eyes like a child, I pulled out a card and read its message: "And the prayer of faith will save the sick man, and the Lord will raise him up; and if he has committed sins, he will be forgiven." (James 5:15)

Tremendously relieved and uplifted by this word, I slept peacefully that night, for the first time in a long time.

A LITTLE OVER SEVEN WEEKS LATER, my father died. The knowledge that he was with the Lord consoled me in my grief and strengthened me to be a support to my mother. She had loved my father deeply, as he had her, and now she was utterly desolate. I spent every dinner and night with my mother in New York City, driving out to Greenwich early in the morning to see the children off to school, take care of the house, and then hurry back to New York. Our many friends from the Stanwich church took over for me at home, when I wasn't there, fixing casseroles for supper, and looking after the children, until Buzz got home.

Each night my mother poured out her heart to me. Overwhelmed with guilt for all the times she had not put my father first in her life, she told me how she had always refused to leave New York, when he had had job offers in various other places. On and on her agony poured forth, and I listened. Occasionally, I would do my best to comfort her, but as I was bereft myself, I had little to offer that would help, resorting to platitudes from the Bible, which were true but had no real meaning in my own life. Mainly, by the grace of God, I had enough sense just to keep still and let her talk, which was the kindest thing I could have done.

It was only after my mother was over the worst that I began to fall apart. For one thing, I had practically stopped eating. At 5'7", my weight dropped to 115 pounds. I never particularly minded being thin, assuming a motive of jealousy when anyone took me to task about it. But one day I looked in the mirror and saw an emaciated, wrinkled old woman looking back at me. She looked to be at least sixty—and I was only forty!

That shook me. At the same time, I was demanding that Buzz fill the void in my life which my father had left. That would have been impossible to begin with, and was doubly so, considering the larger-than-life image I'd had of my father. And now I became angry at God, not only for allowing my father to die, but because He was making so many demands on me that I did not wish to comply with.

I wound up with stomach problems again, this time so acute that I had to be hospitalized. It was not heartburn now, but deeper down in my abdomen. They suspected it might be my gall bladder, but once again the tests revealed there was nothing physically wrong with me. So after a week, they sent me home with some tranquilizers and told me to avoid stress. As that meant avoiding Buzz, I went to stay at my mother's home. Buzz would come over for supper, and then return to our home and the children, who were also more than I could cope with.

One evening, over after-dinner coffee, my mother looked at me with great compassion and said, ''Bel, what would you think of the three of us going up to the Cape and seeing those two women you and Buzz think so highly of? Perhaps they could help you.''

I was startled. For her to make such a suggestion showed how deeply concerned she was; in her day, people did not talk about the things that were bothering them. One had to be strong and manage, and if things got to be too much, you poured yourself a stiff drink and went to bed with a sleeping pill. Years before, my mother had been given sleeping pills, and now she was totally dependent upon them, as were a number of her friends. Money, of course, was an effective buffer; with it, you could control almost any situation, for you could generally get people to do what you wanted, if enough money was involved. And of course, if pressures simply built up too much at home, you could always take a trip, wherever and whenever you wanted. My mother had traveled all over the world, returning most often to Africa, her favorite part of the world.

But she also had an uncanny way of sensing when someone else was hurting and of discerning the exact remedy. Over and over I saw her do this instinctively and spontaneously for others, many times without their even knowing that she was their benefactor. Truly she was a philanthropist. And now it was her daughter who was hurting, who was poisoning herself with dripping despair, and while she herself could do nothing to help, she knew intuitively the perfect antidote...

''We'll drive up in my air-conditioned Oldsmobile,'' my mother was saying, ''and stay a few days and talk with them.'' I had to smile, as she hastily added, ''You two can stay at Rock Harbor Manor; I'll stay at a motel.'' If she were to stay at that Christian place, she might have to miss her pre-dinner drink.

I agreed, for one of my deepest prayers had been that she would come into a personal relationship with the Lord, and Cay and Judy were just the ones to gently lead her there. Focusing on her needs, I was blind to how great my own needs were, nor had I any inkling of the hell I was putting others through.

Buzz called Cay and Judy, who said that they would be delighted to see us, and that there was a vacant room at Rock Harbor Manor. Quickly, we made our plans, and a friend came to take care of the children. The next day we piled into my mother's Olds and headed for the Cape. It was oppressively humid outside, and we were all grateful for the air conditioning; without it, the five-hour drive would have been unbearable. As it was, I remained in a daze most of the way and could hardly believe what was happening.

"Would you like a glass of iced tea?" asked the young woman who greeted us.

We all nodded, parched and dry after the long trip. As we sat comfortably in the gold and white living room, enjoying our tea, my mother looked around. "You know, I like this place," she said with customary candor. "There's something so peaceful about it—maybe it's the wallpaper." Buzz and I smiled and said nothing.

After our tea, my mother went off to her motel before joining us for supper, and Buzz and I went upstairs to our room. Sinking down onto the bed and breathing a deep sigh of relief, I felt more relaxed than I had in months. Slowly, two tears trickled down my face, as I breathed, "Oh Jesus, help me, please help me."

The next morning, Cay and Judy saw Buzz first, and then my mother. They did not see me at all. And the same thing happened the next day. The third day dawned bright and cheery. The heat wave had broken, and a cool, fresh sea breeze was blowing. About eleven o'clock, one of the young women came out on the manor's front terrace and said, "Bel, Cay and Judy would like to see you now."

With heart pounding, I followed her to a little room attached to the garage, where they did their counseling. As soon as I saw their smiling faces, I burst into tears. I felt as if my heart would break.

"That's all right, Bel," Cay said. "Don't try to bottle it all up."

So I kept on crying. At last, my sobs subsided, and I blurted out, "Oh, Cay and Judy, I need help! Please help me!"

They both looked at me lovingly, and Judy said, "We've been waiting a long time to hear that, Bel. We'd love to help you. But we couldn't before, because you hadn't asked. Now is the time. We have much we think God has given us to say to you, but the most important thing is for you to remember that Jesus loves you very much."

I started to talk, and they would occasionally ask a question. Then Cay said, "I read something recently about wealthy families and the collective resentment that comes against them, and it makes a lot of sense. I've no idea whether your ancestors' business dealings were ethical, but there must be a great deal of residual bitterness against them and the whole Rockefeller family. You know the Bible says that the sins of the fathers are visited on the children down to the third and fourth generation, and all of it has piled on your generation's shoulders."

My heart quickened; Cay was getting at something that had troubled me all my life. As a youngster, I never realized that we were different from other families; my friends in Greenwich and at boarding school all had big homes like ours. But as I grew older, I could read for myself the occasional vicious attacks leveled against my forebears, calling them robber barons, and worse. I began to have ambivalent feelings about being a Rockefeller. In a new situation, I was grateful just to be a Lincoln and would never bring the other connection up, wanting to prove that I could make it on my own and be appreciated for what *I* could do. But invariably it wouldn't be enough, and so at the same time I would surreptitiously drop hints that my mother was a Rockefeller, hoping that by some kind of osmosis, I could get all the benefits of the family name, with none of the detriments.

Judy picked up where Cay left off. "No wonder you feel so guilty all the time!" she said. "We've come to know you, and to know how you are always trying to prove yourself worthy and right. It's an impossible task, because no man is worthy or right within himself. All of us have fallen short of the glory of God. We think you—and your sisters and cousins, too—need a great deal of prayer, for only Jesus can release us from these bondages that are put upon us."

I looked at them both with amazement. Never had I heard of such a thing. "We'd like to pray for you," Judy continued, "and cut you off from your past generations, so that you can be free to become the person whom Jesus wants you to be, without carrying the load of fear, guilt, and anxiety that you have been burdened with. You need to be set free from the curse that has been put on your family for all these years, so that you can live your life unto Christ."

I smiled and said, "I'm not sure I fully understand all that, but I do want you to pray for me that way. Would you?"

"Of course we will," they both chimed in.

So they came over and laid their hands on my head. As they prayed, I felt as if an enormous burden had been lifted from my shoulders. It felt the way it used to on a camping trip, when I would reach the end of a portage and could at last take off the heavy back pack I had been laboring under; you felt you were almost floating. That was the way I felt after their prayer.

"Whew!" I exclaimed. "I'm glad I don't have to carry that anymore!"

They laughed and gave me a big hug. We chatted awhile, and then

Judy said, "Bel, what would you think of coming back and staying for a couple of weeks? You really need more help, and we could see you almost every day. We took the liberty of mentioning the possibility to Buzz and your mother, and they thought it would be good for you. But what do you think?"

I burst into tears once more. I had never felt such love, and it was not Cay and Judy's love I was responding to, or Buzz's and my mother's; it was the love of Jesus, and I knew it.

"Of course I'll come," I said gratefully. Everything was going to be all right now. Jesus had heard my prayer.

TWO WEEKS LATER, I arrived back at Rock Harbor Manor, where I was given a small comfortable bedroom with oak furniture and a curious picture on the wall. It was a photograph taken by a Japanese photographer, who, while driving along a snowy highway through the mountains, had been pleading with Jesus to reveal Himself. All at once, he had a strong impulse to take a picture of the melting snow on the mountainside. After developing it, he was gazing at the abstract pattern made by the snow and exposed wet ground, when suddenly he saw a perfect portrait of Jesus—at least, that was what the caption said. But all I could make out was an abstract of light and shadows.

As they had promised, Cay and Judy were able to talk to me almost every day. Sometimes it was fun, and we would laugh a lot and everything seemed light and easy. Other times were more difficult, as they began helping me to face myself. "You are extremely jealous," they said. "It started when you and Cal were little, and intensified until you couldn't stand it and cut off her curls. Now you're taking out that jealousy you had toward Cal, on Buzz." It was complicated, but I could see it, and they had me confess it and ask God's forgiveness.

Next came my self-righteousness. "You think so highly of yourself that you believe you are always right. To admit being wrong is annihilation to you. So where is Jesus in your life? Where is the Saviour who came for wrong ones? How can you claim to be a Christian, when you won't be wrong?" It was true. With my lips I would agree that I was a sinner like everyone else, but in my heart I didn't really believe it—I had a few character flaws, perhaps, but basically, deep down, I thought I was in pretty good shape. Yet all the evidence of my life—thought, word, and deed—seemed to indicate just the opposite. I began to see how much I needed Him—not just once, for salvation, but daily.

After self-righteousness came self-pity. "You're full of self-pity, because you won't admit it when you're angry. Instead of being open and honest, you hide your feelings and sink into the 'slough of despond.' The next time something makes you angry, say so. After all, self-pity is really just anger with no place to go."

On and on they went, each time leading me to the place where I could see my sin, confess it, and ask Jesus to forgive me. And each time, though it was initially a struggle to see the sin, once I had gotten it confessed and forgiven, I felt so much better and freer, it was incredible!

And it *lasted*—this was no temporary exhilaration. As the days passed, I felt progressively lighter. And one afternoon, when I came back to my little room after a long walk on the sand flats, I happened to glance at the photo of the Japanese mountainside—and had no trouble seeing the face of Jesus. Indeed, it was so clear, I couldn't imagine how I had not been able to see it before.

I was alone much of the time during this period, walking or reading on the front terrace of the manor. Sometimes I would stroll down to the harbor and watch the sport fishing boats go out with the tide, each filled with happy, enthusiastic vacationers. Above them, seagulls would glide and bank, following them out to the bay. I seemed to notice all sorts of birds now, and I could begin to differentiate between their calls. At low tide, you could walk out on the flats for more than a mile, and I loved to feel the wind in my hair and the wet sand beneath my feet. I was growing tanner, more so than I had ever been in my life, and I had regained my appetite; my face filled out, and I lost that haggard, strained look. The woman who looked back at me, when I was brushing my teeth, began to look healthy and relaxed and really not much older than I was.

There were others besides myself, staying at Rock Harbor Manor—Corrie Ten Boom, the evangelist, and John and Tibby Sherrill, the husband-and-wife writing/editing team. They were working on Corrie's autobiography, *The Hiding Place*, and occasionally I would happen to come into the dining room for a meal, when one or another of them was there, and we would chat. But mostly I was alone, to read and think and pray—and to hear the still, small voice of God's Spirit, as He helped me to find and come to know myself.

And then came the last day. Buzz and the children would be coming up tomorrow, and we were going to spend a few days in a little cottage in South Orleans. In the afternoon, Cay and Judy asked me to come into the living room. To my surprise, I found Corrie and John and Tibby there, also.

"Bel," said Cay solemnly, "I have asked these people to be here, too, as I think that we have all independently discovered something about you that can change your life, if you're willing to see it. Do you want to?"

I looked at her fearfully, wondering what it could be. Well, everything that God had shown me through them so far, had been a tremendous help—"Yes," I heard myself saying, "I do want to see it."

Slowly, methodically, Cay and Judy started to tell me that I was a liar and full of deceit. I could feel my face getting red, and all I wanted to do was get out of that room and away from the pain of that humiliation. But as much as I wanted to escape, even more I wanted the healing that I knew would come as a result. So I stayed, and asked God for the grace to *hear* what was being said to me.

They asked Corrie and John and Tibby, if they could help me see it, from their own brief experience with me. One after another, they related incidents where I had said one thing to one, and something entirely different to another—about the same matter! "We think," Judy said in conclusion, "that you are self-deceived: you so want things to be a certain way, that you refuse to look at the truth. We think it is also a cover-up for your extreme self-righteousness; you would rather lie than be wrong. We think this is your basic problem with Buzz. If you can be honest with him, truthful and open, and not lie, we think your marriage will be healed."

I nodded, unable to speak. I had heard them—but just barely, and I don't think I could have stood hearing one more word. Never, *never* had anyone spoken to me that way before! They left me to myself then, and I went to my room, threw myself on the bed, and cried and cried. I was alone, deserted, and hopeless. The thought came to me that this was the self-pity that they had been talking about, but that just made me angrier, and I cried all the harder. And then, even as the wailing and whimpering continued, I began to remember things from my past, with almost startling clarity. I could remember *exactly* how I had felt when I cut Cal's curls off—the jealousy and also the deception, as I convinced myself, as well as her, that I was protecting her from bees that were trying to make a nest in her hair. Cay and Judy had been right about my lying and self-deception—and it was monstrous.

As the Holy Spirit brought to mind one vivid memory after another, I got off the bed and down on my knees beside it, begging the Lord's forgiveness, for each sin that He showed me. In the morning, Cay and Judy greeted me warmly, as if nothing had happened, and they had a final word for me, before my family arrived.

"You've asked God to forgive you, and He has. But now you need to forgive yourself. Forgive yourself for being a sinner. Remember, Jesus came for you and us and all the other sinners. He died on the Cross for you. He took your sins upon Him, went down to the grave, and rose again, to sit in heavenly places with His Father. Jesus became the atonement for your sins. And never forget this: He would have died *just* for you; He loves you that much. And He wants you to be free, not only from your sins, but also from your guilt. He wants you to become that new person in Christ that He created, from the very beginning of the world. Now, go in peace."

I was aware then of Jesus' presence, standing right beside me. Again I was speechless, marveling at His being there, and also at these two women, who cared enough to tell me the truth, that I might be set free. To save a marriage, they had been willing to take quite a risk—but it had paid off.

When Buzz and the children came and picked me up, I said to him, "I need to talk to you alone, as soon as we get settled in the cabin." As Tinker was fifteen now, we left her in charge and drove to the nearby shore of the bay. "Buzz," I said, turning to him, "I am a liar and full of deceit."

"But Bel—"

"Please, let me finish," I interrupted him (control was another of my sins). "I want to tell you *all* I've seen about myself." And I proceeded to tell him in detail everything that had happened, holding nothing back, telling it just the way it was. It was difficult at first, but I was surprised to find that as I got into it, it got easier and easier.

Finally, as I wound down, Buzz looked at me with the most tender and loving eyes. Enfolding me in a gentle embrace, he said, "Do you think, after all these years of being married, I don't have a pretty good idea of who you are? But it doesn't stop me from loving you. I love you not because of who you are, but because you're you." He leaned back and smiled at me. "Let's start over."

I nodded, tears of joy flooding my eyes. We sat in silence and watched two gulls climbing thermals far out over the bay. I sensed then that the worst was over, and the best was about to begin.

# *Epilogue*

BUZZ AND I continued to see Cay and Judy for help, coming to the Cape every six weeks or so for the rest of the year. In addition, one or the other of us would come occasionally on their small men's or women's invitational teaching retreats. Meanwhile, other couples were experiencing similar renewal in their marriages and their new walk with Christ, through Cay and Judy's teaching and counseling. In 1969, we joined a prayer group of four such couples, all from Connecticut, and all more or less around our ages. The men were variously employed as a school principal, a nuclear engineer, a manufacturing manager, and a hospital administrator, but one thing we shared: a commitment to live for Christ as much as we could, and to live in openness and honesty with one another.

We grew close in a hurry, and shared many rich times together. The incident that gave our group its name was related by one of the women who had a problem with forgetfulness. One evening, she had gotten so involved on the phone that she had let supper burn up in the oven. In desperation, her husband had bought her a bright green timer, to put on top of the stove. Only in cooking the next supper, she had mistakenly put it *in* the stove, and burnt it up, too. As she told the group the story, we had laughed so hard our sides hurt, and thereafter we were the "Green Timers," which seemed appropriate, for we were realizing that each of us was capable of such acts, and that Jesus loved us anyway.

The Green Timers' first weekend retreat at Rock Harbor as a group came in early December 1969. The first morning dawned bright and clear and cold; sitting at the dining room table in the manor, we could see the Provincetown Tower, 20 miles due north across the bay. Cay and Judy sat together at the head of the table, and the rest of us spread ourselves around, while breakfast—scrambled eggs and bacon and sticky buns—was served by the young women who helped to run Rock Harbor Manor.

Just as we were finishing the last delicious morsels and having a second cup of coffee, Judy put her fork down emphatically.

"There is something special about this group," she said, shaking her head and smiling. "I don't know what it is, but I feel there is such a—*oneness*."

"I agree," nodded Cay. "I think there is a special call on this group."

We looked at each other; what could it be? I was excited, but a little apprehensive. A *group* call? Did they mean that God had a collective call on us as a group, in addition to His individual calls on each of our lives?

It was a question that would have to wait, for we were getting up now, and Cay and Judy were going to take us on a tour of the little community that had grown up around their ministry. Three separate families had bought houses close by the manor, and each had a different story of how it had occurred. But all had come to be closer to Cay and Judy and their work.

Cay and Judy and their own families lived next door to the manor. Cay's husband Bill ran a small construction company, and Judy's husband, also Bill, was a business executive, who commuted to a company located outside of Boston. The two women had met on the Cape in 1958, had become prayer partners, and soon felt called into a joint ministry of counseling, teaching, and leading retreats. Their two families had temporarily moved under one roof in 1962, while Bill Andersen's construction company was renovating the Sorensen summer home. In that pressure-cooker situation, there was bound to be friction, and they had learned much in a very short time about resolving conflicts in Christ—so much, in fact, that they felt led of God to continue the joint living arrangement.

Cay and Judy told us that it was through the trials and tribulations of the two families living together that their ministry received its foundation. For as they struggled together, Christ became more and more real to each of them. They stressed that the primary purpose for their being called together in this way was to bring them more deeply into His life, rather than for ministry or any other purpose.

Halfway through the morning, I grew impatient. After all, I had come for teaching, not a house tour. I wished they would hurry up and get on with it, especially after that dramatic word at breakfast about how our group seemed special. What did seeing other people's kitchens have to do with that?

That afternoon, there was much good teaching, and a lot of sharing, and by the time we had finished Sunday lunch the next day, and it was time to leave, I felt closer to this group of people than to any other group that I had been a part of, and the others felt the same way. We agreed to meet twice a month, at the home of the couple most centrally located to the rest. Cay and Judy were delighted. "God has certainly started something with this group," they said, "and it would be a shame not to continue it."

Just before leaving, we asked them to give us a date when we could come on another retreat together, and checking their calendar, they suggested the second weekend in June, the following summer. Home we went with a song in our hearts, and soon discovered that we had so much to share with one another, two evenings a month weren't enough; we decided to meet every Saturday night.

Toward the end of May, Buzz and I received a beautifully engraved invitation, and I could hardly believe it when I read it. The John D. branch of the family was inviting the William branch over to Pocantico Hills, for the afternoon and dinner. All the descendants and their spouses were being invited. My mother called, ecstatic: It was unprecedented; not in the history of the Rockefellers had there ever been such a gathering of the clan! Everyone on our side of the family, she told me, was thrilled! They could talk of nothing else—what it would be like, what they would wear, and so on. It would be the adventure of a lifetime!

I was thrilled, too! And then my mind registered the date on the bottom of the invitation: June 14, 1970—the very weekend of our Green Timers' retreat at Rock Harbor.

"Oh, God," I moaned, "why are You always making me choose between You and my family? If we don't go, my mother will be desperately hurt. Everyone will be upset. Oh, God, this is terrible! What are we going to do?''

Once again, Buzz and the Green Timers—and God—refused to give me any guidance. It was my family; the decision would have to be solely mine. Finally, I went over to Deer Park to see my mother. I arrived early in the morning, and she was having breakfast in bed. Her bright blue eyes welcomed me, and she looked sweet—and vulnerable—in her pink velvet bedjacket.

My heart was beating fast, and my mouth went dry. I had better hurry and say what I had come to say, or I wouldn't be able to say it at all. ''Mum,'' I blurted, ''I can't go to Pocantico. I've got to go on a retreat to Rock Harbor that weekend. Our group has been scheduled for that date since last December, and I can't change it.''

She turned pale. At last she said wearily, ''Well, I suppose if you must, you must. But it's a shame, because I doubt if there will ever be another. I will be very, very disappointed that you're not there''—and her eyes filled.

Oh, Jesus, I prayed to Him bitterly, could this be any harder? We agreed that she would take Tinker and Bing with her, and when I got home, I wrote a heartfelt apology: ''We deeply regret that, due to a longstanding prior commitment, we are unable to accept the kind invitation of . . .'' How I wished I could have added that I was not at all rejecting the Rockefellers, or what they stood for, but that God was calling me elsewhere, and I had to respond to His call. But they would not have understood; indeed, I barely understood it myself.

As we drove up to the Cape on June 12th, I was still feeling guilty and subdued. Once there, however, my spirits lifted; so strong was the assurance I felt that I was doing exactly what God wanted me to do, that I began to enjoy myself.

''Guess what,'' Cay and Judy greeted us enthusiastically, ''we've just become incorporated! And the Lord has given us a wonderful name—The Community of Jesus.''

The Community of Jesus—I don't think I like that, I thought; it sounds so odd, so threatening. I rolled the words around on my tongue and repeated them over and over to myself—the Community of Jesus, the Community of Jesus. The more I silently spoke it, the more I liked it. The Community of Jesus—yes, I liked it. I breathed a sigh of relief.

Friday evening sped quickly by, and after breakfast Saturday morning, Cay and Judy told us about a house for sale nearby. ''We wondered if your group might be interested in buying it for a summer place.'' We all started talking about it, and at first, each person had one objection or another. But the more we talked about it, the more each one who spoke seemed to feel that we were supposed to buy it. I didn't know how Buzz felt, because of us all, he had said nothing, and I couldn't read anything from his expression.

Finally, one of the other women in the group became impatient with him. ''What do you think?'' she confronted him. ''The rest of us have been talking out our feelings, pro and con, and you sit there like the great stone Sphinx. Well, what's going on?''

''I'd rather not say.''

''*Not say*?'' she exploded, ''For six months we've been trying to live in openness and honesty with each other, and now you would 'rather not say'!''

''Come on, Buzz,'' others piped in. ''We can't go on, until we know how you feel.''

Buzz looked around helplessly. ''All right,'' he said slowly. ''I feel that Bel and I and the children are supposed to move up here and live in the Community permanently. I didn't want to speak, because I haven't had a chance to talk it over with Bel. But if God is calling us here, I don't see how we can share a summer home with four other couples; we'll need a full-time home of our own.''

The group was stunned—and so was I. Everything in me seemed to drain out onto the floor. We had never even remotely thought about moving anywhere, especially so far away as Cape Cod. What would the children say? What would my mother say? And yet, deep down in my heart, with a feeling as sure and real as when I found out that Jesus loved me and had a purpose for my life, I knew that Buzz had heard God correctly. He was calling us to live in and be a part of the Community of Jesus, now and forever.

I spent the rest of the retreat in a daze. When Buzz and I returned home, we could talk about nothing except our call to live at the Community—were we right? Was it truly God's will for us? It had better be, I thought, or nothing that had befallen us in the past would compare with the disaster which lay ahead. If we were wrong, even coming back would be difficult, for in going there to build a new life, we were burning all our bridges behind us.

Two nights later, at my usual Tuesday night Bible Study, we did something we occasionally did, each of us drawing a passage at random from a Scripture box. Mine was Nehemiah 2:20: "The God of heaven will make us prosper, and we, his servants, will arise and build . . ."

The following weekend, Buzz was planning to go up to the Cape on a men's retreat, and we agreed that after the retreat was over, he should ask Cay and Judy what they thought about our moving up to the Community. So he did. "You two know that Bel and I feel called to come and live at the Community permanently, but we never thought to ask you how you felt about it—how do you feel?"

They both laughed. "We've known for a year and a half that you were coming!" Judy said. "But of course, we couldn't say anything."

Cay nodded. "We're just delighted to have you!" They gave him a big hug, and told him to be sure and hug me for them.

Once Buzz had related this to me, I said that we needed to go and tell my mother, and as soon as possible, for it wouldn't be fair to do otherwise. When we told her, to my great surprise she was thrilled. "I've known how unhappy you've been at work, Buzz," she said, "and I can see how much happier you both are, since you've known Cay and Judy. Yes, you have my full approval."

Next, it was time to tell our children. Tinker was excited and couldn't wait; Bing was frustrated, as he had just turned sixteen, and in Massachusetts he would have to wait another six months before he got his driver's license; Lucy was distraught at the thought of moving away from her friends; and Vicky wondered if there were any horses on Cape Cod.

The second weekend in July, we returned to Rock Harbor, to see if we could find a house. We started with our "dream house"—the one we had admired every time we came up on retreat. We discovered that, while it had been on the market the year before, it wasn't now. Nevertheless, when we called the owner, he seemed delighted to show it to us, and we wound up buying it in fifteen minutes!

And so, on September 3, 1970, we left our old life behind us, and moved to the Community of Jesus. One of the first things I would do in our new home was change the spelling of my nickname, Bel, which came from Isabel, to Belle, a name in its own right. It was not so much that I was rejecting the past; I was embracing the future, in the spirit of Jesus' words: "Truly, I say to you, there is no one who has left house or brothers or sisters or mother or father or children or lands, for my sake and for the gospel, who will not receive a hundredfold now in this time . . . and in the age to come." (Mark 10:29,30)

Many trials might lie before us, times of suffering and pain, as well as great joy and thanksgiving. But above all, there would be peace, the peace which comes from being in the center of His will—that peace which passes understanding. As we pulled into the Rock Harbor Manor driveway, I knew that we were home—really home.

Cinderella Rockefeller had at last found her Prince—the Lord Jesus Christ, the Prince of Peace.

# ACKNOWLEDGMENTS

First of all, I would like to acknowledge the help of my editor and brother-in-Christ, David Manuel, without whom this book would never have come to fruition. He encouraged me from the first feeble efforts, helping me to see and expand the story, enabling me to find the truth and reality of my life, and working tirelessly to make this book for the glory of God. I am also grateful to Rosemary McCabe, an English editor of much renown, for organizing the text and making many positive and worthwhile suggestions.

Without the continual loving support of Cay Andersen and Judy Sorensen, the founders and directors of the Community of Jesus, and my dear husband Buzz, who suggested I write my story in the first place, I would never have been able to see it through—especially the parts that were so painful to recall.

I wish Uncle Avery, my mother's brother, could have lived long enough to see the finished book, for he gladly gave me many hours of his time, as we reminisced through the past. So did Chauncey Stillman, my mother's first cousin, and Aunt Hope, my father's sister and the mother of Lee. I would also like to thank the staff of the Rockefeller Family Archives in North Tarrytown, New York, for their great help; Virginia Smith and Betty Murray for their typing; and the support of countless other friends, like Betty Pugsley and Betty Mitman.

Most of all, I am grateful to God, who, through His Son, raised me up out of a personal hell and into His glorious life—to Him be the glory!

ISABEL LINCOLN ELMER
Cape Cod, 1986

# *Index*

211

St. Barnabas Church (near Greenwich, Conn.), 164, 170
Sargent, Tom, 86-87
Senate Stock Exchange Investigating Committee, xiii-1, 57
Shea, George Beverly, 162
Sherman Antitrust Act of 1890, 5-6
Sherrill, John and Tibby, 197-98
Short, Florence Philena Lincoln (Posy), 70-71, 73, 83, 90, 151
Simsbury, Conn., 186, 189
Sinatra, Frank, 83
Skull and Bones (Yale University), 7, 56-57
Sloan, Alfred P., 78
Sloan-Kettering Memorial Center, 78, 93; ILE working at, 98, 99, 100, 102, 109, 117, 121, 135-36, 170, 181
Smithers (F. S.) company, 167
smoking habit, 162, 181, 185-86
*Social Register*, 95, 126
society, New York, 17-18, 93-97
Sons of Liberty, 16
Sorensen, Bill, 202
Sorensen, Judy, 176, 177-81, 182-83, 185, 186, 189, 190-91, 193-99, 201-3, 204-6
Spence School, New York, 141
Stalin, Joseph, 80
Standard Oil Company, 3, 4, 5-6, 12 56; Percy Avery Rockefeller's career at, 7, 55-56
Stanwich Congregational Church (Conn.), 168-69, 170, 175-76, 185, 192
Stillman, Elsie (great-aunt), *see* Rockefeller, Elsie
Stillman, Isabel (grandmother), *see* Rockefeller, Isabel
Stillman, Isabel (great-great-aunt), five Isabels named after, 4, 9
Stillman, James (great-grandfather), 3, 4-5, 6-7, 8, 9, 14, 24, 25, 45, 56, 144; interferences in children's lives, 7-8, 9-10, 31; provisions of his will, 42
Stillman, Sarah Rumrill (great-grandmother), 4-5

Stillman family, 3, 4-5, 112, 128, 167
Stock Dr., 117
Stock Exchange Investigating Committee (U.S. Senate), xiii-1, 57
stock market crash of 1929, 35
suicide, 115-17, 126-27, 165-67
Swampscott, Mass., 176-79

Taft, William Howard, 5
Tarrytown, N. Y., 6, 8, 119, 166
Taylor, Miss, 73, 82
Ten Boom, Corrie, 197-98
The Chapin School, 59, 61-62

Underhill, Gladys Rockefeller (Aunt Glad), ix, 24, 26, 49-51, 61; birth of, 8; celiac disease victim, 10, 17, 27 49, 64
U.S. Senate Stock Exchange Investigating Committee, xiii-1, 57
U. S. Supreme Court, 5-6

Vassar College, 18, 91, 109-10, 132

Washington, D.C., 90-91
Way of the Cross, 177
wealth: burdens of, 194-95; as a trust, 172-73
Westover School, Middlebury, Conn., 12, 13, 17, 86-98, 91, 168
West Point Military Academy, 95, 104 118-19
Whitefield, George, 34
Williamsburg, Va., 42
Wonham, Hopie (Estin), 69, 71, 81
Wonham, Polly Lincoln, 12, 19, 81, 95, 126
Wonham, Stapely, 19, 81-82
World War I, 12, 14, 17, 79, 125
World War II, 79, 80-82, 89, 91, 92, 125

Yale University, 7, 55; Skull and Bones, 56-57; Yale Bowl games, 60-61